Do These Facts Make You Anxious?

- In 1970, most college-educated women bore their first child before turning 30. Now, they have their first child after 30.

- Average age of college-educated brides today—28; average age in the 1960s—22.

- A vast majority of 25- to 35-year-old working women say their professional lives interfere with their personal lives.

- The number of 30- to 40-year-old single women has tripled in the last 30 years.

- More women enter therapy at 30 than at any other time of their lives.

You're not alone. Read on.

Lia Macko is an executive producer at MSNBC and holds a law degree from Georgetown University. Lia appeared on the cover of the September 2000 issue of *Working Woman* magazine profiling "20 Under 30: The Ones to Watch." She lives in New York City.

Kerry Rubin is a producer at CNN and a graduate of the University of Rochester. She lives in Hoboken, New Jersey, with her husband and daughter.

Midlife Crisis at 30

How the Stakes Have Changed for a New Generation— and What to Do About It

Lia Macko and Kerry Rubin

A PLUME BOOK

PLUME
Published by Penguin Group
Penguin Group (USA) Inc., 375 Hudson Street, New York, New York 10014, USA
Penguin Group (Canada), 10 Alcorn Avenue, Toronto, Ontario M4V 3B2, Canada (a division of Pearson
Penguin Canada Inc.)
Penguin Books Ltd., 80 Strand, London WC2R 0RL, England
Penguin Ireland, 25 St. Stephen's Green, Dublin 2, Ireland (a division of Penguin Books Ltd.)
Penguin Group (Australia), 250 Camberwell Road, Camberwell, Victoria 3124, Australia (a division of Pearson
Australia Group Pty. Ltd.)
Penguin Books India Pvt. Ltd., 11 Community Centre, Panchsheel Park, New Delhi - 110 017, India
Penguin Group (NZ), cnr Airborne and Rosedale Roads, Albany, Auckland 1310, New Zealand (a division of
Pearson New Zealand Ltd.)
Penguin Books (South Africa) (Pty.) Ltd., 24 Sturdee Avenue, Rosebank, Johannesburg 2196, South Africa

Penguin Books Ltd., Registered Offices: 80 Strand, London WC2R 0RL, England

Published by Plume, a member of Penguin Group (USA) Inc. This is an authorized reprint of a hardcover edition
published by Rodale. For information address Rodale, 733 Third Avenue, New York, NY 10017-3204.

First Plume Printing, March 2005
10 9 8 7 6 5 4 3 2 1

"A Speed-up in the Family," from *The Second Shift* by Arlie Hochschild and Ann Machung, copyright © 1988 by
Arlie Hochschild. Used by permission of Viking Penguin, a division of Penguin Group (USA) Inc.

Excerpts from " 'You Ruined Men!' and Other Outrageous, Annoying, and Maybe Truthful Things Younger
Women Are Saying About Us," by Suzanne Braun Levine. Reprinted courtesy of *More* magazine.

Excerpts from *Surrendering to Marriage* by Iris Krasnow, copyright © 2001 by Iris Krasnow. Used by permission
of Miramax Books.

Excerpts from *The Feminine Mystique* by Betty Friedan, copyright © 1963 by Betty Friedan. Used by permission
of WW Norton & Co., Inc.

Excerpts from *Married to the Job* by Ilene Philipson, Ph.D., copyright © 2002 by Ilene Philipson. Used by permission of The Free Press, a division of Simon and Schuster Adult Publishing Group. All rights reserved.

 REGISTERED TRADEMARK—MARCA REGISTRADA

CIP data is available.

ISBN 1–57954–867–9 (hc.)
ISBN 0-452-28606-9 (pbk.)

Printed in the United States of America

PUBLISHER'S NOTE
This book is intended as a reference volume only. Mention of specific companies, organizations, or authorities in
this book does not imply endorsement by the publisher, nor does mention of specific companies, organizations,
or authorities imply that they endorse this book.

To my mother, Karen Macko, for truly instilling in me
the belief that Anything Is Possible—Lia Macko

To my husband, Adam Leitner,
for always being my compass—Kerry Rubin

Contents

Acknowledgments

LIA MACKO

Thanks to my wonderful parents, Karen and Mike Macko, who have supported every unconventional career choice I have ever made with full faith in my judgment and the final result—this is a gift of encouragement for which I am truly grateful. A thank you to my effortlessly brilliant brother, James Macko, of whom I am so proud, and who helped me master the art of laughing at myself at an early age.

To the inspiring women in my family of several generations—great-aunts who owned and operated businesses when few women did; my grandmother, Mary Rulli, who supported my own working mother by providing exceptional daily child care; and the next wave of beautiful and talented young women—younger goddaughters and cousins Jackie Bronder; Lexie Stock; Blaise Rulli; and Trina, Molly, and Margo Orlando, who will surely achieve impressive success in a world that will continue to present new opportunities to women.

Thanks to wonderful and supportive friends and readers: Albert Garcia and my Miami family for your support, hospitality, and endless generosity; Teresa Myers for inspiring me in life with your own wise decisions; Sam Hollander for your wit and for your friendship in good times and bad; Jill Robert for your gift for assembling great and fun women for unforgettable weekends and trips; and John Patrick Shanley for serving as a wise guide and loyal friend.

KERRY RUBIN

When I was growing up, whenever we'd watch the Oscars, Ms. America, or any other awards ceremony on TV, my father would always say, "See, [insert name of winner] must be a good person. They thanked their parents first." It is in that spirit that I would like to first thank Eric and Shelley Rubin. I am so grateful for your encouragement, love, guidance, and steady faith in me.

I also would like to thank my wonderful mother, Beverly Joyce, and all of my brothers and sisters (whom I am lucky enough to also call my friends): Josh and Gudrun Rubin, Alexis Rubin, and Andrew Rubin. A few of the other women in my family who continually inspire me deserve special thanks, too: my mother-in-law, Patricia Leitner; my grandmother Hilda Kiok; and my grandmother Dorothy Rubin—the classiest woman I've ever known.

Extra thanks to thoughtful and caring readers whose smart insights have helped me both in my life and with this project: Shelley Rubin, Rochelle Rubin, Gudrun Rubin, and Gail Evans. Also to my collegue, Sue Walsh, for sharing astute observations about our evolving thesis.

A special thanks to all of my colleagues at CNN's *American Morning* and CNN's Central Bookings Department—a group of extraordinarily dedicated journalists, and nice people.

Last but most important, I want to thank my husband, Adam, for showing me the true meaning of support and understanding—and a love beyond my imagination.

SHARED

Lia and Kerry would like to thank some special people together. First, our agent, Elizabeth Kaplan, for her immediate support of the book project—we appreciate your impressive and effective advocacy and thank you for being there for us each step of the way. We would also like to thank Tami Booth Corwin, Rodale vice president and editor-in-chief, for her vision and for believing in the need for the discussion this book seeks to launch. Our talented editor, Mariska van Aalst, kept us on task and provided us many favors and much flexibility; thank you for going above and beyond so many times. And thanks to our publicists, Cathy Gruhn and Louise Braverman, whose enthusiasm and creativity are beyond impressive.

Lia would like to thank Laura Ingraham and Kerry would like to thank Joy DiBenedetto—two long-time and important friends who support us in every part of our lives and additionally provided enthusiastic and enduring support for the book. Thanks for always coming through in every way that counts.

And on that note, we offer special thanks to Marie Brenner, who believed in the project before we did and encouraged and helped us in meaningful ways throughout the entire process.

Finally, we are indebted to all the women who shared their stories with us. We thank our peers for their very honest revelations about their lives, and we thank the women of the New Girls' Club for their equally honest and compelling thoughts about what they have learned.

Midlife Crisis at 30

Why Are Baby Boomers' Daughters Melting Down Instead of Rallying for Change?

EVERY GENERATION HAS ITS OWN STORY, and ours is no exception. Over the past 30 years, somewhere between Joan Baez and Lil' Kim, what it means to be a successful woman has changed completely. Our mothers lit the fuse by battling workplace discrimination and gender politics. They burned their bras, took on Washington, and won women unprecedented opportunities for professional advancement. In order to take full advantage of the doors our mothers kicked open, the women behind them and in front of us—women now in their midforties—took on their "ticking clocks," setting new timetables for childrearing while mainstreaming new heights of achievement among working women. Our generation's story is fueled by both the progress and the unfinished business of the women who came before us. It has unfolded, but it has yet to be told.

From rebellious flappers to free-love hippies, other generations of women have broken rules, charted new territory, and grappled with the results with a relatively unified voice. Now, young women like us are wrestling with a new round of rule breaking and the sociological seismic shift it is creating. But our generation's story is playing out differently than that of our grandmothers, mothers, or older sisters. Our moment of upheaval is a strangely quiet one because women in their twenties and thirties are unaware of the similarities in the obstacles they're facing and oblivious to the fact that their individual dilemmas emanate from a tsunami of shared and profound cultural change.

Over the past two years, we interviewed more than 100 college-educated women, ages 25 to 37, across the boundaries of salary, race, geography, and experience. While the women we spoke to each had a different story, a strikingly similar theme emerged. All of them came of age during or after the women's movement, and all were raised to believe that their futures were defined by *options* rather than limitations. Yet despite how much these women may have accomplished, they all described feeling trapped in one-dimensional lives very different from those they expected to be living by now. From Wall Street traders to teachers in Cleveland, from writers in Boston to lawyers in Alabama, from suburban stay-at-home mothers to Hollywood producers, the women we interviewed shared a sense of bewilderment about why their lives felt so out of sync with their expectations, as well as a deep fear that the paths they had chosen were leading them in the wrong direction. At some point during their late twenties or early thirties, these women all felt that the stakes had changed—suddenly and dramatically. What we discovered was an entire generation of women in the midst of matching—yet individual—identity crises.

Much of the problem can be traced back to this pervasive conflict: Fully 75 percent of 25- to 35-year-old women say that their professional lives interfere with their personal lives, and more than a third say the conflict is very severe, according to a recent Catalyst survey.[1] And while working women have always struggled to navigate the emotional minefields of love and power, career and family, daughters of Baby Boomers are experiencing the conflict differently. For a generation that came of age at a time defined by options and opportunities rather than brick walls and glass ceilings, the juggling act has changed. Our mothers described the stress of balancing work and kids as a slow, steady burn; in contrast, the 17 million women of Generation X are reaching boiling points *very early in their careers,* often even before marriage or children are part of the equation. And the 35 million women of Generation Y, those born between 1977 and 1994, are being set up to experience the same scenario in just a few short years.

Just what is driving this "crunch"? First, the timetable of events defining adulthood has completely transformed over the course of just one generation. In the past, the major milestones in a woman's adult life—marriage, motherhood, and decisions about career—stretched out over the course of a lifetime in fairly predictable ways. Most women married in their early twenties and expected careers (if they had them) to build slowly over multiple decades. But the latest census data measuring new timetables for marriage, motherhood, and women's earning power show that today's young women are getting married, having babies, and making major decisions about the directions of their careers at a very compressed juncture—right around their thirtieth birthdays. At the same time, there are more single women in their late twenties and early thirties than ever before. And finally, recent studies revealing women's conflicting expectations about romantic relationships and professional success add yet more emotional intensity to what is emerging as a significant interval in Gen-X/Y women's lives.

The echoing, pervasive anxiety our peers expressed during interviews is also largely connected to the lingering social and economic contradictions that continue to affect women of all ages—namely, the persistent gap between What Has Changed in terms of women's progress and What Has Stayed the Same in terms of old-school corporate structures and rigid social conventions. What we discovered in our research is that while the empowerment part of the equation has been loudly celebrated, there has been very little honest discussion among women of our age about the real barriers and flaws that still exist in the system despite the opportunities we inherited.

At some point over the past 30 years, a fundamental perspective shift occurred. While women of other generations see the world as a Monet painting, today's twenty- and thirty-something women see it as a bunch of colorful but unconnected dots. In the absence of that bigger-picture understanding, when the clash between What Has Changed and What Has Stayed the Same inevitably presents itself in our lives, women of our age perceive lingering cultural problems as personal shortcomings. Instead of questioning what's wrong with "the system"—if we're not on

our way to having the perfect career, the perfect body, the perfect husband, and the perfect kids by around the time we turn 30—*we question
what's wrong with us.*

Unlike the clear-cut obstacles our mothers faced when they were our
age, the issues currently stalling the speed of women's progress present
themselves in a far more dissipated, subtle manner. Against that backdrop,
not only are young women less likely to recognize remaining vestiges of
age-old inequalities—they are more likely to internalize them.

Certain laws of physics will always apply to mothers and daughters,
hemlines and cultural trends: For every action, there is an equal and opposite reaction. The Baby Boomers grew up at time marked by rigid
gender roles and spent their early adulthoods rebelling against them. Gen-
X women came of age during the peak of the women's movement and
grew up believing that futures without limitation were within our reach,
if not our destiny. Raised to be self-reliant, we have become a practical
generation of do-ers—women who take pride in fixing problems on our
own. But the flipside of that independent spirit is that when things go
wrong, we tend to blame ourselves. For that reason, our cultural meta-
morphosis is manifesting itself as a series of parallel individual meltdowns
instead of a social movement.

The women we interviewed are all searching for practical advice
about how to navigate lives that look very different from the lives of
women of previous generations. Some are seeking guidance about how to
juggle high-level careers and young children at the same time without
sacrificing one for the other. Some are looking for creative parenting solutions that take into account their roles as the sole or primary breadwinners in their families. Others are struggling to come to terms with
new versions of life's fairy tale, in which Prince Charming may come with
two kids from a prior marriage or show up a little later than expected.
This book is an attempt to make sense of the changes of the past three
decades and to acknowledge emerging, valid ways to claim personal and
professional fulfillment. It celebrates the opportunities and independence
we have gained as a result of the smart choices of women who came be-

fore us, yet at the same time, it examines some of the side effects and un-intended consequences of so much choice. Finally, this book outlines our generation's obligation to move beyond our individual midlife crises and work together for some practical collective changes that may make the allegedly unqualified opportunities we inherited more attainable.

All of the personal narratives shared by Gen-X women in the first part of the book address and exemplify these issues. Some are the complete personal stories of individuals. In other cases, we've changed key details in order to protect the identities of the women with whom we spoke. All shared nearly universal concerns; all were experiencing their own version of the Midlife Crisis at 30.

What's clear from our research is that life is cyclical—women do not tend to repeat their mothers' mistakes so much as create *new* problems while inefficiently overcompensating for what they perceive as missing pieces in the life stories of those who preceded them. As a result, each generation has much to learn from the one before it. After our exploration in the first five chapters of how new problems and new permutations of age-old problems are impacting Gen-X/Y women, part 2 of this book—"The New Girls' Club"—features practical advice for incremental life changes from extraordinary, accomplished, and spirited women willing to share with us at 30 what they have learned over the course of their lives and careers. In their own words, the truly successful women featured in part 2 tell their powerful stories of transformation, reinvention, and revelation.

Forget all those Dr. Phil prescriptions and one-note 12-step plans—an authentic compass for crisis aversion is built into the real-world stories of trial, error, and triumph from women who earned respect and success on the front lines of life. Financial strategist and best-selling author Suze Orman explains why she feels she has it all, even though her most valuable possession is a 900-square-foot apartment. *Vogue's* Julia Reed reveals how canceling her storybook Southern belle wedding to the wrong man at 29 allowed her life to take flight in unexpected ways that culminated in a first-time wedding to the *right* groom at 42. And in journalist/author

Marie Brenner's season traveling with the Boston Red Sox, there's a lesson for all of us about striking the balance between courage and class and knowing the importance of "showing up."

Gen-X working mothers with big jobs and small kids can learn a thing or two about balancing work and motherhood from Dr. Bernadine Healy—the first female head of the National Institutes of Health—whose career took off at precisely the same time she became a single mother. And Geraldine Ferraro—a woman with an all-access pass to scores of politicians, business leaders, and influential thinkers—shares the advice from her mother, a woman with an eighth-grade education, that provided her with the courage to live with cancer. These women and many more share wisdom, insights, and humor about issues that define the personal and professional challenges of our generation.

So, this book is not intended to identify rigid and perfect solutions, as the authors now realize that no such things exist. Instead, it is intended to launch a meaningful dialogue about the story of a generation and share with women in the midst of personal crises an awareness of the cultural threads that bind them, while revealing the galvanizing power of that shared acknowledgment.

PART. ONE

The Midlife Crisis at
30:
Why Now?

CHAPTER ONE

Generation Stressed

SOMETHING WAS WRONG.

We (Lia and Kerry) met while working together at CNN on the launch of a new show. Lia had just been featured on the cover of *Working Women* magazine's "The Ones to Watch: 20 Women under 30" special issue. Kerry was a newlywed, head over heels in love. We were two allegedly "together," bright young women who had worked hard and accomplished something. Our lives were "on track" according to the rest of the world. So why then, to us, did things feel so out of control? *What was the problem?*

At first we didn't realize there was a problem, and we certainly didn't understand its scope. When life becomes a haze of empty Diet Coke cans, bad Chinese takeout, and 12-hour workdays, it's not easy to have deep thoughts. The truth is, we were simply too exhausted to grasp what had driven us to our respective boiling points. Instead, we focused on the immediate and bonded like soldiers in boot camp as we commiserated about deadlines, meetings, and workloads.

It was hard to figure out why everything felt so wrong, when on paper, everything looked so right. But part of the problem was obvious— our professional lives were beginning to eclipse our personal lives in powerful ways, and we were starting to recognize the very real consequences.

Kerry had not made it home in time for dinner with her husband in over a month; he was so alarmed that he asked her if she was having an affair, and he was only half-joking. Lia had only had time to go on three dates in six months. The one time she dared to schedule an after-work dinner with a good friend, she was late because of a work crisis and then bombarded with phone calls and pages throughout the meal. The waiter gave her friend free Merlot and told Lia to get a life.

But it didn't take a French waiter's insults or a husband's loneliness to make either of us realize that the nonnegotiable demands of work were interfering with the nonnegotiable and much more important demands of being a friend, wife, daughter, and woman. We knew our lives were horribly out of sync, but beyond indulging in the standard "move to the Caribbean and open a pina colada stand" fantasy, we were too rushed and distracted to devise a responsible escape plan. Although the world of television news is demanding in its own way, we later imagined (and found ample evidence of) millions of women—working as nurses in hospitals, lawyers in law firms, social architects in public interest organizations, traders in the financial world, or small business owners—experiencing similar stretches of the "crunch" we were feeling.

Not so long ago, it seemed as if we had more life options than a Las Vegas buffet. But around our thirtieth birthdays, we each started to realize that the opportunities and choices we had inherited and earned had come fully loaded with some unanticipated trapdoors. Initially, we weren't sure how to name what was wrong or figure out how to fix it, but one thing was becoming crystal clear: If we didn't start to learn how to integrate our personal, social, and professional lives, we were about five years away from morphing into the angry woman on the other side of a mahogany desk who questions her staff's work ethic after standard 12-hour workdays, before heading home to eat moo shoo pork in her lonely apartment.

Then, late one night in Lia's office, we stopped obsessing about our jobs and started talking honestly to each other about what we were feeling. Lia, who was Kerry's supervisor, had just been offered a lucrative contract. She felt incredible pressure to sign, and it was undeniably the "right thing" to do for her career, especially during a recession. At the same time, she feared it would be a legally binding deal with the devil— "your job or your life."

You see, when Lia was in her midtwenties, she was grateful for the professional opportunities and challenges she'd earned and was eager for more. As long as she just kept working hard and moving in the right direction, she figured her personal life would work itself out when she was ready. For some reason, she assumed things would fall into place, oh, sometime around her thirtieth birthday. But as time ticked by, and 30 came and went, very little had changed, and big parts of her life were still not in place. She was starting to feel the way she had back in college after misjudging how long it would take to write a 20-page paper that was due the next day and realizing in a panic that she might have to ask for an extension. But whom do you talk to about an extension for finding happiness and love?

Kerry was happily married, but she felt no less "stuck" or panicked. She confided to Lia that she and her husband wanted to start a family, but she worried that her life was already so harried that unless she quit her job, her kids would inevitably be raised by the TV and babysitters from Monday to Friday, just as she had been. She had no intention of giving up her career entirely, but she just couldn't visualize a reasonable middle ground.

Problem solvers—not complainers—the two of us had already tried and failed before to create the space needed to address these fundamental questions about moving forward. By the time we met at CNN, we had both changed jobs, switched networks, and even moved to different cities in pursuit of something better. Yet we kept circling back to the same starting point and similar feelings of being boxed into futures we didn't want to sign off on. Although we felt as frustrated as Bill Murray in *Groundhog Day*, we also sensed that we were not the only ones feeling that way, because friends who worked in entirely different fields—impressive women who had their acts together—were going through different versions of the same dilemma. We all shared this tremendous sense that we'd outgrown our lives but were stuck running in place whenever we tried to change direction in a meaningful way.

The Problem with No Name

That night, we agreed that the only way to find a solution to the problem was to fully understand how we ended up here in the first place. So we started to look beyond our lives and those of our friends, and we began to approach the question as journalists. As with all serious projects, we started the information-seeking process by naming our mission—"Project I Am Not Crazy" seemed an appropriate starting point in our sleep-deprived minds. Then we spent the following weeks delving into the data and firing e-mails back and forth about our findings. Once we set out to find a context for what we were experiencing, we quickly discovered that there were more questions than answers.

We found no shortage of news stories chronicling the incredible progress women have made in the workplace, but we when we dug a little deeper, we discovered some statistics that have received considerably less attention. Back in the sixties, the average college-educated bride was about 22 years old. Today, she is nearly 28.[1] Timelines for motherhood have gone through a parallel transformation. In 1970, the vast majority of college-educated women had their first babies *before* their thirtieth birthdays. Now, the vast majority of female grads have their first children *after* their thirtieth birthdays.[2] What's more, a remarkably high percentage of Gen-X mothers are quitting their jobs to stay at home with their kids. The 2000 census reported that 30- to 35-year-old college-educated women have sparked the largest exodus of working mothers from the workplace since 1976.[3]

At the same time, the institution of marriage is being challenged. Over the past 30 years, the number of 30- to 34-year-old single women has tripled,[4] and there has been a 1,000 percent spike in the number of unmarried couples living together.[5]

Taken together, these statistics show that something radical has happened over the course of a generation. For Baby Boomer women, major life events—marriage, motherhood, and decisions about career—stretched out across their twenties, thirties, and beyond. But for women

of our generation, all of these milestones and life-altering choices are converging *at the same time*—right around age 30.

While our early research suggested immediately that something
new and significant was happening among our peers, it was clear that the
dots had yet to be connected—especially by anyone who was *one of us*.
Several prominent social theorists of other generations were tackling finite aspects of these new demographic trends, but by and large, the only
people addressing these issues were those with political agendas who
seemed to want to engage in scare-mongering without providing con-
structive solutions.

The scope of our research broadened when we began interviewing
other 25- to 37-year-old college-educated women. Over nearly two
years, we spoke with a large sample of women living across the country—
from businesswomen to stay-at-home mothers, law partners to social
workers, entrepreneurs to graduate students, and office managers to
artists. Most came from middle-class backgrounds, and nearly all were
raised with a healthy, broad view of what their futures as women could
entail.

What gradually came into focus through those interviews was much
more profound and interesting than our early self-revelations, our initial
theories, or any stark numbers on a page. Frankly, the intensity of the
angst we tapped into was surprising and overwhelming; we started taking
tissues to the interviews because many of them ended with tears. But it
was through all of those discussions— in coffee shops and restaurants,
urban high-rises and suburban homes, office parks and playgrounds—that
we began to realize how discouraged and overwhelmed many Gen-X/Y
women felt and how infrequently they revealed their self-doubt and confusion. We're not talking about clichéd frazzled-woman stories but about
a palpable current of real confusion and bewilderment among women of
our age about the direction in which their lives are heading.

It's important to note that ours is not the first generation of women
plagued by a shared but undefined ill. In the 1963 book that, according to
the *New York Times Book Review*, "changed the world so comprehensively that

it's hard to remember how much change was called for," Betty Friedan recognized the power that comes with the revelation that unnamed social
problems inherited by a generation of women are collective, not individual, in nature. In *The Feminine Mystique*, Friedan observes that the liberating quality of this realization lays groundwork for eventual resolution:

> . . . I heard a mother of four, having coffee with four other
> mothers in a suburban development fifteen miles from New
> York, say in a tone of quiet desperation, "the problem." And
> the others knew, without words, that she was not talking about
> a problem with her husband, or her children, or her home.
> Suddenly they realized they all shared the same problem, the
> problem that has no name. They began, hesitantly, to talk
> about it. Later, after they had picked up their children at
> nursery school and taken them home to nap, two of the
> women cried, in sheer relief just to know that they were not
> alone. Gradually I came to realize that the problem that has no
> name was shared by countless women in America.[6]

Thanks to the efforts of Friedan and her contemporaries, women of
our age are now facing a radically different set of collective questions and
concerns. Ironically, part of our generation's new and ambiguous but omnipresent dilemma stems from a shared sense of inadequacy for failing to
live up to the dreams and expectations those inspiring women defined.
Just as good parents provide their children with a fundamental, inalienable belief in themselves, Boomer women bestowed upon us the belief
that anything was possible in our futures. But when rapid-fire decisions
about marriage, children, and career converge on the compressed
timetable at or around 30, otherwise calm and competent women find
themselves at the precipice of panic. Even those with the most impressive
life résumés feel that they are failing to live up to the Anything Is Possible
opportunity for achievement and the work/life symmetry implied by that
promise.

After considering the similarities in stories among at least a hundred women, we realized that we might have stumbled on a new Problem with No Name. After thinking about it for a while, we recognized what it was.

We are a generation in the middle of a Midlife Crisis at 30.

Why 30?

More women enter therapy at 30 than at any other point in their lives. In the book *Seasons of a Woman's Life*, Yale psychologist Daniel Levinson calls "the age 30 transition a uniquely difficult period," a time of "moderate to severe crisis" for young career women. He describes our panic as "not simply a problem in 'coping with' or 'adjusting to' a single stressful situation. It stems, rather, from the experience that one's *life* has somehow gone wrong." Essentially, this is the moment at which earlier fantasies and expectations of what adult life looks like clash with the reality of what adult life *is* like. Thirty is the milestone at which you realize the dress rehearsal is over—this is your real life.[7]

We all know women who are well past 40 but continue to celebrate their *twenty-ninth* birthdays, and they choose that number for a reason. But just in case we weren't painfully aware that we are at a crossroads, Hallmark has an entire line of cards and party favors to remind us. In fact, Lia and Kerry both received the same card from the "Hallmark 30th Birthday Collection" from well-meaning relatives. The front of the card shows a group of friends at a party. With beer raised, one reveler yells, "It ain't over till it's over!" Open the card, see an empty room, crushed cans, droopy crepe paper. The caption reads: "It's Over. Happy 30th Birthday." Enough said.

Of course, biology plays a role in this wake-up call. Until now, the two of us thought any talk of a "ticking clock" was about as retro as a Betty Crocker cookbook. But as we watched our female bosses and older friends melt down because by the time they started thinking about having children, they were too old to get pregnant, we couldn't help but think that maybe there was a point to that dreaded phrase. "From the most primitive society on the grasslands of Africa to the most cutthroat corporation on Wall Street, the peak age for fertility for women is about 25," explains anthropologist Helen Fisher, Ph.D., of Rutgers University in

New Brunswick, New Jersey. "Sometime around then, women's brains are wired to start feeling an urge to reproduce. Young women today—who expected to be both producers and re-producers—are just finishing graduate programs or starting to win real promotions in their late twenties. For them, the clock can be very disorienting—it signals that tug between two worlds."[8]

But we aren't the first to recognize 30 as the proverbial line in the sand. Kerry recently found a photograph of her mother taken when she was in her midtwenties. She was beaming at the camera, a sparkling young beauty with long, wavy hair, wearing a T-shirt that said, "Don't Trust Anyone over 30." Looking at the photo, Kerry wondered how that younger version of her mother would have reacted if someone had handed her a crystal ball the moment after that photo was snapped, offering her a sneak peek at life on the other side of her T-shirt's proclaimed expiration date for Trust. What would she have done differently if she had known then that by her thirtieth birthday, she'd be a divorcee, living alone while her ex-husband raised their two young kids? Kerry would have to be older than 30 herself to understand the conflicts that fueled her mother's decisions.

Like every generation that came before us, we've all sworn we would not repeat our parents' mistakes. But as she thought about her own life and those of her friends, Kerry couldn't help but wonder: By trying to avoid our mothers' mistakes, what new problems did we create on our own?

The Birth of Girl Power

Our inability to name, solve, and conquer what's troubling us is deeply disturbing to Gen-X women, in part because Anything Is Possible was the unqualified mantra of our youth. Our parents told us that. Our teachers told us that. Our soccer coaches told us that. Pre-9/11, beyond a brief video game war in the Gulf region, we lived in a bubble of invincibility where war and economic woes posed a distant, imperceptible threat. Naturally, everyone had their share of individual setbacks and disappointments now and again, but for most of us, there was rarely a problem that hard work or some soul-searching couldn't solve. What's more, our early adulthoods were marked by the Internet millionaire period of "irrational exuberance," with 25-year-olds on the cover of *Forbes* magazine, we had every reason to believe our pie-in-the-sky dreams would come true.

It's important to understand that the Anything Is Possible message was a deliberate one, started early and with the best intentions. Let's rewind back to the 1970s, when many of us were in elementary school. Women were joining the workforce in droves, and the force of 1960s' feminism was toppling the barriers they faced there. Helen Reddy won a Grammy for her number one hit "I Am Woman," Judy Blume's *Are You There God? It's Me, Margaret* provided us with a starter guide for celebrating our budding sexuality, and *Ms.* magazine had its peak subscription rate of 500,000.[9] Against this cultural backdrop, our Baby Boomer mothers deliberately set out to raise us differently than they had been raised, and they were not at a loss for instruction manuals.

Runaway best-seller *Free to Be . . . You and Me* taught us that William could have a doll, it's all right to cry, and Mommies are people (with jobs). A project of the Ms. Foundation, the book sparked a generation-wide sing-along about futures where girls would be Free to Be . . . anything we wanted to be. Critics sang the praises of Marlo Thomas's collection of upgraded, modern fairy tales, too. A *Newsweek* reviewer wrote: "Yes, persons, there is a liberating, consciousness-raising, non-sexist gift for children this year . . . The idea was to free youngsters from the usual sexual stereotypes, and the result is a collection of charming songs and stories for now."[10] By any standard, it was a purposeful and heavy adult message for kids' music.

Also during the 1970s, the women's movement turned its attention to obstacles girls faced in schools. Feminists doggedly campaigned to wipe out the anti-girl bias in math and science classes and to incorporate stories by and about women into assigned reading lists. And though the Children's Television Workshop wasn't officially aligned with the women's movement, *Sesame Street*—first broadcast in 1969—reflected the educational trends of the times. It's no accident that the genders of Grover, Cookie Monster, Big Bird, and Snuffleupagus have yet to be revealed.

At the same time, cultural images of wonder women emerged, linking glamour to power. The stunning and scantily clad Lynda Carter lassoed bad guys with one hand and mastered the art of accessorizing with the other, as she deflected bullets with her magic bracelets. Angie Dickinson and Charlie's Angels looked centerfold gorgeous as they battled crime, while the Bionic Woman's supersonic ear provided enviable opportunities for long-range eavesdropping. Our young minds wondered: If we pledged allegiance to a daily regimen of Flintstones vitamins, might we too possess extraordinary powers someday?

Title IX guaranteed that we would at least be able to perfect our slam dunk. In 1973, the National Organization for Women pushed the envelope even further—they took Little League to court and scored another homerun: the boys-only league was now officially co-ed.[11] The impact of those strategic political and legal milestones is clear and dramatic. Less than 300,000 girls played interscholastic sports in 1972. By 2000, 2.6 million girls were swinging bats, kicking soccer balls, shooting hoops, and running track.[12] Once the ball was rolling, money followed. In 1972, very few athletic scholarships were awarded to girls. By 2002, more than $180 million in scholarship money was awarded to young female athletes, and Division One coaches regularly show up at high school games looking to recruit the next Mia Hamm or Sheryl Swoopes.[13]

The social and cultural ripple effect of Title IX was dramatic, too. Sports fundamentally shaped our thoughts about competition with women and teamwork with men. "There is no question that Title IX started an empowerment movement for women in 1972," says Donna Lopiano, executive director of the New York–based Women's Sports Foundation.[14] "What it promised was evident in the Billie Jean King/Bobby Riggs match—it showed that women will not fold under pressure, and it showed the power of sport. The legacy of Title IX is that a generation of women have confidence in their ability to compete, and that goes far beyond athletics."

But the pro-girl Anything Is Possible message also went mainstream for reasons that had nothing to do with sports, politics, superheroes, or muppets. As the divorce rate more than doubled between 1965 and 1979, mothers didn't need to look any further than the practical realities of their own lives, or those of their friends, to see that grooming us for roles beyond wife and mother was now necessary.[15] In her latest book, *Why There Are No Good Men Left*, Barbara Dafoe Whitehead, Ph.D., codirector of Rutgers University's National Marriage Project and one of the nation's preeminent social historians, writes, "[Divorce] had an impact on the thinking about how to prepare girls for successful adult lives. More than a social trend, divorce was a social teacher. As such, it conveyed one indelible lesson: namely, that marriage is unreliable as an economic partnership and precarious as a life vocation for women. Far from being a safe bet, it taught, marriage is a gamble. Moreover, the gamble was riskiest for traditional wives."[16]

So, with impressive speed and precision, suburban mothers, teachers, Girl Scout leaders, and even grandmothers were soon making conscious efforts to prepare girls for adult lives in which they would enter romantic relationships and business arrangements from positions of strength. With all of these influences converging as we were growing up, eventually Having It All *on our own terms* seemed like a responsible and reasonable plan.

Of course, your average fourth grader had no clue that anything unusual was going on. Playing soccer, learning about Susan B. Anthony, and getting special attention in geology class didn't seem like a big deal. Nevertheless, all of those "consciousness-raising groups" did impact our daily lives in finite terms. Across the country, suburban neighborhoods were dividing into two distinct camps: girls who had Barbie dolls and girls whose mothers thought Barbie's plastic boobs would lead to self-esteem issues. Accordingly, girls like Kerry, who lived in a Barbie-free zone, spent a lot of time sneaking a fix over at pro-Barbie homes, like Lia's.

In our play worlds, Barbie was a Career Girl. One day she was a world-renowned fashion designer, the next, a vet. She was glamorous and cool, and she was always in the driver's seat (both figuratively and literally) in the commercials for her pink Corvette. After an exciting day at the office requiring several outfit changes, Barbie would meet her adoring boyfriend, Ken, for a romantic dinner before heading back to the Dream House. She was a homeowner with a sports car, a great job, and a kick-ass wardrobe. We might as well have been playing Helen Gurley Brown. If this was what adult life looked like, we couldn't wait to grow up!

Barbie would have given two very enthusiastic thumbs-up to our lives in our twenties. Sure, we worked nonstop and neglected some important parts of our lives, but there would be time for that later. We had no doubt that all of the pieces in this brilliant mosaic would fall into place by the time we hit 30.

We had a lot to learn.

The Divorce Insurance Policy

Our generation has the dubious distinction of being the first to grow up while our parents were splitting up. Over the past 30 years, the marriage rate has dropped, and the divorce rate has continued to climb steadily to the depressing levels we are at today, when a 25-year anniversary is about as rare as a bald eagle or a white rhino. For Gen-Xers, the rise of divorce took on the social proportions of a Great Depression or a Watergate. The difference is, the revolution that defined our coming of age happened in the privacy of our homes. There is no brotherhood and sisterhood among children of divorce like there is among war veterans or people who par-tied together at Woodstock. Even those with married parents were left with an uneasy anxiety, the feeling that things that were supposed to be permanent just might change.

We tread carefully here because too many Big Statements have al-ready been made about how divorce affected family and society. The so-called breakup of the family has become the common denominator of all things evil to politicians, pundits, and preachers. We don't want to join that debate or the chorus of whiners who blame their parents for every-thing, because the truth is that each family handles divorce differently. Yet, to really understand why so many of us are becoming unhinged by thoughts of where we're collectively heading, you have to take a look at where we collectively came from.

Since lots of us learned how relationships end before we wore our first training bras, it should come as no surprise that the aftershocks of divorce would come back to haunt women in their late twenties and early thirties—around the time when many are preparing to walk down the aisle. Psychologist Judith Wallerstein, Ph.D., founder and former executive director of the Center for the Family in Transition in California, has studied divorce's impact on families for more than 30 years. In her landmark best-seller, *The Unexpected Legacy of Divorce*, she concludes that children of divorce often experience more intense emotional reactions to their parents' breakups when they are in their mid- to late twenties than when the split actually occurred. Dr. Wallerstein calls this delayed reaction "the sleeper effect,"[17] and in a statement for the press, she said, "Our findings challenge the myth that divorce is a transient crisis and that as soon as parents re-establish their lives, the children will recover completely. That does not happen. . . . It's in adulthood that children suffer the most."[18]

As a generation, the core story we absorbed about divorce was that it happened most often to couples who married too young, had babies too soon, or just grew up and grew apart. Accordingly, we launched our post-collegiate years armed with a big cultural lesson: The route to marrying the right guy for the right reasons was to focus on ourselves for a while. Unlike past generations of women who married young and assumed they would continue to grow as individuals alongside their husbands, the women we interviewed came to believe that living on their own terms *before* walking down the aisle was the best way to ensure that a marriage would last. Essentially, daughters of Baby Boomers have inverted their mothers' game plan. It's as if, consciously or unconsciously, we've all been after some kind of Divorce Insurance Policy, and taking control of our own lives—by focusing on our careers, pursuing personal passions, and delaying marriage—seemed the right way to get it.

In part, the pursuit of a Divorce Insurance Policy explains why women's timetables for marriage have changed so dramatically over the course of just one generation. Kerry's stepmother, Shelley, sums it up well. "I was a hippie when I was in college," she recalls, "but even though my girlfriends and I were the campus radicals, I remember us talking about how we'd better get married before we were 25. Now, if my youngest daughter were to get married at 25, I'd be a little concerned."

Shelley needn't worry, because wedding bells were not on the minds of most of the recent college grads we interviewed. These twenty-something women told us they intended to take care of a few things on their own before contemplating a life with someone else. The slightly older women in our research sample, especially those living in urban areas, told us they didn't even begin to think seriously about marriage until they were on either side of their thirtieth birthdays. Considering that the average woman's fertility starts to decline at age 27, the potential hidden costs of these changed attitudes can't be underestimated.[19]

In her critically acclaimed book *The Divorce Culture*, Dr. Whitehead notes, "The mainstreaming of divorce suggested that relationships—especially those that are binding or permanent—are risky investments. The most reliable form of investment thus becomes investment in the self."[20] In real terms, that "investment in self" most clearly manifests as investment in career, which many of the women we interviewed focused on throughout their twenties. This sheds some light on a recent Rutgers University/Gallup poll: 65 percent of women in their twenties say it's extremely important to be financially "set" as individuals before they marry, and 82 percent say it's unwise for a woman to rely on a marriage for financial security.

Primed for success, we got good at our jobs, too, and many of us shot up the corporate ladder at a rate that would have been unfathomable even a decade ago. As we were motivated by successful Boomer women and inspired by the unprecedented opportunities in the marketplace, the First Commandment of the Gen-X/Y woman's playbook became "Thou shall not squander an opportunity." And we haven't.

But there are unexpected side effects to all that professional diligence. Many of our peers became so busy scheduling meetings, attending obligatory corporate functions, or trying to launch that dream catering company/record label/art gallery that they inadvertently forgot to program "get a life" into their Palm Pilots. This is not because Gen-X/Y professional women are shallow or self-involved. We're not the Jimmy

Choo— and Manolo Blahnik—wearing girls you hear so much about on TV (we were far too busy to obsess over shoes or drink $12 Cosmopolitans every night). Sure, we've had a good time along the way—skiing out West, sailing in Nantucket, and nesting with Mr. Maybe. But weekends and vacations don't add up to a life, and the frenetic pace we've kept as we've earned advanced degrees and chased passions and executive titles hasn't left many of us with much time to nurture meaningful relationships. Even the most happening young women we interviewed spend more Saturday nights alone than you might imagine.

30 Is to a Woman What 50 Is to a Man

Between cheerleading practice, student council meetings, piano lessons, and dance rehearsals for her school's production of *42nd Street*, Lia started logging 12-hour days in high school. She went on to graduate from college magna cum laude and was among the youngest in her Georgetown Law School class. She even tried to ditch graduation to get a jump-start on the legal/television job waiting for her in New York City. Lia was in a *hurry*.

At 29, she was right on schedule: a good job, a growing paycheck, and a fair share of recognition in her industry. But something wasn't right; Lia had been living on fast-forward ever since she was a teenager. She knew that if she didn't hit "pause" now to assess her priorities and life choices, she probably never would. It didn't help that a recession was rolling in like a storm cloud, the ripple effect of which would impact her career path as she approached her thirtieth birthday.

In a round of e-mail negotiations with her middle-aged male boss, Lia stumbled upon a revelation as she attempted to communicate why a particular job wouldn't be right for her. She typed, "Turning 30 is to a woman like turning 50 is to a man." As she hit "send," she began to realize why there was nothing arbitrary about that number. Around 30, Lia and the other working women we interviewed started to search for a sense of clarity about their professional futures, as they began to question how a husband and children might eventually fit into the complex and often demanding professional realities they had created. As a group, our emphasis on independence and self-reliance doesn't mean that marriage and motherhood are no longer top priorities, too: 90 percent of women in their twenties consider getting married and having kids an "extremely important" key to happiness.[21] So, while many of our personal values have remained traditional, there are no clear cultural guidelines about how these values and our professional strides might fit together.

What women are experiencing at 30 mirrors the loss of control a man may feel when, at 50—just as he starts to go gray, lose hair, and gain weight—his sense of power shifts, and he sees younger, eager, qualified (and less expensive) men start to gain on him in the professional arena. He knows that if he'd planned on a stellar breakout career, he'd better be well on his way by now. This sense of narrowing was exactly what Lia felt as she pondered what seemed to be critical next moves. But unlike men her father's age whose midlife crises were rooted in questions about where the time has gone, our midlife crises grow from fears about where the time is going.

The Meltdown

Ironically, part of the reason an entire generation of grounded young professional women are having these premature midlife crises is that in many real ways, the Anything Is Possible message of our youth proved to be true. For the first time ever, there are female law partners, vice presidents, account executives, and senior managers in their early thirties—and a cadre of working women making significant financial gains while they are still in their twenties. Yet regardless of where a young woman may rank on the corporate ladder, our research told us that sometime around 30, college-educated women around the country are universally starting to discover that the Anything Is Possible message has also proved to be too good to be true. Over and over again, the women we interviewed acknowledged that certain aspects of their daily lives were becoming increasingly out of sync with their value systems and deeper goals. Others described feeling as if their professional lives and their personal lives were on a collision course with each other. The prevalence of the Midlife Crisis at 30 phenomenon suggests that we are all dealing with this building sense of anxiety by panicking and searching furiously for the unmarked exit ramp to a better place.

The spirit of self-reliance that's guided the two of us—along with most of the women we interviewed—since we were kids also taught us to solve our problems on our own. In high school, college, and entry-level jobs, this worked. But as we venture into our thirties and collectively confront the inevitable contradictions that are larger than us as individuals—whether they're systemic to an outdated corporate culture or a work/life crunch driven by a gap between expectation and reality—our independent problem-solving ("what did *I* do wrong"; "what can *I* do better?") doesn't cut it and doesn't solve it.

"Children of the Gender Revolution," a study of 18- to 30-year-olds by New York University sociologist Kathleen Gerson, Ph.D., provides some context for why this is happening. Dr. Gerson explains that in certain respects, the world did a 360 while we were growing up. Young women now assume they will have long careers, egalitarian marriages, and children. But while some things have changed, others have stayed the same, and corporate America simply has not caught up with the times. Not only has there been little movement to create new work structures that fit more easily with family responsibilities, but most major companies offer true equal opportunity only to women who are single-minded workaholics. The fact that the workweek is longer than ever before just tightens the squeeze, Dr. Gerson notes.[22]

Our Politics Are Personal

So you ask, why aren't Gen-X/Y women teaming up and fighting for a four-day workweek? A vacation policy as generous as Norway's? A daycare center in every office? Early in our research, it became obvious that our peers were all wrestling with the same issues, yet responding to them by turning their anxiety inward and focusing on their own lives instead of seeing the bigger picture—let alone lobbying for universal changes. The women we interviewed weren't lacking social conscience, but their individual experiences had caused them to assess what wasn't working in their lives from a different vantage point. In an interview, NBC News vice president Cheryl Gould observed this difference between the way her Boomer peers approached problems and the attitudes she sees in young women today: "My generation was far more political. We saw things as a political movement—there were forces at work that had to be changed. And I think that when you realize you are part of a force for that change, it gives you a sense you are on a mission for the future."[23]

Sociologist Bernard C. Rosen, Ph.D., a Cornell University professor emeritus who explored the psyche of Generation X in his book *Masks and Mirrors: Generation X and the Chameleon Personality*, explains, "The Boomers believed they could, in fact, make a difference. The Xers don't feel like they can."[24] A recent Yankelovich survey supports Dr. Rosen's claim: 53 percent of Gen-X mothers say a person's main responsibility is to themselves and their children, not to making the world a better place, while only 28 percent of the core Baby Boomers felt the same way.[25] While Boomers were more optimistic about changing the world, pragmatic Gen-Xers have less faith in the system and instead opt to protect their own.

Of course, ours is a generation that has been given some pretty good reasons to be skeptical of Capitol Hill. After all, we were in nursery school during Watergate, came of age during Iran-Contra, and launched our careers while the country was fixated on the impeachment trial of an intern-chasing president. Furthermore, the idea that the Gary Condits of the world could legislate away the hurdles in our daily lives doesn't make much sense, does it? Wired to question the elites, one can't help but wonder whether there is a place for the common man in modern government when 42 senators—and several of the 2004 Democratic presidential candidates—are millionaires, with 10 percent of the chamber worth upwards of $10 million each.[26] It's also hard to have faith that enlightened CEOs (Enron's Ken Lay, WorldCom's Bernard Ebbers, and Tyco's Dennis Kozlowski come to mind) would acquiesce to our lifestyle needs if only they better understood our problems. Even Alan Greenspan admits that "irresponsible greed" has gripped the boardroom.

The message to us has been clear: We have a better shot at fixing our lives ourselves.

The Expectation Gap

Lia recently attended a Women in Radio and Television luncheon, where Barbara Walters discussed a report about the perceived role luck plays in professional success. High-achieving Boomer women thought most of what they've accomplished could be attributed to luck, but high-achieving Boomer men said luck had very little to do with it. Both Connie Chung and Leslie Stahl laughed as they told the group of women gathered there that they were granted their big breaks in television because of CBS's affirmative action program—"they needed a token Asian, a blonde female, and Bernard Shaw," they joked.[27]

The conversation, lighthearted though it may have been in retrospect, underscores an Expectation Gap between working women of different ages. Unlike the women at the luncheon (and our own mothers), we've never been the only woman in the room, and no one has ever asked us about our typing skills or sent us to fetch them a cup of coffee. In fact, Kerry has had more female bosses than male bosses. Our expectations of how far we could go—and should go—as women are rooted in a very different set of cultural assumptions.

Margaret Mitchell, author of *Gone with the Wind* and someone who knew a few things about hubris and humility, once said, "Life does not have an obligation to give you what you expect." The Boomer women at the luncheon understood Mitchell's truism—they worked hard, but they saw there were things they couldn't control and could even laugh about the role the unforeseen played in their success. That very important detail seems to be lost on women of our generation. Up until now, most of us have been operating on the assumption that we could be X—*if only we were good enough*. Sure, "right place, right time" might help, but in our minds, success is about drive and merit. And we have that part nailed. After all, we've been in Girl Power boot camp since we joined our first soccer team.

But the Anything Is Possible mantra of our empowered youth, however well intentioned, overlooked some systemic roadblocks still looming in our future, leaving us with no one to blame but ourselves when things don't go according to our carefully constructed plans. This is exactly what's happening to college-educated twenty- and thirty-something women, who feel as if all the rules changed at the same time. What's more, the impact of these shifts was exacerbated when they coincided with the unexpected unraveling of the New Economy. As a ubiquitous ticker reminded us that the NASDAQ was tanking, our personal stock was falling, too, in ways we hadn't expected, didn't understand, and weren't equipped to handle. The whole world changed, and we didn't see it coming. The Midlife Crisis at 30 is our collective attempt to regain our emotional footing.

Total Systems Failure

First, there's the bait-and-switch in our personal lives. Single women considered hot prospects throughout their twenties start to feel like spinsters on the other side of 30. As friends start to couple up and get married, it suddenly becomes a lot harder to meet good men. The cool apartments in neighborhoods we're still struggling to afford no longer feel glamorous—they just seem annoyingly small and lonely. City girls begin to long for real homes with more than two rooms. And the same parents who once encouraged us to live independent lives are now calling us to quote scary stats from a book they read about in *Time* magazine, that 8 percent of women earning $100,000 or more marry for the first time after 30; only 3 percent of that group marry after 35.[28]

And, just when we needed a little help from our *Friends*, our pop culture comrades moved on with their lives. Rachel had Ross's baby, and Monica and Chandler were looking to adopt. *Vogue* devoted an issue to motherhood, complete with a cover photo of a supermodel holding her toddler son, and Gucci launched an omnipresent ad campaign featuring the ultimate accessory—a pudgy, smiling baby. At the same time, Candace Bushnell was profiled in the Vows section of the *New York Times*, Patricia Field was designing maternity clothes for Sarah Jessica Parker, and the Olsen twins outranked our contemporaries on both *Vanity Fair* and

Forbes power lists. Bridget Jones and her singleton posse were suddenly about as passé as shoulder pads and leg warmers.

At the same time, many of us lost our jobs, and those of us who didn't have been derailed in other ways that had nothing to do with the recession. Young women regarded just a year ago as the office Golden Girls were having a hard time pulling off the transition from protégé to powerhouse. It's acceptable to be the outstanding "little sister" with big ideas at 27, when you are promising, productive, and —let's face it—relatively cheap labor, but to institutionalize the next promotion in title and salary is another issue entirely. While old-school rules of corporate hierarchy have loosened up, they haven't gone away, and once you hit a certain rung on the ladder, they kick back in with a vengeance in a variety of subtle and not-so-subtle ways. Thus, scores of hardworking young women, who signed up for a decade of 12-hour days with hopes that it would all pay off soon, are finding themselves slamming into a wall of corporate politics they never anticipated. The safe meritocracies they thrived in since graduation no longer feel so safe.

Although not everyone is gunning to make vice president or law partner by 30, the pressure to be ensconced within some kind of clearly defined career path by your early thirties is nearly universal. It may be socially acceptable to spend time searching for a professional calling during your twenties, but after 30, that grace period ends fast. Women who have been trying on different careers since graduation now describe feeling an anxious urgency to find one that fits. The Expectation Gap kicks in around this time, no matter where you stand on the corporate ladder.

Even those of us who steered clear of traditional workplaces during our twenties aren't immune to this pressure. We spoke with plenty of passion-chasing Bohemians who are now feeling the crunch of society-assigned deadlines more powerfully than ever before. A funny transformation of perceptions still occurs for women over 30. Adjectives begin to change—"aspiring" actors/filmmakers/musicians/writers are recast as "wannabes" or dilettantes, especially if they have yet to star in or produce their first feature film, get that record deal, or publish their generation's equivalent of *War and Peace*.

Our generation's Problem with No Name only intensifies after marriage and motherhood. As "children of the gender revolution"—the largest group of daughters to be raised by working mothers—we must be on to new, creative ways to better balance our careers and our kids, right? Wrong. Remember that statistic from the census, about how college-educated Gen-X mothers are veering off the career track in record numbers? That's just the beginning of the story. In the following chapters, we will give names to some new balls thrown into the career-family juggling act and answer a question on the minds of many mothers and daughters (as well as economists, historians, writers, and politicians): Why are so many Gen-X mothers quitting their jobs? Is the surge of stay-at-home moms rooted in market conditions, or are we witnessing a generation-wide latchkey-kid backlash?

Finally, world events marking the late 1990s and the early years of the new millennium created an emotional impact that undoubtedly contributed to our urgent and collective desire to make sense of our lives. In dramatic ways, a generation of *individuals* became schooled in collective failure and loss as we confronted an abrupt economic downturn and the events of September 11 and its aftermath. All of us, irrespective of personal choices, neuroses, fears, or regrets, began to realize at the same time that it was time to get down to the very serious business of getting over ourselves if we intend to make contributions that matter.

It was time to grow up.

Beyond 30

By the time the two of us were in the middle of our own midlife crises, we'd both heard John Lennon's famous adage about life many times—you know, it's "what happens to you when you're busy making other plans." After reflecting on the lessons and events of the past few years, we believe it now. It finally sank in—life is not an orderly event, and there is much to be learned from its messiest parts. But that realization hasn't marked "The End" of the Gen-X/Y Achievement Fairytale or a return to retro principles or Jane Austen-esque angst. Instead, that awakening marks the beginning of a new story, in which young women like us begin to see life as a marathon requiring agility and resilience as opposed to a breathless and dramatic sprint to the never-ending finish lines we've all helped to create.

While we've realized that Having It All is more myth than Holy Grail (at least as we've been defining it), we've also discovered through our research that many savvy, inspiring, and even slightly frazzled women have figured out important parts of the puzzle—and there is much to learn from their stories. Likewise, what we've viewed previously as isolated problems or personal victories are actually moments of revelation that can lead other women to key discoveries or decisions. By giving a name to a new Problem with No Name, we hope this book helps young women better understand why they feel so overwhelmed and confused, even when it appears that they have so much.

Thirty may indeed be a point of self-evaluation and transition, but it's also a time of reinvention and opportunity. At 30, J. K. Rowling, whose Harry Potter franchise has made her a billionaire, was a struggling single mom on public assistance, scribbling a children's story on napkins while her child napped.[29] Nine-time Grammy winner Sheryl Crow was still a backup singer.[30] Madeleine Albright, who eventually became the first female secretary of state and the highest-ranking woman in the history of the U.S. government, was not yet out of graduate school. And it wasn't until she was 34 that Sharon Stone laughed at the youth-focused Hollywood regime when she gained instant (and enduring) celebrity status with the release of the sex thriller *Basic Instinct*.[31]

As certain old habits are sure to die hard, and most of us are still not ready to shake our "thou shalt not squander an opportunity" vow, we shouldn't underestimate the possibilities that may still lie ahead for us. One thing has become abundantly clear: At 30, there is still plenty of time to claim your dreams, provided you have clarity and focus about where you want to go.

Make no mistake about it, though—the stakes couldn't be any higher at this stage of the game. The proverbial open season for life options is coming to an end. In fact, that sense of closing doors was what drove us to write this book in the first place—we didn't possess the practical knowledge we needed to make the necessary, smart, and informed decisions about what comes next. And while we know now that there are no simple answers, we also know that there are certain inalienable truths. In the coming chapters, we will share them with you, and we hope you find them as helpful as we have.

When all is said and done and analyzed and chronicled, the most important thing that we learned from our Midlife Crisis at 30 is that *it happened when we were 30*. There is still time for all of us—the generation of women following feminist liberation and its subsequent backlash—to get it right, as long as we have the courage to trade in control and rigid choreography for improv techniques more appropriate for lives that have their own unpredictable rhythms. If we let go, listen, and learn from women who have learned a few things along the way, we'll claim the Anything Is Possible dream after all—one we will now fully appreciate but have yet to imagine.

2

CHAPTER TWO

The New Glass Ceiling

A FEW MONTHS BEFORE KERRY WAS BORN, her grandmother came to visit her pregnant daughter, lawyer son-in-law, and first grandchild, toddler Josh. An elementary school librarian who had become increasingly progressive as she approached retirement age, Kerry's grandmother was at the center of a mini-scandal at the time for speaking perhaps a little too passionately in the teachers' lounge about books by Ken Kesey, David Viscott, and Betty Friedan.

Midway through the weekend, Kerry's mother and grandmother went to the grocery store to pick up a few things. Chatting as they cruised the aisles, Grandma asked, "What kind of ice cream do you like these days?"

Kerry's mom pulled a box of Breyers, half chocolate and half vanilla, out of the giant freezer and said, "This is what I always get. It's great— Eric likes chocolate, Josh likes vanilla."

"Yes, but what kind of ice cream do *you* like, Bev?"

She didn't get it. "I just told you—this is perfect. Josh likes vanilla, Eric likes chocolate."

Grandma kept pushing: "Yes, but what about *you*?"

Mom, now visibly annoyed, dropped the Breyers in the cart and snapped, "Chocolate for Eric, vanilla for Josh. This is good."

Grandma was feeling very feisty in those days and wasn't going to let her off the hook easily. "Bev—what type of ice cream do *you* like?"

That's when the truth hit: She didn't know the answer. Beyond a vague home-movie memory of eating a pistachio ice cream cone as a kid in the Bronx, Kerry's mother had no idea what type of ice cream she liked anymore. And it was at that moment—in the frozen foods section of a Foodtown outside Albany, New York—that something clicked inside her, and she knew it was time for change.

During the 1970s, everyone from Gloria Steinem to Mary Tyler Moore embraced the idea that the road from ice cream dilemma to women's liberation led directly to the office. That's exactly where Kerry's mother, and 13 million other women like her, would go between 1975 and 1985.[1] Ilene Philipson, Ph.D., a San Francisco–based psychologist and author, writes, "Beginning in the late 1960s, most forms of feminism began to define women's autonomy and, often, liberation in terms of labor-force participation . . . feminists embraced the workplace whole-heartedly. It was there that women could finally discover both equality with men and a kind of self-realization and fulfillment unavailable in the domestic sphere."[2]

Our mothers worked hard so their girls could inherit a world of many flavors, and 30 years later, we have a lot to thank them for. Today, a new gender gap is emerging in education—girls are outscoring boys on most standardized tests, and women outnumber men on college campuses and in graduate schools.[3] And in a literal sign of the times, a billboard for *Cosmo Girl* magazine plastered across a building a few blocks from Lia's apartment reads, "Respect her. She'll manage your portfolio someday." All of this Girl Power is translating to earning power as well. Today, nearly 30 percent of working wives make more money than their working husbands.[4]

Yes, we've come a long way, baby—but the truth is, just as much hasn't changed. The persistent gap between What Has Changed in terms of women's progress and What Has Stayed the Same in terms of corporate structures and social conventions is leading women of our generation to a new crossroads.

New statistics provide a snapshot of the intensity of our peers' daily dilemmas: 75 percent of women ages 25 to 37 say their jobs interfere with their personal lives, and more than a third describe the clash as very severe. Working mothers are leaving the workforce in record numbers. Poll after study after survey repeatedly reports that professional women in their late twenties and early thirties would gladly accept lower salaries and less prestigious titles if it meant they could secure more flexible work schedules. After watching the corporate chiefs who opted out of motherhood and the women with thriving careers who dropped out of the workforce to raise their kids, today's twenty- and thirty-something women are coming to the uncomfortable conclusion that not only can they *not* Have It All—they can have *only* one or the other.

Ironically, we're beginning to see the world in black-and-white terms once again. Chocolate and vanilla revisited.

The New Glass Ceiling

We've hit the New Glass Ceiling—one that keeps women who want a life outside of work from getting ahead and doesn't allow women who are getting ahead to have a life outside the office. While other generations have grappled with ticking clocks and gender discrimination, the unique backstory of our generation—which includes unprecedented workplace opportunity and the world's longest workweek—has led us to a new inquiry and a surprising new ambivalence about our life options. Thanks to women who came before us, Gen-X/Y women don't question whether they can become CEOs, neurosurgeons, or senators; the question confronting us is *at what cost* do women hold these positions?

Kathryn Mlsna, counsel for McDonald's Corporation and an active member of the Northwestern University alumni association, tells us that she's noticed a shifting sense of priorities among the graduating students she mentors. As recently as 10 years ago, the majority of female students asked her the same kinds of questions the guys did—basically, they wanted help landing prestigious jobs at Fortune 100 companies. Now, that has changed, she says, and even the women who graduate at the top of their class are coming to her with a new set of strategic questions and concerns. They want concrete advice about how they can develop a meaningful career that will also allow them to have a life.

Thirty-one-year-old Ellen has been asking herself that question a lot lately. Truthfully, she's the last person you'd expect to be in the middle of a premature midlife crisis. She is effortlessly gorgeous in a lanky California blonde, Cameron Diaz way. She has a great smile and seems intimidatingly hip in her Fred Segal ensemble and Gucci sunglasses. What's more, she's talented. She knows the rules of the Hollywood game, and she has thrived in its competitive, capricious environment for years.

While it's easy to envy Ellen, appearances can be deceiving. She's traveled far enough along Hollywood's yellow brick road to get a glimpse of the (wo)man behind the curtain, and she doesn't like what she sees. Now she's taking a look at where her life is headed, and instead of feeling excitement about her future, she's scared to death.

● ELLEN, 31 YEARS OLD
REALITY TV PRODUCER
Los Angeles, California

I was voted "Most Likely to Win an Oscar" in high school. I used to want to be an actress, but even before I moved to L.A., I realized that what the people behind the scenes did was more interesting, so I changed my mind. I landed my first job in talk shows and eventually ended up in reality television. Now I spot trends and help teams get new shows and series off the ground.

I hate to complain, because on many levels, I know I have it very good. There are lots of talented people in L.A. who are waiting tables, so I am grateful for my paycheck. And even though I haven't found Mr. Right, my friends back home in Petaluma are impressed by the kind of men I've dated—guys with tickets to Lakers' games and movie premieres (and jobs). I've had fun, but so far, nothing has developed into a serious relationship. To be honest, that's probably my fault—I haven't really had time to focus on that part of my life.

After a decade in the business, I've been part of the scene for a long time and have networked pretty successfully. I can jump the line at Sky Bar any night of the week, and I've had more than a few power lunches at the Ivy. Although I'm com-

fortable in Los Angeles, I'm not really happy. This is what I thought I wanted. So why does something feel so wrong? For a while, I couldn't put my finger on what was missing.

It started to hit me when I went to a prestigious industry lunch last year, honoring women in Hollywood. This event is a very big deal—the room was full of women with Emmys and SAG awards, and several even had Oscars. I was impressed. So there I was, sitting at a table with women I'd admired all of my adult life. But as they were serving the gazpacho, I looked around and started to think about their lives. Very few of them were married. Of the three at my table who were married, one was with a compulsive cheater with a reputation for sleeping with every "model" in Hollywood who was trying to transition into film. Another was on her third marriage. As I listened to their conversations, they were full of regrets. The divorced director sitting next to me told me more than I ever needed to know about her fertility treatments. I smiled, nodded, and told her not to worry. "Of course a 42-year-old-woman can get pregnant. . . . Look at Madonna and Iman. You have nothing to worry about," I said reassuringly. As for the women in the room who did have kids, they spent so much time on location, I can't imagine they were able to spend much time with them.

They all wore gorgeous Armani suits and Cerruti mules and looked good from a distance—but close up, these women looked tired. They were beyond Botox, and they were only in their forties. I realized I was on the fast track to becoming one of them.

Then I looked across the room and saw the gang of young, pretty assistants lined up in the outer lobby, staring back at me as they waited for their bosses to finish lunch. These girls were after the same kind of jobs I wanted—they were also making strides, and they were about eight years younger.

I left the lunch and had my very first genuine panic attack.

For the first time, I started to recognize the huge, gaping holes in my life. It's sort of pathetic. I can get last-minute reservations at Euro Chow, but I don't know how to cook. I chose L.A. over New York so I could be close to water—but I haven't been to the beach in two years! I rarely even have time to read anything except Variety or the Hollywood Reporter, and it's been way too long since I've written anything more than a pitch.

On top of it all, the reality-programming craze has really pushed me over the *edge. Now, anyone can have their own television show—aging rock stars, people who eat bugs, adventure seekers, even gold-digging brides and desperate bachelorettes! And some of the people developing these shows for seven-figure deals are young. For the first time, I feel old.*

I'm starting to realize that something has to change. I need to take a break from L.A. or find an assignment with more depth. Though what I'm doing helps me make my mortgage payments, I spend way too much time at the office. Plus, I went to film school to become a screenwriter, and my career has absolutely nothing to do with that. It's time to at least buy a dog and hit the beach, or I am going to become as plastic as the environment I am living in.

Ellen has been on the fast track since she rode her first Big Wheel, but in her attempt to get ahead in the entertainment business, she compartmentalized her definition of success and lost sight of the big picture. She's facing a different crisis than the women at the luncheon faced when they were 30. Thanks to their achievements, Ellen has every reason to believe that she can land one of the top jobs in her industry. At the same time, she now sees that many of the women she thought Had It All actually made giant sacrifices by default. Thus, instead of taking a moment to celebrate her success—to feel good about earning a seat at the table— Ellen is having panic attacks about the potential hidden social and emotional costs of continued advancement.

Granted, the details of Ellen's current predicament might seem a bit glam, but the factors driving her angst are universal. And now Ellen, along with many others her age, is desperate to find a more forgiving road map to success. Michele Mitchell, political reporter and author of the novel *The Latest Bombshell*, expressed similar conflicted thoughts: "While I am deeply appreciative of all that Boomer women have accomplished and I know that the world I am operating in is much broader thanks to their efforts, that does not mean I am willing to make the same personal sacrifices they may have been forced to make in their careers. It's a different era, and women of my age are not going to operate in the same way that older women have." While it's still too early to succinctly sum up how younger women are re-writing the rules, one thing is abundantly clear from our research: The women of Gen-X/Y, the generation poised to claim the feminist dream, appear to be questioning whether the cost of success, at least as it is currently tagged, might be too high.

The Overworked Week

The *Chicago Tribune* reports that the Japanese recently added the word *karoshi* to their language; it means "death from overwork." Although 3,500 new words were added to the *Oxford English Dictionary* in 2002—including *ass-backwards*, *asymmetrical warfare*, *fashionista*, *bling-bling*, *mochaccino*, and *bunny-boiler* (remember *Fatal Attraction?*)[6]—to date, no comparable word for *karoshi* exists in the English language.[7] This is no small irony, since a recent United Nations study showed that Americans work more hours per week than workers in any other country in the world, including Japan. In fact, the average American employee spends a startling 12.5 weeks more per year on the job than the industrious Germans and 6.5 weeks more than the average Brit.[8] As a nation, we make the Energizer Bunny look like a slacker—and thanks to e-mail, cell phones, laptops, and pagers, the workweek keeps on growing, and growing, and growing.

Although Gen-Xers certainly aren't the only ones feeling crunched these days, it's important to recognize that the time bind intensified exponentially while we were coming of age. Free time has fallen by more than 40 percent since the early 1970s,[9] and numerous studies have shown that we are working significantly longer hours today than our parents did when they were at similar places in their careers.[10] For us, it feels as if the dues-paying will never end, especially when market conditions make it likely that we'll never experience the idyll of job security that our parents often enjoyed. In today's competitive environment, even superbly qualified peers in industries ranging from education to technology have already been laid off more than once before hitting 30. Just as other generations struggled through the aftershocks of the Depression or the recession in the 1980s, the overworked week coupled with the economic downturn of the past few years has led many hardworking Gen-X professionals to feel as if the American Dream has become one of those nightmares in which you're breathlessly running as fast as you can, but you're actually stuck in place.

What we, as women, are going through runs even deeper than an epidemic of premature *karoshi*. The ever-expanding workweek and the New Glass Ceiling it has created are replacing gender discrimination as the primary barrier to young women's professional advancement to upper executive ranks. Unlike the original glass ceiling, which was marked by definitive, clear roadblocks, the New Glass Ceiling manifests as a series of subtle trapdoors—and its impact is often couched in deceptive language about "choices."

Let's be honest. Most of the executive women Ellen was seated with at the luncheon did not "choose" to be single or childless, although the number of hours they spend at the office is undoubtedly part of the reason that they are. According to the 2000 census report, the number of childless professional women has jumped dramatically since the 1990s. The group most affected? Women earning more than $75,000 a year.[11] Wisely, Ellen isn't accepting objective success at face value; she's taking time to evaluate whether she might be able to mitigate the price some of her female colleagues have paid.

The emotional impact of such revelations isn't unique to Ellen, and this shared realization has touched off a powerful ripple effect across an entire generation of college-educated women. Female accountants, lawyers, publicists, pastry chefs, and architects everywhere are trying to figure out how to catapult years of experience, with their countless late nights, early mornings, and working weekends, into a position of elevated professional status—without further (or in some cases, fully) compromising the opportunity for a personal life or family.

This particular question was the starting gun for Lia and Kerry's inquiry. What the two of us learned by asking many successful and happy women "How do you make your lives work?" is that balancing professional and personal life is never easy, but it's always possible. In part 2 of this book, "The New Girls' Club," the stories shared by these inspiring women offer pragmatic advice and creative solutions—and most of all, hope.

But the key to breaking through the New Glass Ceiling is to understand that it is supported by issues more complex than the growing demands of our bosses and our jobs. Its roots are a tangled web of social, economic, and psychological influences, and to untangle those knots in a meaningful way, it's important to examine the role we may have unintentionally played in tying them in the first place. As we continue to unravel our generation's collective backstory, it becomes clear that the nature of the New Glass Ceiling is indirectly supported by both Gen-X/Y women's increasingly emotional investment in their workplaces and the rapidly changing social conditions that led us to this new version of an age-old Hobbesian choice.

The Gen-X/Y Neighborhood: The Office

Corporate culture has transformed tremendously over the past three decades, as we've shifted from an industrial to an information-based society. In the past, any worker, whether an engineer at Westinghouse, a salesperson for State Farm, or a physician affiliated with a respected hospital, expected to work hard and pay dues—with a concurrent expectation of corporate reciprocity and job security. As a result, loyal corporate players enjoyed lifelong tenures marked by well-defined milestones: yearly raises, scheduled promotions, lavish retirement parties, and the proverbial gold watches.

Conversely, those who launched careers in the 1990s will change jobs an average of nine times *before they are 32*.[12] Gen Xers entered the workforce during a particularly volatile era, marked by economic swings, ongoing mergers and acquisitions, ubiquitous corporate greed, and the restructuring of our cornerstone institutions (HMOs and privatized education systems are two prominent examples). This New Corporate World has created new pressures, and many of us now exist in a perpetual state of "proving ourselves"—either to win respect and promotions at new companies or simply to keep the jobs we have.

Ironically, although corporations exhibit less of a commitment to us, we are exceedingly committed to them. The workplace has become much more than a place to collect a paycheck. With more young women than ever before delaying marriage and children, and many moving to distant cities in pursuit of professional opportunities, the office has become our de facto neighborhood. When they were our age, our parents may have had spouses, children, and poker games to come home to at night, but for many young women, the office has become the stage where many important parts of our lives play out.

Because the overworked week requires us to spend so much time at the office, it's only natural that we would connect with colleagues about things that transcend our to-do lists. For example, one of Lia's closest friends used to be the host of a talk show she produced at MSNBC in New Jersey. Kerry's matron of honor used to work two doors down the hall from her at CNN in Atlanta. And in places like Washington, D.C., the steady supply of young Capitol Hill staffers has spawned an interoffice baseball league with a game schedule more complicated than a Florida election ballot. Those games, and the outings to local bars that follow them, have become as much of an institution on the Washington social scene as the Inaugural Ball.

While these examples are organic ones, human resources departments are aware of studies that place social connections with coworkers as the strongest single predictor of job satisfaction. In the interest of recruiting and retaining talent, they strive to create corporate cultures that foster a sense of community. This philosophy was perfected by the "early adapters" of the Internet era, when seven-figure deals were made on cocktail napkins and twenty-something workers had sushi for lunch over games of foosball.

While there is less cash to burn in the current corporate climate, Gen-X/Y workers have come to expect a certain level of office camaraderie. As companies continue to look for less expensive ways of promoting this interpersonal glue, it seems nothing is off-limits, even promoting workplace love connections. "It's Love! A Valentine to AOL-TW Couples" was the banner headline across a recent edition of *keywords: magazine*, the Time Warner internal monthly newsletter. Inside the company-wide publication, there are sticky-sweet profiles of five Time Warner colleagues/couples who fell in love on the job, including the story of one lesbian couple's meeting as well as the romance between a supervisor and one of his direct reports. (Good thing they got married, or that charming love story could have been recast as a sexual harassment case.)[13]

All of this esprit de corps is not intrinsically harmful, but it isn't entirely harmless, either. Some very murky emotional territory is created when our personal lives become so intimately linked to our professional lives, and many Gen-X/Y women have come to rely too much on a social network that could collapse with a layoff or change in professional status. Ultimately, many of us inadvertently stumbled into a trap: *Who we are* became too wrapped up in *what we do*, and emotional and financial security has become dangerously intertwined at work.

Lizzie is one of those impeccably well-groomed people who looks put together even during late-night trips to 7-11. An expert bargain hunter with a closet full of designer outfits to prove it, she is drawn like a heat-seeking missile to the cashmere sweater or Tuleh skirt tucked away on the back rack at Loehman's or TJ Maxx. Although she is a classic beauty who projects the casual grace of a Texas blueblood, Lizzie grew up far away from that world and has worked incredibly hard to create a stable life for herself. We met her right after she was laid off from the marketing department of a pharmaceutical company, and she was not taking the news well.

● LIZZIE, 30 YEARS OLD
UNEMPLOYED
Dallas, Texas

I had four job offers when I graduated college. My top choice was with a big ad agency in New York City that specializes in fashion accounts. This was my dream job—but it paid the least, and I had loan debt. I'm the daughter of a single mother who worked two jobs to pay for Catholic school and then college, so I knew it was time for me to be responsible. I did the math: I took the highest-paying job in the lowest-rent city, and I ended up in the marketing department of a company in Texas. Decent pay, good benefits, and low overhead—a perfect formula. I told myself I'd work there for a few years until I could make a dent in my student loans, and then I'd move on to New York or Chicago. That was eight years ago, and I am still in Dallas.

Approaching 30 with a growing collection of bridesmaid dresses, I wasn't too concerned about being single because it was important to me to make it on my own before settling down. I didn't want to have to rely on anyone else, and my strategy was working. I even bought a loft in Deep Ellum. It needs some work, but it's a cool living space in a fun neighborhood—light years away from the garden apartment in the suburbs of the suburbs of San Antonio, where I grew up. When I showed it to my mom, she was so proud. She's always had good taste, but she never had money for things that didn't relate directly to my education. My dad would send us a check every once in a while, but basically, we were on our own.

When I was 29, I loved my job, and I assumed that I would continue to do well as long as I stayed focused and continued to work hard. When my boss would call on a Friday afternoon and ask me to crash a presentation over the weekend, I never blinked. I knew how to make problems with accounts go away, and I always did it with a smile. Management loved that, so early on in my career, I was assigned to lots of special projects, and people took me seriously. I spent most of my time at work, but it really didn't feel that way because most of my friends worked there, too. Even when I worked late, there was always someone else around to grab a drink with after work.

In hindsight, I realize I should have pushed harder for the promotion my employers kept promising me, and I definitely should have cashed in my stock options when they were actually worth something. I shouldn't have assumed things would always stay the same, because in a very short period of time, lots of things changed, and now I feel like my world has unraveled.

Basically, I got screwed. I still can't believe it. I knew that the company was on the block, but everyone told me my job was safe. When I expressed concern, they told me not to worry, that the buyout would provide new opportunities for advancement. It didn't work out that way. After all the sacrifices I made, and all the real success and respect I've earned, I can't believe this is how it turned out.

Everyone scattered after the layoffs, so now most of my friends are gone, too. And in practical terms, the recession is real and there are very few jobs out there. Work has been the center of my world for so long now, I'm embarrassed to admit just how lost I feel without it.

So where am I now? Without a job, the apartment is an unnecessary luxury, so I'm selling it and losing money on the deal. I don't have friends close by, and I don't have a boyfriend. Despite my mom's good advice and my best intentions, I ended up exactly where she was at 30: unemployed and alone. I thought I was doing everything right. I thought I was being smart. And now, I am not sure what to do next.

Harsh though it may be, you may be thinking, "Earth to Lizzie." In the immortal words of an era we thought had passed, it's the economy, stupid. After all, tens of thousands of hardworking, smart, good people have been demoted and laid off over the past few years. Before you suggest that all Lizzie needs is a little perspective or a Prozac prescription, though, dig a little deeper into her story. She is not living in a vacuum, and she is not the only one taking workplace setbacks so personally these days. Psychologist Dr. Ilene Philipson has treated hundreds of young men and women who experienced a powerful sense of betrayal and abandonment by their companies. In her book, *Married to the Job*, she explores why:

> The increasing colonization of our emotional lives by the workplace is not merely an individual psychological issue . . . growing investment in work is a broad social current, one that is insufficiently recognized or understood. Divorce, the loosening of intimate ties, social fragmentation and the decline of the neighborhood, community and civic participation propel us to seek meaning and sociability at work. Identification with one's corporations . . . reliance on coworkers as one's primary source of friendship, tying one's self-esteem to a supervisor's approval, and total immersion in company culture as a substitute for embeddedness in community, increasingly characterize life in the United States today."[14]

Hardworking women like Lizzie, who are searching for financial independence and an informal network of support, are often the most susceptible to professional overinvestment and its hidden costs. Just like

Lizzie, who earnestly dived into work so she could pay off her loans, most young women who fall into this trap start out with the best intentions. Yet somewhere in the midst of all those long workdays, a fundamental perspective shift occurs—their worlds start to shrink, and their jobs gradually take on a disproportionately large role in their emotional lives. As the years tick by, they derive continual approval from their bosses for working late, volunteering for weekend duty, and accepting extra work without appropriate credit or compensation. Eventually, not unlike women who are charmed into bad relationships with controlling men, these women find themselves married to jobs that control too much of their daily lives and their sense of self. This helps to explain why Lizzie had made enough money to buy a condo, yet the closest she'd come to her post-debt dream of moving on to New York or Chicago was TiVo-ing *NYPD Blue* or catching the occasional Cubs game on TV with a baseball-obsessed former boyfriend.

While some might characterize Lizzie as hyperaggressive or driven, we interviewed a lot of women like her, and they simply think they're making diligent and necessary decisions when they opt to work 12-hour days. They don't even realize the potential impact of their sacrifices until the workplace quicksand has completely swallowed them up or something unexpected—like a layoff or a Midlife Crisis at 30—acts as a wake-up call. What's more, women like Lizzie are usually very talented people who become so socially associated with their chosen occupation or individual area of expertise that they literally *become* their jobs in their own minds and those of their peers. They're known as Lizzie the PR Maven, Suzy the Executive Producer, or Kelly the Exceptional Surgeon.

Top trial attorney and former Court TV anchor Rikki Klieman examines this phenomenon in her memoir, *Fairy Tales Can Come True: How a Driven Woman Changed Her Destiny*. "I was a trial lawyer. Put me on a beach, put me on a mountain, that's who I was. Rikki Klieman, Trial Lawyer," she writes. "If you took that away from me, who would I be?"[15]

In an interview with Lia, Klieman further explained that once you start defining yourself through your professional title, it becomes increasingly difficult to separate your personal self and desires from your professional success. "It's good to have pride by defining yourself by job title," she says. "But if you get there by working all the time, and the only thing you are thinking about at night before you go to sleep is your job, your life is out of whack."[16]

Given that the tricky realities of corporate politics are often beyond one's control, Klieman points out, sometimes even the most responsible and dedicated employee will not be rewarded with job security or a promotion. "Though a cliché, it's true—the only reward for hard work is more hard work," she says. "You can work as hard as you want, and the person who pleases the boss more gets the opportunities. Under one management regime you are a bride, under another, a bridesmaid—if you understand that, you are ahead of the game."

Klieman's observations and advice are relevant to professional women of any generation, but they're particularly valid for Gen-X women because of two parallel trends that evolved as we grew up. Family and neighborhood downshifted their central role in American life, with attendance at church services plummeting while the number of TV sets per home climbed as steadily as the divorce rate. At the same time, the number of hours Americans logged at work jumped to world-record levels. As family life felt increasingly out of control, many people responded by diving into work—a place where rules seemed to be more clearly defined.

Thirty years later, the cube wall has become the proverbial back fence. While it's easy to get sucked into the "community" spirit at work—especially when everyone around you wears T-shirts with company logos, goes to office happy hours, and plays on the company baseball team—in the end, it's important to remember that there is a fundamental difference between corporate culture and real community. Corporate cultures are designed to serve the corporations' needs, which inevitably circle back to the bottom line—not to team spirit, romance, or personal growth. Young women need to remember that the office is not a real neighborhood, even when they let you bring your dog to work.

Latchkey-Kid Backlash?

In a 1998 Barnard College commencement address, Joyce Purnick, an alum and accomplished journalist, cautioned an auditorium full of women on the verge of entering the workforce: "I am absolutely convinced I would not be metro editor of the *Times* if I had had a family," she said. "With rare exceptions—in nearly all competitive professions—women who have children get off the track and lose ground. I see it all the time in my business. There is no way in an all-consuming profession like journalism that a woman with children can devote as much time and energy as a man can."[17]

When we read Purnick's speech, we initially regarded her observations as harsh and pessimistic. It can't be *that* bad, we thought—there are plenty of working mothers who seem to manage just fine. But then we took a look at the top-tier personalities and wage earners in our own industry, network television. Oprah Winfrey and Diane Sawyer never had children, and Connie Chung and Barbara Walters adopted kids when they were in their forties. A decade ago, rising star Meredith Viera, then the only female correspondent for CBS's *60 Minutes*, was fired after she asked to work part-time following the birth of her second child. Katie Couric, mother of two, would seem to be the exception among this group of power players. While we do not presume to know the complex considerations guiding the decisions of these women, in an industry where private choices become public stories, it seems that Purnick might have a point.

Veteran journalist and author Peggy Orenstein describes the full spectrum of the nature of these private choices in her book, *Flux: Women on Sex, Work, Love, Kids, and Life in a Half-Changed World*. She asserts that all women inevitably hit a career-baby/work-life conflict at some point, regardless of how much control they *think* they have over their lives. "The bait-and-switch nature of women's choices becomes more intense sometime in her early to midthirties. . . . No matter what she does—whether she is single or married, avidly pursues a career or scales back, has children or does not—the contradiction between a woman's vision of equality and the tug of tradition will get her right in the gut."[18]

Although ours is a generation that came of age during a time when traditional gender roles were challenged in the home and in the office, in courtrooms and in pop culture, Gen-X/Y women are far from immune to that familiar tug-of-war between ambition and tradition. Rather, the women we interviewed have come to develop their own uncomfortable mix of contradictory beliefs about how best to balance work and family—views that reveal the influences of both a Girl Power upbringing and quality time spent with more traditional grandmothers.

"Life's Work: Generational Attitudes toward Work and Life Integration," a 2000 Radcliffe Center for Public Policy study/poll, quantifies some of the cultural confusion we've inherited and illustrates just how wide the gulf between What Has Changed and What Has Stayed the Same remains when it comes to balancing family and career: 96 percent of those surveyed say parents should share childrearing responsibilities equally, yet 68 percent also believe someone should stay at home to raise the children. Realizing that their poll yielded contradictory results, the researchers did another round of questioning and soon discovered that there was very little dispute over who that "someone" should be.[19] So like it or not, the question for us, as it has always been for working women, is how will *we* navigate the emotional mine field of love and power, career and family?

If this dilemma gets us "in the gut," as Orenstein described, Emily is currently doubled over with her own. A 28-year-old with wavy brown hair and bright green eyes that shine through sexy-librarian–style glasses, it's easy to see why she was elected president of her sorority back at Boston University. Emily is a very friendly and decisive person, but lately, she feels like she's lost her footing. On the verge of her first big promotion and trying to get pregnant at the same time, she knows her next career move will have a big impact on her life down the road. From studying abroad in Italy to cold-calling potential clients at work, Emily has never shied away from opportunities. But now, she's confused about which path to follow. "It's like when you place your order at Starbucks and there are all these options. . . . Normally, I might try something with vanilla, cinnamon, or extra foam, but lately the choices and decisions in my life have become so overwhelming, all I want is the reliable decaf."

● EMILY, 28 YEARS OLD
S ALES A SSOCIATE
Boston, Massachusetts

I watched a lot of television as a child. I know this sounds strange, but I think that some of my most well defined childhood memories are the story lines of '70s sitcoms, soap operas, and cartoons. The Brady Bunch and the Jeffersons were my surrogate families, and I actually remember running home from school to watch Luke and Laura get married on General Hospital.

I was a latchkey kid. Every day, I would take the late bus home from school, let myself into the house, make a peanut butter and banana sandwich, and sit in front of the television until 7:30 P.M. Then I would go upstairs to my room so when my mom came home at about 8:00, she'd think I had been doing my homework all afternoon. I always got good grades, but the truth is, I never had to work too hard to get them. I spent much more time watching television than studying.

My parents signed me up for all kinds of activities. I was a tree in the Brownie play, in the chorus for the school musicals, and played right wing on the soccer team. I never had a room full of trophies, but still, my parents dutifully came to all the big games and recitals, and they even framed some of the paintings I did in art class. And trust me, those paintings were very "experimental."

When I was a kid, I had a vague sense that my mom did Important Things at work—but I didn't understand she was breaking glass ceilings and all of that. All I knew was she wasn't around a lot. Neither was my dad, but my friends' dads weren't either, so that didn't seem so strange.

I remember one time I got sick at school. I threw up all over my desk. All the kids were making fun of me; it was really awful. They sent me to the nurse's office and I just cried and cried because I felt so sick and because I knew I was going to be called barf-breath or something like that for the rest of the school year (which, of course, I was). Anyway, to make a long story short, I remember hearing the school nurse calling both of my parents' offices over and over again, but for some reason, neither of them was around. I remember sobbing into the scratchy yellow paper pillow so the nurse wouldn't hear me. Eventually, our neighbor Mrs. Maranowski came and took me home. Turns out, I had appendicitis, and I spent four weeks recovering from surgery.

I am not going to whine on and on about how tough my childhood was, because it wasn't. I love my parents. The fact that my mother worked made me very independent, and I am honestly very proud of who she is and what she has accomplished. But on the other hand, I know that I was a really lonely kid, and there is a part of me that can't help but feel that I got the raw end of the deal. On some level, my mother put her career ahead of my childhood, and deep down, I can't help but resent that every once in a while.

My husband and his sisters were all raised by a stay-at-home mom. I find myself being jealous of their closeness, their endless hours of home videos chronicling family togetherness, and all of their funny jokes and inside stories. Ironically, my sisters-in-law view their mother's life as repressed, so they are marching off proudly to show the world and their mom and dad that women belong in the workforce.

Jack and I are trying to have a baby. We are so excited about it, and I just can't wait to be pregnant. Every time I think about us actually having a little baby, I just tear up. It's hard to put it all into words, because I have just never felt this way before. I've never wanted anything so badly.

And now, as I ogle every passing stroller and linger at the window of every Baby Gap on the street, I am thinking more and more about leaving my job and becoming a stay-at-home mom. I want to create what I didn't have.

I sell mutual funds. I like it, and I'm good at it. Now I am on the verge of the big promotion and title change that I've wanted for a long time. I know that my parents are proud of me, and my husband is, too. And I'm not going to lie— the cash and benefits will allow us a pretty nice life for a young couple. But honestly, something is shifting within me, and now I am confused about where I want to be.

I know my mom and my sisters-in-law will judge me if I pass on the promotion or quit my job; they won't understand my choice. They are very politically correct, but I know that they don't have a lot of respect for women who work part-time or stay at home with kids. I sort of floated the idea at Thanksgiving last year, and they practically took my head off—they said I would be wasting all my education and would become boring and Barney-obsessed.

I can't help but feel guilty about it. I mean, people invested in me, and I invested in myself. If I just give up my career now, why should any company invest time and money in young working women? If our endgame, whether we know it or not, is just to throw it all away just when it's about to really count, what was the point of all of those 60-hour workweeks?

My husband says that this is all my choice. He says he will support whatever I want to do, and of course, I really appreciate that. But here's the thing—I don't know what to do. On one hand, I want to start building a life that is more kid-friendly. This promotion will mean longer hours and more travel, which is exactly what I don't want. On the other, I have been working toward this job for such a long time. More than anything, I'm just really afraid that whatever I do, a few years from now, I'm going to say to myself, "I had so many opportunities. How did I end up here?"

Emily's dilemma has become as familiar a maternal rite of passage as a baby shower. The struggle to find solutions consistent with both her individual beliefs about childrearing and her financial realities is an internal wrestling match every working mother can relate to. In fact, a Google search for the phrase "work-family balance" yields nearly four million more hits than a search for "breastfeeding."

But our generation's shared backstory infuses new layers of confusion into the conventional conflicts between work and family obligations. The disconnect between the unqualified Anything Is Possible mantra of our youth and the untidy complexities of what it actually takes to balance career and children has left many of us feeling guilty for not feeling capable of living up to our own expectations. Additionally, our research found that many young women today feel a surprising, uneasy ambivalence about their own working mothers' choices as they set out to clear paths for themselves and their families. On one hand, adult daughters of ceiling breakers (and women like Emily) experience a brand-new "daughter of" guilt that inspires second thoughts about a decision to leave the workforce. On the other, lingering latchkey-kid memories tug these same women in the other direction.

This may be part of the reason that the latest census report shows that Gen-X mothers may relate more to June Cleaver than to Murphy Brown when making the career decisions that directly impact their ability to spend time with their kids. Thirty-something mothers are veering off the career track in record numbers; the past few years have seen the steepest decline in the labor force participation of mothers with infants since 1976. The number of women who stayed in their jobs during their first pregnancies also slipped for the first time since 1961. (It's important to note that this workplace exodus is concentrated among married mothers between the ages of 30 and 44 and with at least one year of college.)[20]

Given the realities of the biological clock, the majority of mothers responsible for changing the direction of the census are closer to 30 than to 44, and chances are, they experienced their own share of crises before making the decision to stay at home with their kids. While it's still early to project where this emerging trend may lead, this research underscores an emerging value system shared by most Gen-X mothers, regardless of socioeconomic status: When the demands of a job require too many sacrifices at home, women of our generation will opt to quit or reduce their work schedules—*if they can afford to.*

"Stopping Out" and Starting Up

Young women married to men whose paychecks are big enough to support both of them are not the only ones driving this trend toward temporary career hiatuses. High-achieving young professional women—those poised to eventually land top jobs in their fields—are leaving the workplace in droves and beginning to question the meaning of "success."

In *BusinessWeek* magazine, Stanford MBA director Sharon Hoffman says the ranks of stay-at-home moms have swollen so much that she invented a new term for them: *stop-outs*. Similarly, a recent study, conducted by Harvard Business School professor Myra Hart and reported in *BusinessWeek*, found that of the women graduates from the classes of 1981,

1986, and 1991, only 38 percent were still working full time.[21] The B-school's alumni bulletin summed up the results of the study with an illustration of a briefcase-toting executive rushing out of her office. The sign on the door read "Back in 5 Minutes," with "Minutes" crossed out and replaced with "Years?" If actions speak louder than words, a wave of ambitious young women must be wondering why How to Have it All—At the Same Time wasn't a required management course at their Ivy League business schools.

Some may not view this trend so favorably. At a cursory glance, these "stop-outs" may look more like yuppified copouts to the women who fought so hard for our workplace rights. Still, the burgeoning trend doesn't necessarily represent backsliding or surrender. On the contrary, it may represent the evolution of workplace gains for women, since the trend is increasingly visible at the highest levels of business. Of the 108 women who have appeared on Fortune magazine's "Most Powerful Women" list over the past five years, at least 20 have left their prestigious positions—most voluntarily. They include former Pepsi-Cola North America CEO Brenda Barnes, who moved home to Illinois to focus on her family, and former Fidelity Personal Investments president Gail McGovern, who took a job in slower-paced academia.[22] Following a two-year sabbatical of her own, Ann Fudge, chairman and CEO of Young and Rubicam, was described as "announcing a mission" during a recent interview. "We need to redefine power," she exclaimed from her office, and she followed with the $6 million question: "Do we have to follow the boys' scorecard?"[23]

Fudge has a point. If the goal of feminism was choice, strategic breaks from the workplace could be the first step in a long process of redefining success on broader, more complex, female terms. Since the first wave of workplace change emerged from a movement undeniably rooted in gender "sameness" and equality, it makes sense that the next step might more readily accommodate gender distinctions or individual preferences. Moreover, we may be approaching a day when values beyond title and salary—such as "independence" and "flexibility"—might also be accorded equal respect: 26 percent of women at the cusp of the most senior levels of management don't want the promotion. Even some of *Fortune* magazine's most-powerful-women-in-waiting now claim they do not want to be the next Carly Fiorina, nor do they aspire to run huge companies.[24] At this rate, one has to question whether the editors will soon have to invent a new matrix for ranking power players.

Certainly, many working women will continue to strive for success as conventionally defined at the highest levels of corporate America. But on the other hand, even industry giants like General Electric are beginning to recognize that it's becoming difficult to retain female talent without offering family-friendly policies and more flexible routes to upper management positions.[25] At the same time, accounting firm Deloitte and Touche has more than doubled the number of employees on flexible work schedules over the past decade, while quintupling the number of female partners and directors—from 97 to 567—in the same period. IBM has recently followed suit, now guaranteeing its employees up to 156 weeks of job-protected family time off.[26] CEO Sallie Krawcheck, number 14 and the fastest mover on the "Most Powerful" list, notes: "If corporate America could somehow figure it out and let women get to the top without requiring them to charge hard their entire careers, we may get there someday."[27]

Until these kinds of policies become the norm rather than the exception, mothers who want to continue working seem to be choosing Plan B—self-employment—whenever possible. The number of businesses owned or co-owned by women has jumped 11 percent since 1997, nearly twice the rate for businesses in general.[28] The story behind those numbers is that many of the working women who are quitting their jobs are not abandoning their ambitions; they are merely rejecting the often rigid rules of corporate culture. And by rewriting *those* rules—on their own terms—female entrepreneurs are beginning to redefine the way businesses are structured.

From Girl Power to Mother Power

A "Mommy and Me" class in suburban New Jersey is not the typical image that comes to mind when one imagines what the next stage of women's progress might look like. Yet in many ways, the group 33-year-old Lisa belongs to is a microcosm of our generation's emerging story—one where women are challenging the one-or-the-other nature of their "choices" by attempting to chart more individualized courses to professional success. She told us that her classmates include Mary Ellen, a former public relations executive who now consults part-time from her home, and Zara, a former stockbroker who just opened a clothing boutique in a neighboring community.

And then there is Lisa—a prosecutor with a sharp mind, quick wit, and an impressive track record for felony convictions—who did not return to work after maternity leave. Like many of the stay-at-home mothers we interviewed, Lisa doesn't see her time in the home as a permanent choice. Because she has an established conviction record and is respected within her professional community, she is fully confident she will be able to reignite her career a few years down the road, after her son heads off to school. "I realized that my career will always be there, but I can't rewind time," she said. "That's why I'm staying at home with Ben now. I do just enough networking and consulting to keep my name out there, so I will have options later on. I don't feel like I checked out of my career—I just put it on hold for a while."

We'll have to wait and see whether the various gambles Lisa and her classmates have taken pay off, but our interviews with the women of the New Girls' Club provide a clearer sense of the odds. Rooted in the realization that life is long and careers can play out over time, many of the women we interviewed—from former vice presidential candidate Geraldine Ferraro to author Judy Blume—stayed at home with their children when they were young and didn't launch break-out careers until they were well into their thirties. The lesson women of our age can draw from their experience is not that we must rewind the clock and have babies early and careers later like these successful Boomer women did. But there is an important lesson to be learned from their long-range view of life, guided by a fundamental understanding that sprinting is not the *only* way to reach the top of your professional game. If Ferraro didn't even begin to practice law until she was 38, and if Blume didn't publish her first children's book until after her thirtieth birthday, why should a woman who has already established herself by working for more than five years in her chosen field doubt that it would be safe to step away from a traditional career trajectory, at least for a while?

Admittedly, many of these ideas about restructuring work sound nice as theoretical constructs, but there is another, very critical issue in play—namely, money. Although the prospect of creative career paths is promising, "stopping out," starting up, working part-time, or taking professional risks that could affect their earning power are simply not realistic options for the majority of women who don't have the financial leverage of an MBA or a rich husband, a progressive boss, and a hell of a lot of guts. For most Gen-X families, the debate over whether mothers should work is simply a nonissue because, more often than not, it takes two reliable incomes to afford a comfortable middle-class lifestyle.

So while we are grappling with all of these workplace changes, there is a parallel question most of us face in our personal lives: Why do we put so much pressure on ourselves to be full-throttle in all aspects of our lives, all the time? If all of this premature midlife confusion is a sign that Gen-X/Y women are in the midst of redefining what it means to be successful women, the good news is that we seem to be considering the question in full range. Not only are we reconsidering what it means to be successful professionals, we are also beginning to reject adulated icons of perfection on the home front in ways that might allow for the eventual, rational melding of both worlds.

'Cause I'm a Woooo-man

Remember that Enjoli perfume commercial from the 1970s, with the glamorous working mother in the power suit and sexy stilettos who fried bacon with one hand and cradled her baby in the other? Back then, that you-can-have-it-all poster woman who could bring home the bacon and fry it up in the pan became the ultimate female fantasy. That commercial was intended to target Baby Boomer women, and it worked. Not only did women buy the perfume, they also bought into the ad's Superwoman image and message.

As kids, we watched our mothers, aunts, and neighbors try to have it all and inevitably fail to pull it off with the same sexy, self-assured ease the lady in the commercial embodied. Now that we daughters of Baby Boomer moms have become mothers ourselves, we've developed a different female fantasy of our own—one customized for a more practical generation. The updated Superwoman archetype living in our collective psyche is a real working mother who has accomplished amazing feats such as finding terrific child care and an interesting, lucrative job with a flexible schedule. Our Superwoman leaves work early so she can watch her kids play soccer—and while she's there, she doesn't worry about the unfinished project on her desk or feel the need to answer her ringing cell phone. Conversely, while she is at work, she doesn't worry about her kids because she knows they are in good hands. Women who can pull *that* off are quickly becoming the new sex symbols for pragmatic and aspiring mothers who fantasize about real-world answers to their real-world concerns. Forget about the bacon—the new "Enjoli woman" moves between both worlds, guilt-free.

But the reality of most of the mothers (and fathers) we interviewed is largely shaped by the struggle to structure professional lives in a way that limits the number of hours their kids log with babysitters and TV sets Monday through Friday. This leads us back to that persistent gap between What Has Changed and What Has Stayed the Same for working women: Despite the fact that there are more than 15 million working mothers in their twenties and thirties, the widespread institutional changes that would make compressed workweeks, telecommuting, meaningful part-time careers, or "stop-outs" standard viable options have yet to occur on a broad scale. And for each company that makes *Working Mother* magazine's "100 Best" list, there are dozens more where mothers get the evil eye when they stop what they're doing to check on their kids at 3:00 P.M. or, worse yet, dare to leave the office at 5:00.

Even though many Gen-X mothers are struggling with similar problems, as a generation, we tend to focus on our own lives instead of rallying together for collective change. Contrary to some assumptions, this individualism doesn't come from self-absorption; rather, it arises out of years of training. We simply assess what's not working and how to fix it from a different vantage point than our parents did. Sociologist Bernard C. Rosen, Ph.D., a Cornell University professor emeritus, explains, "Many in Gen-X feel they missed out on something growing up. They complain that their parents were too busy to pay attention to them. . . . They are not so interested in changing the world, and that should mean more home life." "Life's Work," the Radcliffe College study mentioned earlier, echoes Dr. Rosen's observations. Boomer women ranked "having a job that makes a difference" as a top priority, whereas Gen-X women ranked "having a work schedule that allows for time with family" as a much bigger concern. In short, we have our heads down, focused on doing right by our own families, and we can't see that all around us are women just like ourselves, silently struggling and wishing for more.

Having It All vs. Having Enough

At or around age 30, the women we interviewed—regardless of whether they were single or married or mothers—each faced similar unsettling moments where questions about identity, career, and family converged and overlapped. And often for the first time in otherwise self-sufficient lives, they described feeling frozen in their tracks by the choices that loomed in their immediate futures. For a generation of independent women used to solving their own problems, panic sets in upon realizing that some roadblocks are *systemic* and, in many cases, beyond any individual's capacity to overcome on their own. We are paralyzed by the potential ramifications of chocolate-or-vanilla choices that could lead to one-dimensional realities.

The first step in moving forward in a meaningful way is to recognize that the well-intentioned "you can do anything" promise has a tendency to transform into an unrealistic "you should be everything" brand of guilt at 30 and beyond. One way to mitigate this Expectation Gap is to leave behind the airbrushed, clichéd myth of Having It All and replace it with an updated mantra—one rooted in having the confidence and self-awareness to recognize when you Have *Enough*. That doesn't mean lowering standards or downgrading dreams; it means having focus about what is important to you and devising a creative, realistic plan for achieving it that acknowledges existing obstacles.

For Ellen, the path from the New Glass Ceiling to Having Enough might be transitioning into the writing career she's always dreamed about, even if it means leaving a safe job and reliable paycheck behind—at least for a while. For Lizzie, it might mean seeking guidance regarding negotiation techniques so that when she hits the pavement to look for her next job, she will ultimately strike a deal that honors her abilities. It could mean continuing a career in sales for mother-to-be Emily, where she can work the phones from home instead of joining the managerial ranks, where face-time counts. All of these scenarios involve short-term sacrifices, including possible pay cuts, temporary lifestyle changes, and additional rounds of dues-paying or interviewing. But for Ellen, Lizzie, Emily, and the millions of other young women like them, the deliberate efforts they make to realign their career paths now will ease their immediate anxieties *and* broaden their long-range professional options.

Midlife career transitions are never easy, especially as most corporations are currently structured. As we note in this chapter, many of the best emerging trends for women seeking to balance work and life—such as "stopping out" and starting new businesses—can still become realities for only a select few. Yet the fact that so many individual women poised for conventional gains are beginning to question the very meaning of power and success suggests that something more profound is afoot.

Across this century, every generation has pushed and pulled and ultimately reshaped the cultural idea of what it means to be a successful, modern woman. Back in the 1950s, success looked like Donna Reed. In the 1970s, it was Gloria Steinem in a Diane von Furstenberg wrap dress. In the 1980s, it wore a power suit. And in the 1990s, Carly Fiorina and Hillary Clinton once again reframed our image of what it looks like when a woman flexes influence. What is driving the Midlife Crisis at 30 is nothing short of the burgeoning seeds of another round of change, where women are once again redefining what success looks like.

The Gen-X/Y women's round of change will be trickier to identify because it will no longer revolve around one or two iconic visions of success based on age-old assumptions that frame a patriarchal, hierarchical world. This time, "change" is not only about expanding access to existing choices, it's also about adding new definitions of success to the existing lexicon. Not unlike what *Fortune* heard from the female executives they interviewed, many of the women we spoke to described accomplishment in much broader terms. Instead of talking exclusively about making partner or having a corner office, they also included in their discussion of success far more descriptive words, such as *fulfillment*, *influence*, *balance*, and *control*.

Based on these conversations and our research, it seems it is our generation's collective responsibility to carve out small and large ways to make life within "the system" more forgiving and professional opportunities outside the system more accessible. As complex and individualized as these emerging visions of success may be, striving to create them is exactly what will help bridge the gap between What Has Changed and What Has Stayed the Same. Former Enron executive and whistleblower Sherron Watkins has said, "Power will not change the nature of women. Women will change the nature of power."[29] All the studies and statistics indicate that our generation is primed to go further in this regard than any before it, so the only remaining question is, "What are we waiting for?"

CHAPTER THREE

The Bitch vs. the Good Witch

A YEAR AFTER LIA AND KERRY FIRST MET AT CNN, things were taking a turn for the better. Having just emerged from a meeting with a thirty-something publishing executive who was going through a premature midlife crisis of her own, we could sense that the book project resonated with her. In a post-meeting huddle a few steps outside the lobby of a midtown skyscraper, our agent of 10 days told us to expect a book deal within a few weeks. Accustomed to working long and hard for everything we earned, we were absolutely stunned at how quickly things were moving. Overwhelmed with excitement, gratitude, and a little bit of shock, we scoped the neighborhood for a place that served champagne. After tapping flutes, Kerry called her husband and Lia called her boyfriend; we planned to share the good news with our families and close friends when we returned to our respective homes.

But our moment of celebration was followed by an awkward mutual admission. We implored one another not to tell any of our colleagues about the possibility of closing a deal until the ink was dry. Our shared reticence was not motivated by superstitions about tempting karma or by an unfounded sense of paranoia. The truth is that while we were confident that most of our peers would be happy for us, on more than one occasion, we had also witnessed firsthand the damage that can occur when just one vicious or jealous person decides to take action against you. Under normal circumstances, we might not care so much, but we were committed to the project and didn't want to jeopardize it in any way. After 10 years in the working world, we had become realists.

Once the deal was signed and the book under way, we began to uncover research that confirmed our suspicions and validated our experiences. Have no doubt—there is real polarity in the way women treat each other at work. They can either be your best friends and most strategic allies, or they can be your worst enemies. But it's hard to predict who will become "the Bitch" and who "the Good Witch" because, unlike those old Hanna-Barbera cartoons, no hovering angel and devil will duke it out over the shoulder of your would-be saboteur or savior, weighing the pros and cons of every ethical dilemma. The real-world motivations for support and sabotage among peers or supervisors are not always so clear.

Actions, on the other hand, often *are* clear. Popular culture has many examples. There is no shortage of female authors and pundits who revile Hillary Clinton and have built careers around deconstructing her marriage and psyche. But the former first lady has just as many equally passionate supporters who appear on TV at a moment's notice to defend her leadership skills and political contributions. Similarly, when allegations against Martha Stewart surfaced, some women expressed glee at her demise, while others rushed to her defense, wearing "Save Martha" T-shirts.

Professional role models like Geraldine Laybourne, founder and CEO of Oxygen Media, have made it their life's work to make a win for them a win for their female colleagues. Laybourne told us, "When I got into the executive ranks at Viacom, I did everything I could to try to get another woman into the group with me, because I knew it would be good for the company. We had almost a silent pact between women—we would make sure that everybody's ideas got reiterated and were assigned as to whose they were. And that changed the whole operation of our company."

The deliberate efforts that progressive Boomer businesswomen like Laybourne have made over the past 30 years have played out in dramatic ways. The gender dynamics our peers face in the office today are very dif-

ferent from those our mothers faced when they were our age. Yet just because there are very few "first woman to . . ." slots left unfilled, that
doesn't mean the playing field has been entirely leveled. If the challenge
for our mothers' generation was to figure out how to secure a lone seat
at the boardroom table, the challenge for our generation is to figure out
how to creatively channel our competitive impulses into developing an
environment in which women can have an enduring influence on the way
major decisions are made—at every rung on the ladder.

Gail Evans, former CNN executive and author of the best-selling
book *Play Like a Man, Win Like a Woman*, gives lectures across the country
to women of all ages and business backgrounds, talking about how to get
ahead in the corporate world. During an interview, she told us that every
time she would go out to give a speech, 15 or 20 women would come up
to her and tell her tremendously discouraging stories about "how hard
they worked, how much they cared, and how they could not understand
why the guys were getting ahead more than they were." Evans says it frustrated her until she realized one day that we are all so busy trying to improve ourselves as individuals, we missed something very basic. "We
cannot make ourselves smarter. We have maxed out there. We have done
as much as we can do," she says. "We've tried to act like men in the workplace, and that doesn't always work, either. We've tried everything else,
and clearly it has not worked. The answer is simple—it's time for us to
team up as women and work together, because we are not helping and
supporting each other. And that is one part of what the boys do that we
have totally missed."

What Evans was saying—and what was driving the anxiety the two
of us were feeling at the bar—is that some women still think of success
primarily in individual terms. Despite the best efforts of the Good
Witches of the world, there is still no collective unspoken pact among
professional women to look out for each other. On the other hand, there
is daily anecdotal proof in the pages of the *Wall Street Journal* or the
opening salvo of the evening news that the Old Boys' Club is alive and
well. Just read between the lines of stories about the designated players
in IPOs, mergers, and acquisitions or the spinning of corporate and po-

litical scandals. One can even look to culture bibles such as *Vanity Fair* for articles chronicling the influence of the male Gay Mafia in Hollywood. And although *Time* magazine recently named female whistleblowers the Persons of the Year, and we routinely celebrate the Madeleine Albrights, Condoleezza Rices, and Carly Fiorinas of the world, there is still no co-ordinated female power base equivalent to Bohemian Grove.

Why is it that even the most competitive of men know how to look out for their own, yet most women still feel like they are in it on their own?

The Office Bitch

Women used to fear other women stealing their husbands, and influential femmes from Pamela Harriman and Slim Keith to literary heroines like Scarlett O'Hara did quite well for themselves in this trade. As women moved from the home to the workplace, though, new brands of undermining emerged.

The Office Bitch has now officially joined the Virgin, the Whore, the Evil Stepmother, the Fairy Godmother, and the Crazy Ex-Girlfriend/Wife in central casting's roster of standard female characters. But unlike the other stereotypes that most thinking people realize live only in fairy tales and soap operas, a recent American Management Association survey indicates that most women perceive the Bitch as real: 95 percent say another woman has undermined them at some point in their careers.[1] Perhaps this helps explain the findings of a similar survey from Gallup: 60 percent of women 18 to 29 years old would rather work for a man than a woman. Another national survey reports that woman-on-woman office sabotage has increased by 50 percent during the past 10 years, indicating that some women are hurting each other instead of helping each other as they gain more power in the workplace.[2]

But perceptions don't always reflect reality, and the full story behind these dramatic numbers also stems, in part, from lingering confusion about what motivates competitive women. In other words, sometimes the Office Bitch is a Bitch, but *sometimes* she's a decisive leader who is misunderstood. Phyllis Chesler, Ph.D., a best-selling author and psychotherapist, explains in her book *Woman's Inhumanity to Woman*:

We live in strange times. On the one hand, an increasing number of women compete against each other in direct and aggressive ways, both physically and verbally, in sports, business, law, journalism, science, medicine, and the arts. On the other hand, even today . . . women remain ambivalent about or continue to disapprove of the women who compete in direct and visible ways. This gets many good female CEOs, politicians, or professional athletes in quite a lot of trouble.[3]

When Senator Kay Bailey Hutchison first ran for the Senate, Gloria Steinem called her a "female impersonator," columnist Molly Ivins called her a "Breck girl," and the media never seemed to tire of reminding voters that she had once been high school cheerleader. In an interview with Kerry, she reflected on the lingering double standards applied to women with power. "A man can be irascible and it's even not described at all, or it's described as a neutral to positive trait," she says. "But if a woman is irascible, it is almost always portrayed as negative. I have seen that time after time after time. There is no leeway given for a woman to be tough, and when we are, there is a different way of describing our effectiveness." Despite the fact that most twenty- and thirty-something women played sports as kids, competed like thoroughbreds for spots at exclusive universities, and have, for lack of a better word, "aggressively" planned their careers, we are just as guilty of this misconception as anyone else.

Girl Power Gone Bad?

Theories on the roots of this female vs. female aggression have fueled a wave of best-sellers, including Rachel Simmons's *Odd Girl Out* and Rosalind Wiseman's *Queen Bees and Wannabes*. These books argue that because girls have no socially approved outlet for anger, they take their conflicts underground and engage in sophisticated psy-ops against each other. This "hidden culture of aggression among girls" plays out through ritualized rumor spreading, practiced doses of the silent treatment, and the formation of rigid cliques that routinely gang up on an "odd girl out," making her life a living hell. Wiseman says, "Our best politicians and diplomats couldn't do better than a teen girl does in understanding the social intrigue and political landscape that leads to power."[4]

If you're having any trouble understanding what all this means, just close your eyes and think back to junior high school. Alternatively, think about real events you hear about in the news, such as the elaborate and highly publicized girl-on-girl hazing ritual that took place in 2003 in an affluent Chicago suburb and led to the criminal prosecutions of 12 teenage girls.

The social Darwinism we learned at recess has had a profound influence on the women we have become. After conducting an in-depth investigation of workplace power dynamics, psychologist Donald Sharpstein concluded that women are far more likely to use gossip for revenge than men are.[5] Instead of leaving this juvenile behavior behind at the playground or prom, it seems that many of our peers are stuffing these sophomoric tricks into designer briefcases and acting out adult versions of preteen politics at work.

Can Women Be Sexist?

It's been 20 years since Melissa was unceremoniously banned from the "popular" table at Woodrow Wilson Junior High School, but she still worries that cliques and rumors are hurting her reputation. A stylish blonde vice president at a New York investment bank, Melissa felt an icy chill from some of her female colleagues when she was promoted. At first, she thought she was being paranoid, but that changed after a disappointing encounter in the office bathroom.

"I was putting on some lipstick, and I overheard two of the analysts gossiping about me from behind the stalls," Melissa recalls. "They said, 'The only reason Melissa got the job is because she is sleeping with Jim.' They went on and on about how my skirts are too tight and my heels too high, and they said that I flirt with my married boss. Obviously, none of this is true—I worked very hard to get the promotion and am more than qualified for the job.

"In addition to pissing me off, the comments just make me sad because I thought Rose and Melinda—two accomplished colleagues with MBAs—were beyond that type of petty gossip. The whole thing reminded me of my days as a high school cheerleader. At some point in your life, you really hope to get beyond it."

Although there are plenty of women working in the financial world, the testosterone-drenched trader culture famously depicted in the book *Liar's Poker* remains very real. For every Melissa, Rose, or Melinda competing in the financial marketplace, there are dozens of guys who still view the trading floor as a frat house. Given the ethnography of their professional environment, it's especially surprising (and disappointing) to hear such a typical locker room remark coming from a *female* colleague. Has Gordon Gecko submerged Girl Power among Gen-X/Y women? We wondered, Just how hard are women making it for other women to get ahead at work? Are women guilty of sexism?

We sent out a mass e-mail posing these questions to friends, colleagues, and all the women we had interviewed during the course of our research. It took us about 5 minutes to realize that we had hit a nerve. Before long, our in-boxes were flooded with controversial responses of dueling extremes. For every nasty war story, we (happily) received an equally passionate response defending the good name of working women, with examples of female mentors who routinely helped others move up in the ranks. Once again, it was the intensity of all the responses—the complete absence of ambiguity—that struck us as most significant. When we followed up with phone calls and listened to story after story of both bona fide sabotage and inspiring female solidarity, we couldn't help but relate to both prosecution and defense.

We also couldn't help but notice a disturbing pattern that emerged during our conversations with new mothers. More than a dozen described similar scenarios in which supervisors made subtle comments about "priorities" when their pregnancies started to show; others detailed a downgrade in work assignments or exclusion from important meetings after they came back from maternity leave.

Pregnancy discrimination is nothing new—Lia's mother went through the same thing 30 years ago while teaching art in a public high school in Mount Pleasant, Pennsylvania. Back then, working through the late stages of pregnancy was actually a firing offense, and as her stomach grew bigger, she began to get concerned. She couldn't afford to lose her job, because Lia's dad was in law school at the time, and she was supporting their family. So she did some legal research of her own and discovered a state law on the books that trumped the local ordinance the school board had been using to keep pregnant women out of the classrooms. With this knowledge on her side, Lia's mother taught through the school year before giving birth to Lia at the end of June. Her efforts became known informally as the "Macko Amendment" and paved the way for other women to continue working through their third trimesters when it was still far from the norm.

Yet one very important difference exists between what Lia's mom went through and the scenarios our peers described. The earlier perpetrators of this brand of discrimination were usually men. This time around, the perpetrators are also women—in many cases, those past their baby prime who happen to be single and/or childless.

Baby Envy

A colleague responded to our inquiry with a very detailed, upsetting description of a run-in she had with her boss—a woman who is a legend in our business, with an office full of Emmys and other prestigious awards to prove it. Our friend had just returned from maternity leave to her job as an associate producer on a highly esteemed network newsmagazine show. Although there were many women on staff, the department culture was such that this new mom questioned whether putting a photo of her baby on her desk would make her look bad. Within her first week back on the job, a story was assigned about dog safety, focusing on dogs and infants. The reporter was on a tight deadline, and as luck would have it, our friend had an infant and a golden retriever, so off the team went to her home to shoot some footage of Fido and the baby. Back at the office later that day, our friend's boss screened the tapes, took a close look at the shot of the baby, then turned to her and said "Wow, you have a gorgeous dog!" No mention of her newborn.

While that comes nowhere close to meeting the legal definition of discrimination, the obvious omission marked an icy welcome back to work and a changed dynamic between employer and employee.

We wanted to believe that the stories we kept hearing were isolated incidents, but in good conscience, we consulted several well-respected employment lawyers and asked for their opinions. They told us our informal survey had tapped into an emerging phenomenon, one in which a significant and growing number of young women are reporting acts of discrimination by female bosses during pregnancy and/or after maternity leave. One attorney described the perpetrators as women who felt they had been forced to make an either/or choice about career and family. And now—often unconsciously—they assume that by getting pregnant, their direct reports have made their choice and are no longer committed to their careers.

Our peers are far more likely to understand their legal rights than most women were 30 years ago, which in part helps to explain why Equal Employment Opportunity Commission data indicates a dramatic increase in pregnancy discrimination lawsuits filed over the past decade. It's also important to recognize that the number of complaints filed against female bosses has increased, at least in part, simply because this is the first time that two (and sometimes even three) generations of professional women find themselves working together in the first place. Yet, one would think that an increased awareness about what constitutes pregnancy discrimination, combined with an increased number of women working together, would lead to a *decrease*—not an increase—in cases filed. However, recent studies from American University's Center for Gender, Work, and Family argue that frank and open statements by employers reflecting the view that "new mothers don't belong in the workplace" are driving a new wave of gender discrimination—from women as well as men.

Terri, an attorney in Oregon, encountered a fierce and unexpected bout of "baby envy" after the birth of her first child and her shift to part-time status at her job. This composed redhead wasn't about to let herself get bitch-slapped, however. She fought back.

● TERRI, 33 YEARS OLD
ATTORNEY
Portland, Oregon

As a child advocacy lawyer for an agency designed to help women and children, I never expected to encounter any bias at work after Sydney was born. However, my supervisor—a 50-year-old woman who routinely works a 6- to 7-day week—informed me in my one-year review that as long as I continued with my new 3½-day schedule, my career would suffer. This was true, she argued, despite the fact that I still had just as many clients as most of my full-time colleagues and am one of the most experienced and respected attorneys on staff.

After I returned from maternity leave, my boss routinely excluded me from high-level meetings and often made remarks about my decision to have a baby. In one memorable conversation, when we were discussing the evolving nature of alimony and child support laws that are routinely part of general consulting work we do, she helpfully informed me that if my husband and I should ever divorce, she would testify for me regarding the "harm" inflicted on my career by my choice to have a baby. The awfulness of that comment—on so many levels—affected me profoundly. After that conversation and my review, I realized that things were not going to improve, and I had a choice to make: I could let this woman make me feel guilty about wanting a family and real professional aspirations, or I could refuse to accept it and find a better part-time alternative.

I chose the latter. It would have been easy to stay, suck it up, and just write her off as crazy. The pay was good, the benefits were better, and the hours allowed me the quality time with my little girl that was the point in the first place. But I thought I deserved better, so I braced myself for the energy, dedication, and risk required for a covert job search in a small, specialized legal market—in the middle of a recession.

Terri acted wisely and aggressively, with precision and without emotion. She consulted an employment attorney so she knew how to protect herself if the workplace aggression escalated or if her job search was discovered and she encountered any retaliation. Then she conducted a quiet and strategic job hunt by first approaching former colleagues for "advice"—colleagues who happened to love her work and value her as an employee. One of them offered to hire her, but instead of committing immediately, Terri countered with a proposal that provided a flexible workweek and responsibility for the budget and management of a special projects division. Now Terri is writing groundbreaking reports with her own byline, and the projects she oversees are generating meaningful dialogue among leaders in her area in her state. And she's only been at the job for four months.

I was grateful for an opportunity to escape, but I didn't want to make a parallel move. I learned the hard way that at a certain point in your career, working part-time can make you vulnerable, irrespective of how hard you are working or how well liked you are, unless you are directly accountable for your own projects. Sure, I still have some trouble juggling responsibilities, and the new job requires more travel and a longer commute, but I am extremely grateful I was able to create this type of opportunity for myself—finding a job like this is almost as impossible as finding a needle in a haystack. And not to sound like a jerk, but part of me revels in taking my skills to a competitor. I hope it makes my former supervisor reconsider her actions the next time she's managing the career of a promising lawyer—and mother.

The Office Generation Gap

While not all interaction between Gen-X/Y women and their Boomer bosses is so extreme, there are tangible differences in the way women of different ages approach projects and define professional expectations. If you consider the bigger picture, this makes sense. What it means to be a successful woman has changed so dramatically—in such a compressed time frame—we are in the midst of nothing short of sociological whiplash. The speed of these changes has created friction between Boomer and Gen-X/Y women in the workplace, often leaving us to feel more divided then perhaps we really are.

Yet even in the most collegial of environments, Gen-X/Y women are not always picking up the baton from Boomer women and running beside them in the same race. Young working women have developed their own set of the workplace "do's" and "don'ts" that often clash with Boomer women's rules about competition, productivity, and ambition. We are experiencing office generation gaps about everything from timetables for promotions to facility with new technologies. The tension has started to boil over: many human resources managers report workplace conflicts between younger and older have outpaced conflicts between the genders.[6]

During a recent interview, Gloria Steinem admitted, "A woman in her twenties or thirties and I are almost in parallel universes. We have different references, as if we are in two different countries." We interviewed women in their forties and fifties who perceived their younger colleagues as selfish, and we found that some women in their twenties and thirties compare their Baby Boomers colleagues to nagging mothers-in-law. Some Boomers consider us disrespectful of the breakthroughs that they fought hard to achieve. Some Gen-X/Y women say, move over, we are ready for our next promotion.

Suzanne Braun Levine explored these emerging generations gaps in the *More* magazine article, " *'You Ruined Men!'* And other outrageous, annoying and maybe truthful things younger women are saying about us." She writes:

> "I see our complaints are mirror images: They think we are p.c., victim-oriented, domineering, and no fun. We see them as cavalier about the breakthroughs we fought so hard for and entirely lacking in social conscience. They claim we put self-fulfillment ahead of family. We counter that they put self-indulgence ahead of efforts to change the system . . . their complaints play into our regrets and even, deep down, our twinges of jealousy. . . .But we're not about to admit our second thoughts, just as they are not about to let on how often they, for all their big talk, sometimes feel insecure."[7]

Carole Hyatt is a best-selling author, speaker, and career specialist who has devoted her career to helping women succeed in business. She describes the generational backlash and misunderstanding that begins when women reject the choices of their working or non-working mothers. "My mother was a true 'professional mother,'" says Hyatt. "Her life was about entirely about being a mother—she was there for me after school, packing lunches, making dinner, helping with homework. And I couldn't stand it, couldn't wait to get away from her. I remember that I was so excited to join the Brownies. I show up and she has a surprise— she is the Brownie leader! She had so much energy and she put it into her children.

"So I determined early that I would be a working mother. It is not that I wasn't around, but I bought into the message of 'quality time.'. . . I thought it would be great to appear on weekends and to travel with my daughter, yet it turned out that wasn't perfect either. No matter what choices we make, what we still haven't figured out is how our children— and especially our daughters—will accept the balance we chose to create," Hyatt concludes.

One mother/daughter duo, who attended one of Hyatt's workshops, continues to discuss how they've overcome some of these moments of generational conflict and how their differences play out in their life choices. Anne Janas is a 56-year-old vice president of corporate communications for Hachette Filipacchi Media. Her daughter, Sterling Eason, is a 35-year-old who has already mastered a myriad of professions in a number of geographic locations, from managing stage productions in London theaters, to directing experiential brand campaigns for high profile clients in New York.

ANNE: I got married when I was 20 and had Sterling when I was 21, so those first years were about survival. It was a matter of going out and getting a job and making enough income to pay for her father to finish his undergraduate and master's degrees. So in the beginning, I did not even perceive work as anything more than an opportunity to bring money into the house. The first 6 or 7 years I worked as a secretary because I knew how to type, and in the late 1960s that was a reliable, good paying job with benefits. So the sacrifice that came from my end was two-fold—the largest was not being able to be a

stay-at-home mother in those early stages of her life. The second was
that what I really wanted to be was an artist.

STERLING: Most of my friends' mothers did not work when I was growing
up; they were not "career moms." Most of my friends went home
from school and their mothers were there with cookies. I wanted
my mom to make sandwiches for me and cut the crust off and make
perfect little triangles. But instead, I often had Indian leftovers for
my lunch! Eventually, it got to the point where I really liked that; it
was only early on that I wanted more traditional things, because I
saw other kids having them.

When Sterling was 6 or 7 years old, Anne decided to integrate her
artistic interests into her professional life. She took some graphic design
courses and, based on the portfolio she created, she was hired for a creative position at a television station. "Once I started seeing how much fun
it was to go with her on the job, it really changed," Sterling recalls of the
occasional days and working weekends she spent with her mom on the
job. "She tried to make it fun. If you are in that situation, you have to try
to adapt. If she were a stay-at-home mom in the afternoon, she would
have played games with me, but she was a working mom so she played
games with me at her work."

As adults, these two women acknowledge the differences and similarities regarding the challenges of their respective generations.

ANNE: One of the things about my generation—we were often the only
woman at that table. That became a real personal challenge to me.
I really wanted to break through those barriers—it was a game, it
was a challenge. It was very satisfying to me to see that one woman
at the table turned into two, turned into three, turned into four. I
really didn't see it as every woman who came to that table as taking
away from my situation. I was a feminist with a capital "F," but still
very proud of it, and I feel that rather than your generation having
any sense of entitlement, part of it might be that the legacy is in fact,
there is some flexibility on your part.

STERLING: I think they have set the bar high. We are there to meet it and set it even higher, and I think everyone expects that. These women were fighting the image of June Cleaver; we are fighting the image of Britney Spears. It's all the same, just a different place in time.

Sterling adds, however, that while some aspects of the mission are the same, women like her mother support choices that were different than their own, especially when it comes to new timetables for family and children. "I feel like my mother's generation has given us a supporting hand in saying, 'It's okay if you guys want to wait. We get it. We did it early and it was hard and we are envious of your ability to choose more freely than we did.'"

And Sterling is right—the choices women are making today about their careers are very different than those our mothers made, and everyone is not as enlightened as Sterling and Anne about these differences. After all, consider just how much has changed in the last 30 years. If you were to have asked the average suburban mother in 1973 to define "work-life balance" or "family-friendly company," you'd get a blank stare not unlike the one you'd get today if you asked your grandmother to define "bling-bling" or "asymmetrical warfare." Three decades ago, someone with Sterling's diverse professional resume might have been profiled by *Ms.* magazine. In today's world where women nearly outnumber men in business schools, gutsy women like Sterling remain impressive—but their accomplishments have been mainstreamed. What has not been mainstreamed, however, is what they will do next—and how it will affect the direction of their careers and the quality of the lives they choose to lead.

From Glass Ceilings to Jagged Shards

What is clear from this discussion is that twenty- and thirty-something women are operating in a working world that's radically different from the one our working mothers faced when they were our age. While certain tradeoffs may still be necessary, our choices are of an entirely different breed than those available to our mothers and grandmothers, and for this, we should be endlessly grateful. However, when a glass ceiling breaks, the floor underneath becomes littered with tiny, razor-sharp shards. The hurdles we face may be less visible than the ones our mothers faced, but the intensity of the lingering dissonance regarding women and power is still causing considerable damage.

One thing is abundantly clear: Women have real power over other women. We think it's time to use that power to generate a collective call for the workplace changes necessary to allow more than a lucky few the ability to pursue lucrative, high-impact careers while still enjoying meaningful personal lives and/or motherhood. If the women of our generation don't initiate meaningful dialogue—and make a pact to identify an incremental plan to close the ever-expanding gulf between What Has Changed and What Has Stayed the Same—the workplace will invariably continue to demand more. Make no mistake, feminism's gains are clearly at risk; if things progress at the same pace, the pendulum of women's progress may eventually swing backward to the point where a fulfilling personal life and a successful career are mutually exclusive pursuits—and our choices will be black-and-white again.

CHAPTER FOUR

Happily Ever After, Revised

ONE OCTOBER EVENING, Lia had a blind date and nothing to wear, so she went to the boutique around the corner from her apartment for some emergency shopping. All she wanted was a new sweater, but when it was discovered she was prepping for an evening out with a mystery man, the salespeople mobilized assistants into action. A storewide "strategy session" ensued, and before long, everyone was involved in the cause. "Wear this shirt (low cut), this skirt (tight and black), these boots (thigh high)—Do what we say and he'll marry you. Good luck!" Lia found the episode amusing and joked that she must be getting old if people were so earnestly wishing her "good luck" and treating her blind date with a friend of a friend of a friend as such a special occasion.

On a deeper level, however, the shopping incident illustrates important aspects of the undertow pulling so many of us toward a Midlife Crisis at 30. For the past decade, both the internal and external pressures to get married have been largely overshadowed by the momentum we felt to establish ourselves as independent women. But at 30, those pressures move center-stage, and many young single women have a wake-up call inspired in part by an unexpected onslaught of contradictory cultural messages. And these messages are far more pervasive than some "helpful" fashion tips from saleswomen working on commission.

"A Woman Needs a Man Like a Fish Needs a Bicycle" was plastered across many a bumper sticker, T-shirt, and lapel button when we were growing up. More recently, *Time* magazine put the stars of *Sex and the City* on its cover and made the same point all over again in a headline that asked "Who Needs a Husband, Anyway?" Sarah Jessica Parker, Candace Bushnell, and Gloria Steinem answered that question by walking down the aisle and saying "I do" in their real lives, reinforcing the confusion among a generation of women who are realizing just how much they want a man in their lives—even if they've been socialized to believe they don't *need* one.

This confusion quickly escalates to panic when the same women who were celebrated during their twenties for their accomplishments, independence, and degrees are suddenly hit with a wave of unsettling encounters on the other side of 30. Dermatologists start to suggest early Botox treatments, and everyone from Aunt Sylvia to the accountant starts to ask probing questions about your "life plan" and whether it includes a husband and children. Anxiety builds as it becomes obvious that the average thirty-something is more likely to encounter someone who knows that the dictionary once defined *spinster* as an unmarried woman over 30 than to meet someone who knows the average age of first marriage for college-educated women is close to 28.

It's also at this crucial interval that many single women realize that Mr. Right is nowhere in sight, and begin to second-guess all of their choices of the past decade. Thirty-two-year-old Pam explains, "My career is on track and I have great friends, but when it comes to love, I'm totally behind in the program. The main question I keep coming up with—and I've been asked it by others, too, which is a rather awkward question to answer—is, 'Why am I still single? Why hasn't anyone snapped me up?'" Millions of other attractive and happening young women join Pam in her inability to figure out the answer.

But single women aren't the only ones feeling ambushed by conflicting cultural directives and the shifting emotional priorities that kick into gear around 30. Many Gen-X brides, settling into life after the honeymoon, also struggle to close their individual Expectation Gaps between the fantasy of Happily Ever After and the "what are we having for dinner tonight?" reality of married life. New mothers go through a similar re-alignment after inevitably realizing that their angelic infants trigger not only maternal bliss but also unexpected tradeoffs and new pressures.

From dating to marriage to motherhood, Happily Ever After is in a state of flux. The findings from our research were very clear: Around their thirtieth birthdays, regardless of what life threshold they're crossing, Gen-X women are becoming deeply confused about why key relationships in their lives look so different from the way they thought they would look—and they blame themselves for failing to live up to outdated (and often inflated) expectations. Knowing that the Midlife Crisis at 30 is often more painful and bewildering when it comes to our personal lives, we set out to examine the gap between What Has Changed and What Has Stayed the Same through a different prism: how we look for love and what happens after we find it.

Single by Choice?

As we venture into our thirties, Gen-X/Y women have developed a view of love that's a strange brew of romantic ideals and cynicism. In a recent Gallup poll of single 20- to 29-year-olds, nearly all the women surveyed agreed, "When you marry, you want your spouse to be your soul mate, first and foremost."[1] The belief that a soul mate is "still out there" is also close to unanimous.[2] Yet, while this faith in the existence of a perfect partner is nearly absolute, there is less confidence that a perfect union can be sustained: 68 percent say it's more difficult to have a good marriage today than it was when their parents were married.[3] In short, the survey says we are true believers in Prince Charming, but we have a decidedly less romantic vision of the Happily Ever After part of the fairy tale.

Part of our inability to bridge the gap between romantic expectations and real-life commitment comes from the fact that it takes many of us a long time to get serious about dating and even longer to get to a place within ourselves where we are honest about our individual expectations for our romantic futures. To really understand just how much has changed in the way we look for love, consider how normal it was for women of our mothers' generation to go to college for their "MRS" degree. Today, the 21-year-old co-ed who frets about a finding a husband is as out of place on campus as Jerry Falwell at an Eminem concert. Twenty-something women's attitudes about sex also reflect this changed point of view: 84 percent of college-educated single women ages 20 to 29 agreed, "It is common these days for people my age to have sex just for fun and not expect any commitment beyond the encounter itself."[4]

All of this sexual sampling and unintentional romantic procrastination is further complicated by the Girl Power lessons of our youth, which instructed us not to "settle" in any part of our lives. Not surprisingly, these views have also come to shape our belief in a soul mate and the unconscious desire to hold out for the perfect person with whom we have the best chance of lifelong happiness. But despite all this optimism and the impressive statistics that suggest America's 40 million women have more collective consumer and political clout than the AARP, very few women would describe themselves as single by choice. At the end of the day, most women still want a faithful partner, who's legally required to be there through the good and the bad, much more than new Santa Fe tiles for the kitchen or that next big promotion. And even with our admirable independence and our good intentions, the vast majority of empowered single women at 30 and beyond are confused about why they are alone and how time managed to slip away.

The Sequential Success Trap

Celine has clear blue eyes, steady hands, and the street smarts of a native New Yorker. Although her Brooklyn attitude has served her well in the competitive world of professional kitchens, her close relationships with her sister and her childhood friends have always been her real source of strength.

Celine thought her life was very much on track during her twenties, but when she hit 30, she began to question whether the path she chose had led her in the wrong direction.

● CELINE, 33 YEARS OLD
CHEF
New York City

I remember days in my early childhood when my mom and I would sit around and watch Julia Child episodes, one after the other. Though I can remember other people telling me that I should be a chef, my parents raised me with the credo that if you expose your children to enough experiences, they will drift toward what they like, toward what they are good at. I think that's the best way to describe my career ladder, as a series of drifts.

I spent a year at college, spending too much money on much too free-form an education. I left for Paris shortly after completing a year of my BA to really test myself in the culinary world. At the time, it seemed like I was also trying to get a bug out of my system, to cook and to travel. One really allowed for the other in my mind—and the idea of a profession that could be translated into any culture, language, or country was a great draw and continues to motivate me in the field.

In those early professional days, I had to be strong because more often than not, I was the only woman in the room. While I never really thought of myself as a feminist, my career led me right into the belly of the sexist beast. I was trying to be a chef when women were still few and far between at the professional stove.

A typical night was me in chef uniform—sweating, yelling, working at a clip to keep up with my own ego and those of my male peers, making mindless small talk with the other cooks on the line that I'd stand next to every day in a 10-foot space. The conversation was limited because their days consisted of little more than just coming and going to work, like myself. The wee hours off were spent drinking for free at the bar where we worked—and the cycle was complete.

For years, I was just as good at trash talking as the next guy, and my experiences backed me up. I thought only of the next step up my career ladder, about experiencing what I like, about traveling even if that meant being alone. I dated a lot of men over that period, mostly thinking that there are as many good men as bad out there, as many Mr. Wrongs as Mr. Rights, and that I could only find one of my soul mates if I kept trying. My schedule made it difficult to develop a consistent relationship, and at the time, I didn't mind.

After a few years of cooking, I burned out. I left the daily kitchen grind and instead, I stayed alive by catering freelance while I completed a BA in film at Hunter College back home in New York. Gradually, the late nightlife that I had cultivated for years succumbed to early study nights and busy study weekends— that is, in between catering jobs. I had a Big Love in my life then, someone that I lived with. Unfortunately, when I changed my life to go back to school, he couldn't change with me. When I realized that being in a relationship meant compromising things I felt I needed to do, I realized I wasn't willing to sacrifice to be in a couple—not yet, at least.

When I turned 30, all of this changed. My sister had kids, and friends started having children, too. My thoughts began to fall less and less to work and more to what was in my life when work was finished. So . . . I approached my thirtieth year fraught with regret and confusion. What had I done all those years? After all those dates and living situations, I saw fewer chances of meeting "the one" and more the chance to meet someone who "isn't as bad as" or someone "I could live with." I was also haunted by my mother's choices—at my age, she already was married and had my sister and me. In comparison, my past was starting to seem like a mindless waste of time.

Like Celine, many of the women we interviewed shared a key unspoken assumption: They viewed a certain level of success and personal development as a *prerequisite* for a marriage of equals that would last "until death do us part." As if through some mythological voodoo, most young women today believe that the more exotic life experiences we collect, the more likely we'll encounter and recognize Mr. Right, a sensitive knight in shining armor who respects our careers *and* wants to take care of us. As long as we stay away from the trap-a-husband shenanigans of "The Rules" girls, the general consensus has been that the right relationship with the right man will materialize at precisely the right moment, at the snap of our perfectly manicured fingers.

As far as marriage goes, the beliefs of most of the Gen-X/Y women we spoke with can be summed up as "all good things come to those who wait." A Gallup poll echoed our research, finding that 87 percent of single women in their twenties believe they will find their soul mates "when they are ready."[5] And unquestionably, "ready" means very different things to different women. For some, it means finishing grad school, law school, or med school. Others can't imagine settling down until they've gone on a few *Lonely Planet* world adventures or completed a tour of duty in the Peace Corps. And "ready" sneaks up on plenty of us after making a first unquestionably adult purchase, such as a couch that isn't a futon, expensive lingerie, a car, or a home. But what only a very few of the women we interviewed anticipated *before* their thirtieth birthdays was that maybe there is no such thing as perfect timing, and perhaps the most reliable "ready" barometer has nothing to do with external events.

You see, until now, most Gen-X/Y women have built adult lives rooted in one very basic premise. Unlike our mothers, who believed that a career could come *after* marriage, we believe a career must come *before* marriage. Many of us have been guided by the powerful, unspoken assumption that life would play out in finite stages, in a New Sequential Order. Stage One: work and individual development. Stage Two: marriage. Stage Three: kids. Of course, it's incredibly presumptuous to think that life could ever unfold in such an orderly fashion, yet the real reason so many of us feel like we've hit a wall is that somewhere along the way, we forgot to connect the dots. Both as individuals and as a larger culture, we've compartmentalized our visions of success into rigid categories that are, by their very definition, on a collision course with each other.

By the time women like Celine finally grew up enough to realize that what they really wanted was stages one (work and personal development), two (marriage), and three (children) all at the same time, it was too late for a quick fix. They were already entrenched in patterns that didn't allow much breathing room. About this time, that Perfect Plan began to feel like a prelude to dysfunction.

Lia fell right into this trap. At 29, she thought she had the whole life/work/love situation figured out. She had been able to control her professional success via a steady wave of promotions, and she had no reason to believe this would not continue. At the rate she was going, she would be able to shift her focus to love, marriage, and children "in a few years," after arriving at a more secure professional perch.

Lia dated some wonderful men and fell in love a few times during her twenties, but when those relationships ended, she actually felt relief instead of despair. This is not to say she didn't have her fair share of Ben and Jerry's after disappointing, heart-wrenching breakups or that she didn't feel there was something profound missing from her life. But somewhere along the way, Lia intercepted a message about independence that became a defining myth: Because she had no intention of "settling" in the relationship department, she thought she was *supposed* to become as "evolved" as possible before she could even consider the possibility of a soul mate. She thought this meant she needed to do more, learn more, and achieve more before she would emerge as an equal to an exceptional partner.

But Lia now sees that her theory was embarrassingly naïve. In the personal arena, it overlooked the fact that people often grow more together than they do on their own. In the professional sphere, it failed to take into account that certain aspects of life can never be controlled. And as Lia approached 30, she realized that with each move up the ladder, she had won less and less control over her life and found herself in jobs increasingly removed from her professional goals.

Days before her thirtieth birthday, she left her job. She was committed to the pace of her profession but realized that the grind had distracted her from her true goals and desires. She wanted to move forward with focus and regain some clarity before committing to another contract or long-term project. Hitting "pause" at this particular moment seemed like a good idea.

The Sequential Success Trap and the Divorce Insurance Policy have led Gen-X women to similar ends via different means. As we have illustrated in previous chapters, the Divorce Insurance Policy has led many women to focus on financial and emotional independence *before* marriage as a conscious (or unconscious) act of self-protection from the fallout of divorce. But whereas the Divorce Insurance Policy has evolved as an emotional response to a social problem, the Sequential Success Trap has grown from an entirely different set of circumstances. The women who fell into the Sequential Success Trap found themselves there because they simply focused on self-development and careers for a decade or more while they attempted to make good on the Anything Is Possible promise.

As a generation, we have inherited unprecedented professional opportunities, but we still lack a guidebook for how to take advantage of them in a way that also acknowledges our parallel desires for marriage, motherhood, and an otherwise fulfilling life outside the office. And in this lies the missing link in the true evolution of the empowered woman. We have learned how to succeed like men, but we still have not figured out what it means to succeed on our own terms. The issue is not that Boomer women didn't run far enough down the field with the ball, but rather that by sprinting to finish first in our own lives, we stopped working as a team to complete the unfinished business of the women's movement. And ironically, those who are now paying the highest price are the Gen-X/Y women who most enthusiastically embraced the Girl Power message.

Searching for a Soul Mate

Kerry met 31-year-old Rebecca at a dog park for their interview. As they watched her Labrador puppy, Rufus, tirelessly attempt to get the attention of a blasé Great Dane, Rebecca opened up about her love life. "My twenties vis-à-vis relationships were about experimenting, impulsive decisions, adventures—though that sounds more glamorous than it was," she admitted. "Up until now, dating has been more about self-discovery than finding someone to settle down with. It's a whole different game."

The Sequential Success Trap certainly has not stopped young women from falling in love, but it has changed the way they look for it. On some fundamental level, many of us have been approaching dating as research for figuring out who we are and who we want to become as much as (if not more than) figuring out who we want to marry. Dating has become part of the process of shaping who we are as *independent* adults, essentially acting as a kind of mirror to help us envision what we might want our futures to look like as individuals. In many cases, the desire to become someone in our own right before becoming someone's partner has transformed dating into part of Stage One (personal development) rather than a preface to Stage Two (marriage). But what many Gen-X women haven't anticipated is that there might be a downside to all that romantic meandering.

Thirty-six-year-old Betsy is a tall blonde with a gentle Southern accent and a lot of charisma. She runs marathons and performs stand-up comedy in local clubs in her spare time. When you spend any time with her, you find it easy to understand why she's so good at closing difficult deals with cranky clients—it's tough to say no to her.

Betsy has enjoyed the freedom of being single—until recently.

● BETSY, 36 YEARS OLD
TALK SHOW PRODUCER
New York City

You know those times when you are bored or don't feel pretty, so you go buy a new outfit? Something wild, something daring, something sexy or rockstar-ish? It makes you feel transformed for a minute, like someone other than yourself. I have done this all my life with men. I wanted to try different ones on, like a new pair of jeans, to make myself feel new or pretty or cool or alive.

There was John, the long-haired, rich, good-looking, standoffish jerk. Duke, the simple-minded, cute house builder who loved me but talked too much, too soon about building us a house so we could have lots and lots and lots and lots of babies right away. Bud, the fast-talking, chain-smoking sales guy. Kirk, the musician who took me to almost every concert there was in Atlanta. Phil, the tall Jewish genius who looked like Kramer, loved to talk world politics, and flew me with him wherever he went—except I barely kissed him once in two years. Todd, so good-looking I couldn't stand it, except he never spoke unless he was talking dirty in bed.

I have always said I would never "settle" just to settle down. I wanted to make sure I married the right guy, and I think that's why I have dated so many different types of men. I always knew I wanted to be with a guy who made me laugh, but beyond that I've been pretty fuzzy about what an ideal husband would actually be like. Now I am realizing that I have spent a lot of time chasing passions and not enough time really looking for love. While I do believe that my soul mate is still out there, I'm starting to worry that I may be facing a really lonely future. Maybe in all this looking for Mr. Right, I have been secretly afraid to really find him.

Like most red-blooded women, Betsy yearns for a relationship that is full of passion, romance, and excitement. But after dating for more than a decade, she is now realizing that can't-eat/can't-sleep infatuation doesn't always translate into enduring love. And though Betsy need not compromise passion, it is time for her to separate the fantasy of what she thinks she wants in a man from the reality of what she really wants from a committed, long-term relationship.

The Romantic Expectation Gap

Since macho *Homo heidelbergensis* flaunted his superb hunting skills in Europe and Africa more than 600,000 years ago, women have been hardwired to look for mates who will be good providers. But as women gained opportunities to provide for themselves over the past few generations, expectations have changed. Instead of thinking of matrimony as a practical union, today's women expect their "evolved" mates to provide more than basic necessities. In "The State of the Union," a *Ladies Home Journal* special report, University of Texas sociology professor Norval Glenn, Ph.D., explains, "People now believe that a relationship with one person should meet all their emotional needs. In most cases, that isn't going to happen."[6]

Plenty of the Gen-X/Y single women stuck on Stage One's Have-It-All treadmill are holding out for these perfect partners—and not surprisingly, they are having a tough time meeting men who are in step with their romantic expectations. Case in point: A recent *Time* magazine poll reported that 66 percent of single women say they would get married only if they met the *right* man.[7] And what does the right man look like? Kate, a 34-year-old small business owner, says, "I don't need someone to support me financially or provide me with a feeling of purpose or, as they say, 'complete me.' UGH! I am whole. I want to find a man to be my best friend and my equal partner in everything. I have become very choosy about who I date. If he isn't going to be my soul mate—what's the point?"

As we mentioned earlier, the term "soul mate" comes up a lot when you talk about love with Gen-X/Y women. Like Kate, most of the women we interviewed insisted that they were not looking for a Prince

Charming—then, without missing a beat, they described an equally un-attainable ideal. It's ironic that we've developed such lofty expectations of our potential husbands at a time when nearly 50 percent of marriages still end in divorce. Perhaps settling for nothing less than an equal-partner-in-everything/best friend/soul mate is another manifestation of the Divorce Insurance Policy: Whereas marriages between mortals may fall apart, a marriage between soul mates is bulletproof. It's no accident that the phrase "soul mate" has an almost spiritual ring to it, too. After all, if God can't guarantee a marriage made in heaven, who can?

Anthropologist Helen Fisher, Ph.D., of Rutgers University in New Brunswick, New Jersey, has devoted her entire career to examining the history, biology, and social dynamics of male-female relationships. For her latest work, *Why We Love: The Nature and Chemistry of Romantic Love*, she hooked up hundreds of couples to MRIs and discovered the brain chem-istry of love. "*Soul mate* is a lovely term, but it's hard to find and hard to keep," Dr. Fisher says. "As women have become more independent, we have gained the luxury of becoming wildly romantic about love. We live in a society where you can obtain material things with ease and exert a lot of control over career and health. But at the same time, community and family have become highly unstable.

"The human animal will always look for a sense of connectedness, but those instincts are now being directed toward one person, which is an unprecedented demand on a basic partnership. Although romantic love existed in even the most primitive societies, the search for a soul mate is a truly modern dilemma. The word *intimacy* did not even exist in Shake-speare's time."[8]

We may not be the first generation of women to realize that a good man is hard to find, but the cultural gold standard for what makes a man "good" has become pretty steep. Our movies, love songs, and bridal mag-azines reinforce the idea that love is always magical, while our earthly ex-perience indicates otherwise. Any honest, *happily* married woman would admit that her soul mate/husband is guilty of a laundry list of choice im-perfections. Journalist Iris Krasnow pulls back the veil in her best-selling book, *Surrendering to Marriage*:

A successful marriage has little to do with sustained bliss and everything to do with surrendering to the grind. When you ask yourself, "Is this all there is?" about the spouse you've been sharing a bathroom with for 10 or 30 or 50 years, there's a good chance the answer is yes, this is it—jackhammer snoring, a man who watches too much sports, a husband who will never change. But if you look hard at what you also have—great kids, a loyal partner, a family unit as an anchor—usually you will discover that all that is yours, however imperfect, is more than enough.[9]

For Betsy, the big question is not whether her soul mate exists but whether she will still be able to recognize him as such when their relationship naturally evolves over time.

Let's pause for a moment to clarify something. We do not believe that "pickiness" is why the number of single women with college degrees has tripled since 1960.[10] We aren't implying that Gen-X/Y women should make extraordinary compromises for the purpose of snaring a husband, or that women who never marry are destined to have lonely, depressing lives. After interviewing young women around the country, however, this is what we know for sure: There are a lot of smart, attractive, kind, single women out there whose honest concern that they may never meet that Great Guy is causing them considerable angst. And when that angst coincides with other manifestations of the Midlife Crisis at 30, it creates a perfect storm of sorts, putting a lot of single women who consistently make good decisions about their lives at risk for making bad decisions about men. Some women panic and start to lower their standards, while others become frustrated by the whole dating process and start to feel confusion about what it is they even want from a partner.

A meaningful romantic relationship remains so elusive to Betsy and other women like her in part because, despite her well-rounded dating résumé, she remains quite unclear about what she's looking for in a mate. In the absence of a realistic vision of what that "soul mate" might actually be like, it's easy for a fantasy to set the course of your romantic compass.

Antoine de Saint-Exupéry once said, "Love does not consist in gazing at each other, but in looking at each other in the same direction." To that end, the *Time* magazine poll cited earlier posed the question, "If you could not find the *perfect* mate, would you marry someone else?" It's interesting to note that the results indicate that single men are significantly more open to compromise than single women are.[11] Despite the influence of porn, swimsuit models, Britney Spears, and the Dallas Cowboy Cheerleaders, men apparently have an easier time understanding that their future wives will probably be imperfect, real women who will *not* Have It All.

Training Wheels for Love

Not all women without wedding bands are waking up alone. Prenuptial cohabitation is quickly replacing marriage as the first shared household experience, and it has become a de facto "starter marriage" for growing numbers of young women. Over the course of just one generation, "living in sin" has gone from the scandalous to the mainstream. The number of heterosexual unmarried couples living together has jumped from under 500,000 in 1960 to close to five million in 2000.[12] Attitudes about shacking up have also changed considerably, as more than half of all Americans now see living together as a morally acceptable lifestyle. These shifts in the social landscape were not lost on Kerry's mother. "If I had moved in with your father with no ring on my finger, my mother would have absolutely killed me. Actually, scratch that. I wouldn't have ever even *thought* of doing something so unrespectable. It just was not an option; it would have been like saying 'Hmmm, should I take that express shuttle to the moon?'" she recalled. "But when you moved in with Adam, there I was heading to Pottery Barn to buy you guys a tablecloth. Times have definitely changed."

Barbara Dafoe Whitehead, Ph.D., codirector of Rutgers University's National Marriage Project, has spent her entire professional life examining just how much times have changed in regard to relationships and marriages. In her book *Why There Are No Good Men Left*, she notes, "In Western societies, a system of romantic courtship and marriage has governed mate selection for centuries." With the anthropological precision of Dian Fossey, Dr. Whitehead observes that unlike societies that practice arranged marriage, Western European and American cultures established a highly standardized dating process marked by well-defined rituals— ranging from the grand balls of the Victorian era to the sock hops of the 1950s—to ensure the road to marriage was a linear one. But as women have become more independent from men in recent years, the "romantic courtship system" has lost its grip, and a new "relationship system" has emerged that is far less marriage-oriented than the traditional system. Dr. Whitehead observes that "as marriage is the signature union of the established system, cohabitation is the signature union of the emerging relationship system."[13]

Even though each couple's decision to move in together is undoubtedly motivated by a variety of romantic notions and practical considerations, the fundamental allure of the "relationship system" is rooted in our generation's backstory. In many ways, the dramatic number of young unmarried couples living together is a direct response to the rampant divorce and unprecedented home front instability that marked our coming of age. Furthermore, many of us with indelible memories of messy divorces, flawed custody arrangements, and angry or depleted parents have unconsciously come to perceive living together as an opportunity to attain the benefits of marriage, with fewer risks. This helps explain the findings of a recent Gallup poll: 62 percent of Gen-Xers believe living together before marriage is the best way to predict if a relationship is built to last, and 43 percent say they would marry someone only if they lived together first.[14]

Jennifer is a striking 26-year-old Brown University alum who crunches numbers by day and moonlights as a hip-hop performance artist by night. She thought living under the same roof with her boyfriend of four years would provide some clarity about their prospects for marriage. "Divorce scares me," she says. "I don't see it as an option for my life. For that reason, I am extra-cautious when it comes to committing to the right person. Living together was a test that allowed me to experience what a life with John might be like."

Jennifer's situation didn't lead to wedding bells, but it did provide her with an opportunity to learn more about herself and what she wants from a committed relationship. It also enlightened her about some of the perils of viewing living together as a Divorce Insurance Policy.

● JENNIFER, 26 YEARS OLD
RESEARCH ANALYST
Chicago, Illinois

When my then-boyfriend moved in with me, it was somewhat understood that this was the make-or-break factor of our four-year relationship. We had our share of existing problems, but for some reason, we felt that living together might solve some of them. So I cleared out my smallest closet for his suits and ties, emptied out the bottom drawer of my dresser, and condensed my cosmetics into just two shelves of the medicine cabinet to make room for him in a very, very tiny studio apartment.

The first three weeks were pure bliss. We would come home from work and cook dinner together in the teeny, tiny kitchen, watch TV, brush our teeth together. It felt comfortable and secure and domestic! We laughed about how it felt like we were playing house.

After the moving-in-together honeymoon period ended, things got tough. While we still talked about the possibility of marriage in the future, we also got complacent because we were already living together, and neither one of us was challenging the other to move to the next stage anytime soon. Also, by living together, neither one of us had to make a concerted effort to see the other person—it was too easy, and it made us lazy. And when past problems resurfaced, living together was making it more difficult to make a clear and thoughtful decision on what to do with the relationship. It was even difficult to talk on the phone with my girl-friends about my relationship problems, since I had very little private time in our shared apartment. I felt trapped.

My gut was telling me that I should end the relationship, yet my practical side was telling me that I'd lose the roommate who was paying half my rent! The roommate who had dinner waiting for me when I got home. The roommate who was comforting to have around 24/7. There was definitely a temptation to continue with the relationship in spite of its imperfections.

Seven months after first moving in with me, he moved out—at my request. I felt relieved that I had made a decision but upset that our "test" had failed. However, I do feel fortunate to have made the realization that we did not belong together before we walked down the aisle. I have now made a commitment to myself that I will never live with another man unless we are engaged, because I feel like I just got divorced without ever being married.

Thirty years ago, chances are that Jennifer would have been a divorcee for real. In half the divorces filed in 1970, the wife was under 30 years old. Today, nearly half of women under 30 will have lived with a boyfriend without being married.[15] Living together has replaced first marriages for our generation, but while shared rent and steady companionship make living together attractive to cautious women like Jennifer, studies examining marriage trends reveal that cohabitation can actually be dangerous for those searching a for a long-term commitment.[16]

In a survey commissioned by the U.S. Department of Health and Human Services, 30- to 34-year-old women were asked about the outcomes of their first living-together experiences. The survey reported that 5 percent of the relationships were intact, 33 percent had broken up, and 60 percent had led to marriage. But three out of every five couples who married after living together had separated or divorced soon after they walked down the aisle. So although most of us presume that living together is a reliable litmus test for the viability of a marriage, the numbers tell a very different story. Instead of providing a Divorce Insurance Policy, cohabitation prior to marriage actually increases the risk of breaking up *after* marriage.[17]

Unmarried couples who live together also have lower levels of happiness than married couples.[18] One reason is that partners often have very different expectations about why they moved in together in the first place. Without socially acceptable guidelines or real rules for living together, there's a lot of room for misinterpretation. The default mode seems to be one in which the woman sees living together as a prelude to eventual marriage, while the man regards it as a chance to have sex and companionship on a regular basis without the ties of a long-term emotional or financial commitment. Yet moving in together with a plan that includes ongoing honest conversations about where the relationship is heading can help mitigate some of the shortcomings of the arrangement. "This is where we went wrong," says Jennifer. "It was understood that this was the vague next step leading to an eventual engagement, but we didn't have lengthy discussions about it when we decided to move in together. Interestingly, my boyfriend was the one who was more intent on getting engaged; I was feeling so uncertain about things that the thought of being engaged frightened me. Regardless of who is pushing for marriage more, being on two different levels about it while living together is dangerous. It just makes everything more tense."

While living with her boyfriend did help Jennifer determine whether the relationship was built to last, it also made the breakup more emotionally devastating. When marriages dissolve, there is a legal framework for dividing shared assets and an expectation of emotional support from religious institutions, group or individual counseling, and concerned family members. But when people who live together separate, the absence of cultural conventions that could soften the blow and facilitate the closure of the relationship often extends the recovery process, exacerbating the pain of the breakup.

Retro Renaissance?

The overall absence of guidelines for the full spectrum of modern romance—from dating to living together to moving out/breaking up—has left many Gen-X/Y women longing for the simpler, less ambiguous days of the "romantic courtship system." Whether you perceive it as a values renaissance or a retro backlash, considerable anecdotal evidence suggests that a burgeoning number of young women are approaching dating in way that can only be described as "old school."

In "Not Their Mothers' Choices," a *Newsweek* magazine essay, author and journalist Marie Brenner provides context for these trends: "Every generation resists the one before it . . . Susan Faludi has observed that we have seen a 160-year panorama of women advancing and retreating; Elizabeth Cady Stanton's and Susan B. Anthony's progress was threatened by late Victorian political and religious mores which accused women who postponed childbearing of triggering 'race suicide.' As the flappers advanced and women voted, the 1920s and '30s also saw a new wave of labor and federal laws that forced thousands of women out of work. There were fewer women doctors in 1930 than in 1910."[19] Against this backdrop, it should come as no surprise that some very modern young women are approaching romance the same way their grandmothers did.

Twenty-five-year-old Monica, a DJ at a Philadelphia nightclub, exudes cool. To spend time with her is to feel a sudden need to check your hair and makeup and question your entire wardrobe and CD collection. When it comes to her thoughts on dating, though, Monica is more Doris Day than Eve. "For so many of my friends, dating means going out to a club with a bunch of friends, then pairing off and hooking up at the end of the night," she says. "I do things differently. If a guy wants to go out with me, I expect him to take me on a proper date. He'd better call by Wednesday if he wants to take me out on Saturday. If I really like the guy and the date has been amazing, I'll give him a kiss good-night, or maybe on the dance floor. But nothing else.

"There are no one-night stands in my book. I would never, ever, ever live with a man before we got married. My grandmother says, 'Why buy the cow if you get the milk for free,' and I think she's right."

If you've already given away the milk for free, so to speak, don't worry—it's a renewable resource. The gravitational pull toward tradition strikes different women at different points in their relationships. Kerry would never have described herself as a "Rules Girl," but when she sensed a lack of clarity about her prenuptial living-together situation, she responded in a way she never would have imagined: She gave Adam a marriage ultimatum.

Kerry and Adam had been dating exclusively for 4½ years at the time—2 years of dating long distance, 2 years of dating in the same city, and six months of living together in a loft apartment around the corner from Frank Sinatra's childhood home. Things were good. They were dizzy in love, and the living-together experiment was clearly a success. But while they both assumed they would eventually marry, neither was in a rush to walk down the aisle. That changed for Kerry when her thirtieth birthday approached.

Her Plan was to bring up the topic of marriage in a heartfelt, loving conversation over a romantic candlelight dinner. Instead, she chickened out and did what most women in her situation do—she dropped hints. Big hints. But after Darling Adam gave her earrings for Christmas and a necklace for Valentine's Day, it was becoming crystal clear that he was clueless, and she was starting to get pissed off. The tension grew until one random day in the car, Kerry boiled over and unceremoniously blurted, "We have to either get married or break up!" Adam was thrown by Kerry's intensity and didn't say much at all at first. (Okay, there was dead silence.) Kerry felt like she was going to throw up.

Later that evening, they ended up having that heartfelt, loving conversation Kerry had imagined months earlier. Then, on Kerry's thirtieth birthday, Adam got down on one knee in their living room and proposed. He now describes that ultimatum as "a much-needed push that I am forever grateful for."

The Good Mother Marathon

By the time most women hit 30, they've come to terms with the reality that they will never be supermodel thin or Hollywood gorgeous. Then motherhood comes along, fully loaded with an unexpected new barrage of unrealistic images to absorb, images that glamorize the joys of motherhood while downplaying its inevitable struggles. The Expectation Gap between the warm, fuzzy daydreams of parental bliss and the exhausting reality of its more difficult moments is often filled with a heavy dose of maternal guilt, causing many young mothers to feel like failures (or even worse, Bad Mothers) when they clearly are not.

As we have pointed out, studies indicate that a significant number of women are putting off having children until after they've established careers. Many of those new mothers—women who came of age at work—are now approaching childrearing with the same intensity that propelled their professional lives.

At the same time, the requisites of being a "successful" mother have expanded over the past 30 years. Now, in addition to basic nurturing, the Good Mother is expected to be a creative playmate, a developmental psychologist, an education expert, and a ready volunteer. Cultural messages emanating from the *Today Show*, TLC specials on child development, and the 25 different parenting magazines on display at Barnes and Noble newsstands tell parents that they aren't getting the job done unless they engage their children in activities "with purpose." This has spawned an entire cottage industry of "enriching activities" that can make a five-year-old's schedule as harried as that of a sought-after neurosurgeon whose off-hours are packed with tap dance classes and scuba diving lessons.

All of this cultural pressure led many of the new mothers we interviewed to question themselves, to feel as if they were somehow failing their children. Naomi Wolf is the author of the best-selling *The Beauty Myth*, which helped to launch a new wave of feminism in the early 1990s and was named one of the most significant books of the twentieth century by the *New York Times*. In her latest book, *Misconceptions: Truth, Lies, and the Unexpected on the Journey to Motherhood*, she writes, "There is a powerful social imperative to maintaining our collective belief in the 'natural bliss' of new motherhood . . . . Because of the power of that image, many women feel permitted to ask few questions; we to often blame ourselves, or turn our anger inward, into depression, when our experience is at odds with the ideal."[20]

Thirty-five-year-old Julie refers to *Martha Stewart Living* as "my porn." Even in her swinging-single days in Atlanta, she was a domestic goddess —she made throw pillows for her couch, stenciled an indoor garden on her kitchen tiles, and covered every surface of her tiny apartment with pictures of friends and family. Julie was hosting dinner parties where the wine matched the food when most of her friends were still considering pizza a food group.

Now married with a one-year-old daughter, it's no surprise that Julie has navigated some of the challenges of contemporary motherhood with aplomb. Yet, even she was thrown off her game after confronting a new breed of monster lurking in the suburbs—the competitive Alpha Moms.

● JULIE, 33 YEARS OLD
Stay-at-home mother
Roswell, Georgia

Stay-at-home moms can be some of the most intense, ambitious women on the planet. I should know, because I just quit the playgroup from hell!

Let me start at the beginning. After Maddy was born, I quit my intense job. It was hard to do, but Brian and I decided we wanted a simpler life, so we left the city and moved to the suburbs. The loss of income hurts, but it feels like this is the right thing to do, and we'll get by with some sacrifices. For now, I love having a house—I am really excited about creating a home for us.

When I was working, I had lots of friends at the office, but I found it was a lot harder to find stay-at-home moms I could talk to about un-baby-related things. When I stumbled into this playgroup, I really thought I had hit the jackpot. There were four moms and five babies—me and Maddy, Jennifer and Hunter, Rachel and Kristina, Lesley and Jack, and Dianna and her twins, Aiden and Chelsea. All of the moms left corporate jobs at Coke, Delta, or CNN to raise their kids. I thought I had found a new group of best friends—smart, cool, women I could bond with while raising my child.

At first, I was thrilled to get their advice. These women seemed to know what they were doing; most of them had other children already. We are totally in love with Madison, but I'm not going to lie to you—figuring out what to do with a baby has been a little overwhelming at times. The owner's manual for children did not automatically download into my brain after giving birth. We are learning as we go.

It didn't take long for me to realize these mothers were a little over the top. They became weirdly competitive over things like new teeth and crawling. When Aiden said his first word, I swear to God, Dianna was gloating. And then there was the pressure to join a million classes. I have always been a "joiner," a doer, but this was ridiculous. There was Mommy and Me, Baby Gymboree, Water Babies, Baby Yoga, and Baby Sign Language—all this before Maddy was even a year old! I had not dealt with this kind of intensity since cheerleading tryouts in high school.

It was my husband who figured it out first—these moms had channeled into

childrearing all of the ambition and competitive energy that had once made them
rising stars in the corporate world. They loved their kids, but on some fundamental
level, they saw motherhood as a job, and their babies became the Big Account. They
tracked every development like spreadsheets.

Madison isn't a great sleeper, so I was exhausted all the time, and with this
new list of activities, I was wrecked. I stopped working full-time so I would be able
to spend a lot of time with our kids and do everything possible to make sure they
were happy and healthy. But here I was, with Maddy all the time and constantly
feeling guilty that I was not doing enough. The whole point of my staying at home
was to simplify our lives—but the baby and I were busier than ever. No matter what
I did, I felt like we were behind, and I started to question whether I was good
mother.

Many of the single Gen-X women we interviewed had internalized
Holy Grail visions of Having It All. When their lives and relationships inevitably fell short of their inflated expectations, they blamed themselves.
Julie's "playgroup from hell" illustrates how motherhood transforms that
search for the unattainable ideal, leaving many mothers with the unspoken
belief that the route to Having It All is Doing It All for their kids. Journalist Peggy Orenstein writes about the pressure mothers put on themselves in her book *Flux: Women on Sex, Work, Love, Kids, and Life in a
Half-Changed World*:

> The impossible standards they [mothers] set for themselves,
> shared by so many women, remind me of the teenage girls I
> used to interview, who, no matter what their weight, saw
> themselves as fat. I don't know whether there's a Perfect
> Mother equivalent to an eating disorder, but I wondered:
> How good does a mother have to be before she feels good
> enough?[21]

But to fully understand what's driving this hyperparenting trend, it's
important to examine the social context of our own childhoods. Gen-X
women came of age during the Me Generation, a time that Senator Daniel

Patrick Moynihan famously described as the first moment in history when children were not put first. During the 1970s, no-fault divorce passed, women went to work in droves, and the phrase "latchkey kids" entered the collective lexicon. Popular culture was not at all kid-friendly, either. The entire "human potential movement" essentially ignored the human potential of children. Erica Jong's best-seller *Fear of Flying* neglected to mention that *children* were often the natural by-product of all those "zipless fucks." Popular self-help books such as *Feel Free: How to Do Everything You Want without Feeling Guilty* argued that obligation and responsibility were synonymous with repression and unwillingness to change—and many children got lost in the shuffle as their parents tried to "find themselves." Hollywood, never known for its subtle interpretation of societal trends, cashed in with horror movies such as *Rosemary's Baby*, *The Exorcist*, *The Exorcist Two*, and *Damien*—all of which portrayed children as the Devil.[22]

While all parents swear they are going to raise their kids differently than they were raised, studies show that Gen-Xers are twice as likely as Boomers to say they don't have good role models for childrearing.[23] Perhaps the pressure that young women feel to be Perfect Mothers, and the intensity with which many of us are currently approaching parenting, is in part an overcompensation for what some of us believe we didn't learn by example.

The key to making peace with the pressures to be the Perfect Mother is to accept the reality that even Perfect Mothers have some limitations. Thankfully, Julie figured this out on her own.

The other morning, I took the Dr. Spock book off the shelf to look up something about crawling. I noticed again that the first sentence of the book is, "You know more than you think you do." And it finally sunk in: I do know what I am doing—and if I don't, I will figure it out. That's when I realized that I didn't need all of the advice from those moms. I am doing just fine on my own.

Now, I'm finally starting to enjoy the rhythms of life at home with Madison. I'm looking for a new playgroup, with mothers to whom I can relate. We quit a bunch of the classes, too. The baby can't tell the difference, and I am finally feeling less sleep deprived. But we still go to Water Babies because I don't want Maddy to be afraid to swim in the ocean—plus, I noticed it was the only class she really seemed to like.

Boomer women said they would bring home the bacon and fry it up in a pan. It's time for us younger mothers to just be honest and say "We can't do it all. We're just too tired."

Amen.

Modern Love

Whether we're conducting anecdotal research at a downtown bar or suburban park or poring over census data and academic studies, one question keeps emerging: Mothers, grandmothers, and friends, as well as demographers and social scientists, want to know why it is that so many smart, attractive, and otherwise successful thirty-something women have yet to accomplish the husband and/or baby aspect of their life dream? This mystery confounds Celine, Betsy, Jennifer, and all of the other single women profiled in this chapter who can't seem to solve the puzzle either. While the answer is complex, one thing is very clear: It is not *their fault.*

Women are competing at higher levels for top jobs and creative posts, and more are achieving undergraduate and advanced degrees than ever before. Thirty years ago, less than 1 percent of dental school graduates were women; today, 40 percent are. Thirty years ago, 6 percent of degrees in veterinary medicine were awarded to women; today, nearly 70 percent are. Women now receive well over half—57.2 percent—of all bachelor's degrees, and social scientists predict that gender gap will continue to grow.[24]

As young women have stayed in school for years longer than women of prior generations, it should come as no surprise that the structure and timetable for relationships and families has also fundamentally transformed. Yet instead of encouraging women to embrace these advances and build upon them constructively, a flurry of retrograde books, articles, politicians, and pundits seem to be encouraging women to do what we do best—blame ourselves and second-guess our choices. In Danielle Crittenden's *What Our Mothers Didn't Tell Us*, an attempt to explain why happiness eludes the Modern Woman, she questions the integrity of the independence we have achieved: "Gloria Steinem once joked we have become 'the husbands we wanted to marry.' But maybe the truth is that we are in danger of becoming the husbands we left behind: bulky, self-absorbed, and supremely sure our needs should come before anyone else's. And no matter how entitled some women feel to such behavior, it will hardly help us to achieve the lasting, happy marriages most of us still profess to want."[25]

The cultural response to women's progress remains a game of one step forward, two steps back. One step forward—then there's a marriage panic instigated by a1986 *Newsweek* cover story proclaiming that a 40-year-old college-educated single woman in her thirties is more likely to be killed by terrorists than to get married.[26] One step forward—then there's a baby panic sparked by economist and writer Sylvia Ann Hewlett's finding nearly half of the highest-achieving women are childless, although only 14 percent planned to be. In a *New York* magazine cover story, Vanessa Grigoriadis quotes a woman she interviewed about the baby panic that Hewlett's book *Creating a Life* sparked among Gen-X women: "It's as though a disease broke out, and everyone's trying to alert you. 'Emergency Broadcasting System: Your eggs are declining!'. . . . If I want to have children . . . I need to have them when I'm younger and worry about my career later." The problem is, she continues, "it's contrary to everything I've been brought up thinking."[27]

What we've been brought up thinking is that delaying marriage and motherhood will ultimately make us better wives and mothers, and that message is not entirely wrong. Studies show that couples who marry in their early thirties are less likely to divorce than couples who marry in their early twenties.[28] Also, children with older parents are less likely to be raised in poverty.[29] While the ultimate destination of marriage and children has remained the same, it should be clear by now that there is no one official path to happiness—and for many modern women, it's okay to take the long way home.

Hallelujah—there's no finish line to cross by 30, and it's all right (and perhaps wonderful) if you end up in a relationship that's very different in structure from the one you may have expected. You certainly won't be alone. *BusinessWeek* magazine reports that married-couple households—the dominant cohort since the country's founding—have decreased from nearly 80 percent in the 1950s to just under 60 percent today.[30] Demographers predict a growing number of women will become stepmothers before they become biological mothers, and the number of women who will live Brady Bunch–style, raising children from two previous marriages under the same roof, is also on the rise. Furthermore, many women are choosing to become single mothers through artificial insemination, and of the 51,000 children placed in homes through public adoptions in 2001, 30 percent were adopted by single women.[31] All of this means that women today have more options, not fewer, for creating a family. It's time for us to acknowledge that the socially accepted definition of *family* is simply much broader than it has ever been before.

Back in 1897, feminist and activist Charlotte Perkins Gilman observed, "We have so arranged life that a man may have a house, a family, love, companionship, domesticity and fatherhood. . . . We have so arranged life on the other hand, so that a woman must "choose"; she must either live alone, unloved, uncompanioned, uncared for . . . or give up world service for the joys of love, motherhood, and domestic service. . . . A broader reordering might ensure that women are no longer forced to make these difficult choices."[32] Now, more than 100 years later, as the defining dynamics of marriage and the nature of women's professional choices continue to evolve quickly, many of life's key relationships will be reordered on terms broader and more flexible than even our mothers, let alone Gilman, could have imagined.

The proportion of couples in which the woman is the chief breadwinner has increased so markedly that nearly 1 in 3 working women have bigger paychecks than their husbands, compared with fewer than 1 in 5 in 1980.[33] The trend is particularly pronounced among the most highly educated women, nearly half of whom have incomes higher than their spouses. And if trends start at the top, it shouldn't be lost on aspiring professional women that leading corporate mavens are, perhaps by necessity, discovering new ways to enjoy success at the office and on the home front: one-third of the executives profiled in *Fortune* magazine's 2002 list of the most powerful women in business have stay-at-home husbands who have set aside their own careers to take care of the kids, support the working spouse, and generally fulfill the other traditional wifely duties.[34]

The common denominator of this portrait of the Modern Family is that many women discover their complete, fulfilled personal lives after 30—and they do so by following the natural course of their individual journeys in progress, not by suddenly shifting gears in a state of panic. Based on these significant paradigmatic shifts, it should be clear to us that the "answer" for Gen-X/Y women lies not in looking backward and attempting to resurrect anachronistic white-picket-fence norms of Ozzie and Harriet or Ward and June Cleaver but rather in looking *forward* to lifestyle choices more consistent with a broader worldview that we may have yet to imagine. Instead of cobbling together scary statistics that make Happily Ever After seem elusive and on the retreat, we should be celebrating the possibility of new and expanding opportunities for happiness.

The first step to getting to our own redefinition of happiness is to tune out the cultural noise that encourages us to view our future paths as choices of finite, false extremes. We are more than the aggressive career woman whose ambition obliterates her maternal instincts, the earth mother who has traded in all her professional goals for Gymboree, or the *Sex and the City* gal who is happy as long as she has a martini in her hand and Manolos on her feet. Isn't it time we recognize that these are just archetypes and caricatures and that life never falls into these neat boxes? Why should we want it to anyway?

Carly is an example of someone who found marriage and children when and where she least expected it, after more than a decade of focusing on her career and personal goals. As an oncologist at a prestigious women's hospital in Pittsburgh, her eight years of intensive postcollegiate training didn't leave Carly much time for dating or a personal life. At 34, she had a brilliant career and an impressive salary, and she owned a small home in a tony suburb of the city—but her personal life was in an absolute rut. Her schedule didn't allow her much downtime, and when she did get lucky enough to enjoy a random break, she was at a loss when it came to meeting men. "I was way beyond the bar scene and was not ready to resort to personal ads," she recalls. "It was unbelievably grim."

The one thing Carly always did make time to do, though, was ski. Originally from Colorado, she grew up on the slopes, so she would hit the local hills or take week-long trips out West each February. On one of her local trips to Seven Springs, a Pennsylvania ski resort, she met Mike, a skiing enthusiast and lawyer from D.C. with two young sons. They hit it off right away and skied together all morning while his kids took snowboarding lessons. They met up the following weekend, too, but that time Mike got a sitter, and they went out for dinner. When she did meet Mike's 10- and 12-year-old sons, she bravely strapped on a snowboard for the very first time, thoroughly impressing both father and sons as she made her way down the mountain. The couple met every weekend for three months, and because they could ski together for at least part of the day, Mike didn't have to compromise his weekend custody obligations. Not a conventional courtship, but it worked.

Fast-forward to two years later: Carly and Mike are married, and they have his boys most weekends and on holidays. She is now working in Washington, living with Mike in a wonderful home in the suburbs and getting ready for their annual family trip to Vail.

"This isn't exactly how I imagined the 'husband and children' part of my life," she says, "but somehow it seems just right for me."

Happily Ever After, Revised

As we write this chapter, Kerry is popping prenatal vitamins and Lia is considering moving in with her boyfriend (the prelude-to-marriage type of living together). Although we are both excited and "ready" for these new stages, we are also full of anxiety about what we're on the verge of leaving behind. A 35-year-old mother of twins helped us see things more clearly. "On some level, no matter how independent you are, I think our whole lives are leading up to the moment we have children," she told us. "By being women today, we'll have the option of raising biological kids, stepkids, or adopted kids with any type of partner or nonpartner that we want to. But there is one constant. With every birth comes a death—it's the natural cycle of things. Yet this is where so many of us get stuck, because it's tough to understand the full spectrum of what that really means."

When we began to write this book, we had both lost touch with the full spectrum of just about everything beyond eat-sleep-work. And after listening to more than 100 young women describe various shades of the same problem, we realized that we were not alone in our confusion. We also learned something much more profound.

We are a generation of women raised to value independence, but ironically, we have lost touch with what that really means. Up until now, most of us have been busy chasing the individual goals that we each believed would propel us forward, toward lives as Independent Women. But while collecting experiences and achievements translates to an interesting life résumé, the result of what we've been up to doesn't automatically equal independence, better prepare us for modern marriage and motherhood, or protect us from heartache and divorce. Real independence is not the result of external events—it's the result of internal ones.

In her book *A Short Guide to a Happy Life*, Anna Quindlen writes, "You are the only person who has sole custody of your life. Your particular life. Your entire life. Not just your life at a desk, or your life on the bus, or in the car, or at the computer. . . . Not just your bank account, but your soul."[35] What we learned is that real independence means trusting that your "soul" will remain the same, regardless of whether your life plays out in sequential order or not. Real independence means knowing that soul mates who Have It All and mothers who Do It All are fantasies, but loving partners and caring parents are real. Real independence silences that metronomic ticking clock by stretching and sculpting and adding color and shading to the picture of what a happy family can look like.

When Gloria Steinem said, "A woman needs a man like a fish needs a bicycle," she intended to inspire women who were raised to be dependent on men to envision a different kind of life for themselves. Despite the fact that we were raised very differently than our mothers and grandmothers, plenty of young women today are still pursuing independence of the fish-bicycle variety. The challenge facing Gen-X/Y women is to allow our vision of independence to evolve to make room for a vision of *inter*dependence. Once we recognize the difference, we will be "ready" to embrace the organized chaos of a Happily Ever After that's rooted in reality.

CHAPTER FIVE

The Men's Room

WOMEN CARE WHAT MEN THINK OF THEM. Period.

It makes no difference whether we are executives, secretaries, artists, or homemakers—interpreting how we look through the eyes of men inevitably comes up when women get together. We would wager that there is not one woman reading this book right now who hasn't asked a man a variation of the question, "What are you thinking?" at least once this week. We certainly have.

Evidence that women care what men think of them surrounds us, from self-help books and plastic surgery to stilettos and thongs. And given that women still make up less than half of the workforce—and only 12 percent of upper exccutive ranks[1]—any woman who thinks she can get ahead in business without considering how men perceive her at the office is working for either Lily Tomlin or the Lilith Fair.

Yet somewhere between Betty Friedan and the new millennium, most female writers of serious nonfiction books about women neglect to acknowledge this one simple truth without judgment. And they aren't the only ones. Plenty of female radio talk show hosts, professors, rappers, and empowerment-drenched girlfriends dismiss caring about What Men Think of Us as a sign of weakness, repression, or depleted self-esteem. The truth of our lives is more complicated than that. Thanks to the hard work of our mothers and their mothers, Gen-X women were raised to play with the boys, both literally and figuratively—whether they liked it or not. We recognize that our lives are completely intertwined as a result of this shared foundation. So for us, writing a book about the lives of young women without including the voices of young men seemed as disingenuous as creating an anthology of the history of music without mentioning Mozart or Bach. After all, we share tools, experiences, and insights based on our common past, and we have enough common sense to admit that to build the futures we want, what men think of us *does* matter.

If men are from Mars and women are from Venus, young men and women might be more cosmically aligned than many of us realize. The good news is that we share a mutual desire to create balanced lives. A recent Radcliffe Center for Public Policy study indicated that the priorities of Gen-X men and women are more in tune than our parents' are. Of Gen-Xers questioned, 80 percent of the men and 82 percent of the women said they would gladly trade a bigger paycheck for more time with family and friends. When the same question was posed to Baby Boomer men and women, there was a 20 percent spread between genders.[2]

As we've discussed, however, the bad news is that despite our best intentions, the lives we are living are out of sync with the lives we want to live. Furthermore, young women are not the only ones who struggle to Have It All and then blame themselves when their lives fall short of expectations. Our male counterparts, being from Mars, are even guiltier of remaining silent or being dishonest with each other—and with us—about their parallel confusion. Discussing these issues over beers and *Sports Center* isn't a very "manly" thing to do, so by and large, they don't.

Just as what it means to be a successful modern woman has changed dramatically since our mothers' thirtieth birthdays, what it means to be a successful modern man has also transformed since our fathers were in their thirties. "My dad is a doctor, and in the small Ohio town where I grew up, he is considered a great success story," says Jesse, a 35-year-old investment banker. "But the truth is, I barely know him. He gave his whole life to his business. He was a good provider, but he has never been emotionally involved with my life—still isn't. I inherited his work ethic, but other than that, we are really different. I play soccer, I ski; these are things I look forward to doing with my kids one day. My dad never developed any real interests outside of medicine. I love my job, too, but our ideas about the meaning of success are very different."

Suzanne Braun Levine, a founding editor of *Ms.* magazine and author of *Father Courage: What Happens When Men Put Family First*, notes that the first half of the feminist vision was to bring women into the workforce. The "second half of the revolution" was to integrate the men back into the family.[3] The Man in the Grey Flannel Suit and Ward Cleaver have plenty of female colleagues these days, but beyond that, the game plan for the Feminist Vision: Part 2 remains largely uncharted territory. And today, many Gen-X/Y men find themselves wrestling with their own Problem with No Name that has even less of a social context than our Midlife Crisis at 30.

"Society recognizes the changing nature of women's roles, but there is zero support for the changing nature of men's roles," explains Roland Warren, president of the National Fatherhood Initiative. "There are organizations that support working mothers. There are organizations that support stay-at-home mothers. But there is very little social support for men trying to expand their vision of fatherhood and manhood. [Gen-X/Y] men are suffering in silence because although their ideas about what it means to be a 'successful man' have grown, society continues to measure a man's success solely by the size of his paycheck."[4]

Now that it's our generation's turn to untangle and reshape the dynamics of relationships, it's crucial that we try to better understand the men we want as equal partners in dating, marriage, parenthood, and work. If our goal is to become independent *and* interdependent women, it's time to break down the barriers that keep our shared confusion and common goals so elusive to each other. We asked dozens of Gen-X/Y men what they thought about Gen-X/Y women and what they were going through around their thirtieth birthdays. What we learned will surprise you.

The Ideal Woman

Most twenty- and thirty-something men enter each stage of a relationship—whether it's dating, marriage, or parenthood—with clear views about love and the balance of power. Just as the phrase "soul mate" came up a lot when we asked Gen-X/Y women to describe their ideal men, Gen-X/Y men consistently used the phrase "equal partner" when we asked them to describe their ideal woman. Mark, a 36-year-old bachelor from New Jersey, says, "If I have to choose between an absolutely gorgeous woman who doesn't have aspirations beyond becoming a trophy wife and a not-so-gorgeous woman who could be more of an *equal partner*, I am going for the latter. Hands down."

Jason, a 36-year-old father of two from Maryland, expresses similar views: "In a good marriage, 'mine' and 'yours' is replaced with 'ours.' You should be each other's best supporter and *equal partner* in life."

A divorced 33-year-old lawyer from Alabama concurs: "The best relationships are *equal partnerships*, with shared decisions in pretty much everything."

Jamal, Kenneth, Alex, Raoul, Thomas, and the dozens of other Gen-X/Y men we interviewed also used strikingly similar language to describe their vision of the romantic ideal—a true marriage of equals. But whether they (or we) know what that really means remains to be seen.

Certainly, part of the reason for the echoed sentiments can be traced back to the fact that, like us, men in their twenties and thirties have been thrashing around in the gender wars and their aftermath since they were kids. They have emerged—for lack of a better description—very carefully trained. In a *More* magazine article that profiled the kind of sons Baby Boomer mothers raised, one Gen-X guy commented, "Growing up, there was this undercurrent of 'My boy is great, but guys in general are scum.' When you are a kid, you go 'Yeah. Okay. Whatever.' But then you get older and you think, 'Wait a minute. I am a guy!'"[5]

After boyhoods full of conflicting messages about manhood, our Gen-X male counterparts went off to college during the late 1980s and early 1990s, just in time for politically correct educational trends to grip campuses. All these guys wanted to do was drink beer, play foosball, join a fraternity, have sex, and get a degree. Instead, Angela Davis joined Plato on the required reading list for Western Civ, and they were lectured for another four years about the evils of the male patriarchy.

Author and former presidential speech writer Peggy Noonan once said, "To be a man in this world is not easy."[6] In many ways, she was right. The confusion for guys continued well after graduation. One dismayed twenty-something bachelor told *More*, "All our lives we were told about women's equality and freedom. We were ordered not to open doors and pull out chairs. Now women our age want us to do exactly that."[7] Which brings us up to the present, where we find Gen-X/Y men scratching their heads once again, trying to fathom why all of their otherwise well-adjusted female friends are having these premature midlife crises at or around 30.

So when all of the men we interviewed enthusiastically claimed to want equal partnerships, we pushed them to tell us what that really means. We soon discovered that somewhere between good intentions and the practical realities of everyday life, the definition of an "equal partnership" becomes hazy, and even the most progressive Gen-X/Y men and women are still struggling to figure out the ground rules. That omnipresent gap between What Has Changed and What Has Stayed the Same that has led so many of us to a Midlife Crisis at 30 has left men feeling unclear about where they fit into our lives and how we want to be treated. It's also led many young couples into a web of contradictory ideas about how modern marriage actually works. The truth about "equal partnerships" is a lot murkier than any of us would like to admit, and to some degree, most young couples are still unintentionally sliding into socially traditional roles despite their professed desires not to do so.

Flirting with Disaster

One place where equality definitely exists is in the confusion among "independent" women and "evolved" men about the rules of engagement for finding and keeping modern love. For Gen-X/Y daters, the confusion goes far beyond questions about whether the man makes the reservation, pays for dinner, or opens the door for the woman. Rooted in our shared history are also fundamental questions about expectations of potential mates. With a mutual backstory honoring independence and self-reliance, who can say whether Gen-X/Y men and women are really looking for casual sex, a live-in lover, or a long-term relationship? How are two people with booming careers going to have the time it takes to invest in building a foundation for a committed relationship? And as increasing numbers of women out-earn their male counterparts, are Gen-X/Y men nervous that they may become the Second Sex in love?

Although in the end, most of our relationship goals are strikingly similar, many Gen-X men and women have learned the hard way that getting past this social ambiguity to the second date can be tricky. Because we're all feeling our way through a period of social flux, with no real guidelines for initial communication and behavior, only guesses and good intentions guide our actions. Add first-date nerves and mutual work-related stress to the picture, and there is more room than ever for missed cues and misinterpreted gestures.

Never was this clearer to us than when we decided to play matchmaker the old-fashioned way: Lia took her friend Kelly to meet Kerry's friend Mike at a reliable and trendy French bistro in Soho. We thought Kelly and Mike would be a good match because they are both fun and smart, and they share common interests, from skiing and tennis to sailing. Plus, they were both tired of the dating game and were looking for a serious relationship. Waiting for Kelly to arrive, we enjoyed a round of Merlot and chatted with the friendly after-work bar crowd. We were almost ready for a second round by the time Kelly came through the door, 15 minutes after the appointed meeting time. It wasn't a big deal because it's sometimes difficult to calculate the commute from midtown to downtown, but when Kelly explained that a last-minute business call had delayed her, Kerry saw Mike squirm.

Once we were seated, Mike asked Kelly about her job as a public relations executive at a midsize Madison Avenue firm. Things quickly went downhill from there. Thinking that she was projecting confidence, Kelly rattled off details about a string of high-profile accounts and an upcoming travel itinerary that included two trips to trade shows in Europe. After about 20 minutes, Kelly asked Mike about his job as an investment banker. When he provided a cursory answer (because he didn't want to seem like the self-absorbed guys he knows women love to bash), Kelly probed for more information. She thought she was showing interest with her follow-up questions; he thought her line of questioning showed aggression and an unsettling interest in his earning potential. Before the steak fritte and the second bottle of wine, Kelly had to excuse herself to return a page from her boss, who had a pressing question about a presentation he was about to make in Los Angeles.

When Kelly returned, she didn't miss a beat. During the course of the evening, the prospective couple both laughed a lot and discovered common ground regarding everything from mutual colleagues to favorite Indian restaurants to shared travel and language interests. They exchanged numbers, and Kelly thought for sure they would see each other again. She had no idea that Mike had no intention of calling (especially after she checked her Palm Pilot at the table and said she didn't think she had another evening available for at least 10 days). "She was very pretty, and she seemed nice, and we had some things in common," Mike told Kerry later. "I just don't think it's worth it if she is going to be working so hard and traveling so much. She couldn't even make it through a first date without interruptions. I'm looking for someone who has more available time and less preexisting obligations."

The exchange between Kelly and Mike is a great example of a situation that tests the authenticity of many of the key values we claim to embrace as a generation. Like the majority of men we surveyed, Mike told us that he wanted to be with an "independent" woman and even thought "it would be cool" to be with someone who makes more money than he does. Yet his *expectation* of what that actually looks like was completely out of sync with the reality of Kelly's situation, leaving us to ponder whether we are a generation that is truly enlightened, politically correct, or merely confused.

"I don't care how much the woman makes. I have no problem with that and I would love to be with a successful and accomplished woman," says Justin, a 32-year-old cable executive. When we asked Paul, a 35-year-old journalist, to describe his ideal woman, "solid ambition toward career or vocation" was at the top of his list. When we drilled down on the issue of independence with follow-up questions about a woman's potential for work-related travel, weekend and overtime hours, and frequent office phone calls, our male peers began to morph into reluctant Archie Bunkers, retracting or qualifying their answers as they fumbled intellectually with how and when they would fit into the relationship equation. Other male peers who praise the independent woman admit they are intimidated by her seemingly unlimited range of opportunities for social and professional advancement. "Before I met my wife, my guy friends and I—all in our twenties—felt that a good woman was very hard to find," says Kevin. "And mind you, this was in D.C.—a town reputed to have a 3:1 ratio of women over men. But the numbers didn't seem to make a difference. There was so much out there for a woman to get that finding a man and taking the time to cultivate a relationship seemed low on the totem pole. It was hard to shine through all that clutter."

Before we relegate our friend Mike to caveman status for his snap judgment of Kelly, it's important to take a closer look at what transpired between these two hardworking Gen-Xers. Remember the Sequential Success Trap? Like Celine, the chef we profiled in chapter 4, Kelly believes that focusing on her personal development (which translates to her job in practical terms) is a prerequisite for a real marriage of equals. She has been operating under the assumption that her life would play out in a certain sequential order, where independence (Stage One) should come before intimacy (Stage Two).

Although Mike is actually applying the same guiding principles in his own life, Kelly's attitude is still a bit jarring to him because, as Georgetown University linguistics professor Deborah Tannen, Ph.D., notes in *You Just Don't Understand: Men and Women in Conversation*, Kelly's behavior defies centuries of male expectation. Dr. Tannen explains that intimacy has traditionally guided the behavior of women, and it is what all men— even Gen-X men—have come to expect from us during key social interactions. On the other hand, in the male world, status is a guiding principle, and *independence* has always been key. "Though all humans need both intimacy and independence, women tend to focus on the first and men on the second," continues Dr. Tannen. "It is as if their lifeblood ran in different directions."[8] But Kelly's time in the workplace has reconditioned her responses, and her default mode of communication often expresses independence instead of desired intimacy, leaving a guy like Mike confused about her level of interest and availability. When Kelly arrived late, spoke at length about her career, admitted to a full schedule in the coming weeks, and insisted on picking up half the check, she sent the message that she was too wrapped up in her own world to contemplate a relationship that had room for two aspiring, goal-oriented partners.

Is Mike's analysis fair? He might have asked for a second date and tried to learn more about Kelly's motivations and goals. Although she has a job where the demands sometimes continue past 6:00 P.M., Kelly really isn't obsessed with work. There's a fine line between self-absorbed and overwhelmed, and anyone who knows Kelly—a generous spirit who volunteers at the animal shelter on weekends and sends handwritten thank-you notes after attending dinner parties—knows her as exceptionally other-focused and considerate. But this scenario helps to illustrate the new dimensions of confusion that Gen-X/Y daters encounter as we begin to explore the severe, unanticipated social impact of mutually demanding professional lives.

The "Independent Woman" Tipping Point

So where does this leave us? While it's true that modern men don't want fully domesticated wives, they do—like Mike—tend to erect self-protective intimacy shields when they sense potential neglect. Andrew Hacker, Ph.D., professor emeritus at Queens College in New York and author of *Mismatch: The Growing Gulf between Women and Men*, cites sociological research indicating employment among married women is a significant predictor of divorce rate, as employed wives report thinking about divorce more than wives who do not work outside the home.[9] One interpretation of these stats—beyond the obvious fact that employed females have more bargaining power and financial independence in relationships—is that professional stress imposed on the individual partners can, over time, interfere with the goals of a marital *partnership*. This theory is bolstered by a Cornell University study that analyzed the marriages of 1,700 working couples and found that those in which both spouses work more than 45 hours a week reported the lowest quality of life. What's more, "power couples" (in which both partners are professionals or managers) reported the highest levels of conflict.[10] Conversely, couples in which both partners work full-time, with predictable schedules and 40-hour workweeks, reported the highest quality of life—even higher than families where one spouse worked part-time.[11]

Could this mean that there's a quantifiable tipping point when it comes to dual-career couples and marital bliss? After all, we have only so many hours in a day/week/year, and if both people are besieged by obligations of never-ending workdays, it's easy to grow apart. There are no easy solutions, but the good news is that while men of prior generations may have balked at the possibility of a partnership with a career woman like Kelly, Gen-X/Y men accept, praise, and adore the Independent Woman, at least in *theory*. Our remaining challenge—and it's a significant one—is to figure out how to transform all of these good intentions into realistic partnerships among Gen-X/Y men and women inhabiting mutually competitive and demanding professional worlds.

Love, Power, and Vacuuming: Dirty Secrets about Marriages of Equals

Three years ago, when Katherine and Greg shared their first dance as husband and wife to John Lennon's "Imagine," they both imagined their marriage would look different from their parents' relationships. "Greg and I wrote our own wedding vows and pledged in front of God, our friends, and our family that we would always be each other's *equal partners* in life. We even used those words," recalls Katherine. "And today, that's the case in many important ways. We make all major decisions together. But when it comes to practical, daily-life stuff—like cleaning the house, grocery shopping, making dinner, running errands—there is nothing equal about what's going on.

"Even though we both have demanding careers, somehow I am in charge of everything that my mother was, too—and she was a full-time housewife. I have no idea how it ended up this way. I mean, he went to Oberlin College—they had a women's studies graduation requirement, for god's sake!" Katherine crosses her legs and shifts uncomfortably in her seat and then continues, "He should know better, shouldn't he?"

Katherine and Greg certainly are not the first to wrestle with these issues. In her memoir, *24 Years of Housework. . . . And the Place Is Still a Mess*, Pat Schroeder, former congresswoman from Colorado, writes at length about her supportive husband. She sings his praises in chapter 1: "My husband, Jim, didn't want me to leave the House of Representatives. He liked the role of House Spouse and had almost single-handedly defined it. He's been my biggest booster ever since the frigid January day in 1973 when I stood under that pristine white dome with my right hand in the air, being sworn into the 93rd Congress."[12]

But deeper into the memoir, Schroeder paints another picture of their day-to-day reality. When a reporter asked Jim how her political career had changed his life, he said he pitched in more with domestic things, like taking the kids to the doctor. Upon reading this, Schroeder "immediately ran to the House cloakroom and called him . . . 'For $500,' I asked him, 'what is the name of the children's pediatrician?' Knowing he was busted, he coughed and said, 'Oh, I was misquoted.' Jim was way ahead of his time, but he wasn't Mr. Mom."[13]

Twenty-four years ago—when women made up about 42 percent of the workforce[14] and were well on their way to becoming equal partners at the office—sociologist and University of California-Berkeley professor Arlie Hochschild, Ph.D., began to research whether men were in turn becoming equal partners on the home front. What she discovered was that women were still doing the vast majority of child care and housework, even when they worked outside the home. In her landmark book *The Second Shift*, she writes:

> Just as there is a wage gap between men and women in the office and the factory, there is a "leisure gap" between them at home. . . . It was a woman who first proposed to me the metaphor, borrowed from industrial life, of the "second shift." She strongly resisted the *idea* that homemaking was a shift. Her family was her life and she didn't want it reduced to a job. But

as she put it, "You're on duty at work. You come home, and you're on duty. Then you go back to work and you're on duty." After eight hours of adjusting insurance claims, she came home to put on the rice for dinner, care for children, and wash laundry. Despite her resistance, her home *felt* like a second shift.[15]

Many of the young men we spoke with were aware that their mothers worked "second shifts" as they were growing up. Some even had remarkably vivid memories of harried mothers pushed to the breaking point as they tried to bring home a good paycheck, drive carpools, cook dinner, and keep their marriages alive. Twenty-eight-year-old Jonathan recalls, "My mother was stressed out all the time, and I knew it. My dad did not do much around the house, and they would fight about it a lot— it was brutal. Once, when I was about 8, I vacuumed the entire house and then lied and told my mother that Dad did it, to help keep the peace. They divorced when I was 10. Obviously, as an adult, I realize they didn't break up over who did the dishes. But as a kid, I really thought the fact that my dad was a slob was a big part of problem."

This brings us to the question: Is our generation—one raised by working mothers, intent on creating equal partnerships, and populated by more dual-career couples than ever before—sending the "second shift" off to the dustbin of history? Sixteen years after Hochschild's book first hit the best-seller list, are Gen-X/Y men finally picking up their dirty laundry? Simply put, the answer is (drum roll, please): sometimes. A dramatic, earth-shattering conclusion? No. An accurate one? Yes.

A 2001 University of Michigan study quantifies the power dynamics of modern marriage, as manifested in the unglamorous yet telling debate over who takes out the trash (the study measures only chores, not child care). What they found was that while the chores gap is narrower than it was 30 years ago, it still exists and is getting worse instead of better.[16] A recent Gallup poll shows that there is a Mars/Venus perception gap when it comes to housework, too: 73 percent of husbands said they pitched in with the cooking, but only 40 percent of wives said their spouses ever touched the stove. Eighty-nine percent of husbands said their homes had a fair division of labor, an assessment shared by only 55 percent of their wives.[17]

As anyone in a relationship and reading this now probably knows from personal experience, this dirty little secret is disturbing the peace—and the daily routines—of Gen-X couples as well. During our interviews, it became clear that even when tasks are shared evenly, the woman is still the manager of those tasks. Thirty-five-year-old Rick has the goofy, gentle demeanor of a modern Jimmy Stewart, and his fiancée has a matching sweet personality and good nature. As Rick explains, though, things get tense when it comes to housework. "Bonnie expects it to be 50-50 on everything from cooking to wedding planning. I couldn't agree more—in theory. I have to work on the practice," he admits. "I do the work, but only after she's pestered me, and she hates that. Half the time, I am playing catch-up. It's like I know she's right, but I have amnesia and re-peat my mistakes. The problem is, she's very energetic in terms of errands and chores. I'm more apt to put something off until the last moment, while she'll notice things like the dwindling supply of Windex. A dirty apartment doesn't affect me too much, but it casts a shadow over her moods. We have this conversation all the time; it's my downfall."

Remember Jason: "What's 'mine' and 'yours' is replaced with 'ours'"? Even he sheepishly admits that he and his wife are not exactly equal partners in everything. "I have a greater threshold for messiness than my wife does, so she often takes the brunt of the housework," he says. "I hate this topic. Can we please move on to something else? Let's just say, I follow the mantra, 'I do what I'm told.'"

Blaming the guys for this entire mess would be wrong. Experts note that for generations a woman's power was directly connected to her being in control of the way the house looked. Just as a man can still be reluctant to give a woman a seat on the board, a woman can still be ambivalent about sharing her traditional power in the domestic sphere. Thus, although most working women claim they want their husbands and boyfriends to be equal partners in housework, many of us don't really mean it. What we really want is an executive assistant in charge of specific chores—and plenty of us still unconsciously continue to flex our muscles as CEO of the home every time we give our spouses explicit instructions on how to Windex the mirrors.

In the classic movie *African Queen*, Katharine Hepburn tells Humphrey Bogart, "Nature is something we are put on this earth to rise above." So don't give up hope entirely when you look across the room and see your "evolved" man putting his beer on the table without a coaster, despite the fact that you've told him a million times it will leave a ring. As a practical generation socialized during one of the most dramatic periods of social change in modern history, there is reason to believe that we actually may rise above our respective natures when it comes to housework—although reprogramming our internal Martha Stewarts and Pigpens will not happen overnight. As a place to start, try having an honest and very practical conversation about how you can clean up your act as a couple. If that doesn't work, remember that a housekeeper is cheaper than a therapist or a divorce lawyer.

Fatherhood in Flux

While we were busy growing up, our parents were pushing the boundaries of traditional gender roles, challenging the standard breadwinner/homemaker family structures that by and large had framed their own childhoods. As Bob Dylan described it, the times were a-changin', and our mothers'—*and fathers'*—experiences during that time have profoundly influenced our generation's approach to parenting. Just as our shared backstory is shaping Gen-X/Y women's views on balancing career and family, it is also profoundly affecting Gen-X/Y men's approach to fatherhood. Although there is nothing new about sons setting out to raise their families differently than they were raised, a slew of studies, surveys, and polls show just how different Gen-X men's attitudes about fatherhood are from those of previous generations. In a recent national survey on parenting, one Gen-X father expressed the sum of decades' worth of research by demographers, social scientists, academics, writers, educators, and psychologists in a sentence: "Among Baby Boomer dads, you were really cool if you were involved with your kids;

now, if you're a dad and you're not involved with your kids, you are just lame."[18]

As a generation, our fathers' involvement with our collective upbringing is a study in extremes. On one hand, millions of us were raised in homes where our fathers did not live. During the 1970s alone, the divorce rate doubled, as did the number of children living in single-parent households.[19] Research shows that Gen-X children raised by single/divorced mothers logged more hours watching TV dads like Mike Brady, Bill Cosby, and Howard Cunningham than they spent bonding with their real-life biological fathers. On the other hand, a very different story emerged within intact families. Over the past 30 years or so, the amount of time married fathers spend with their kids has doubled, increasing even more dramatically in families where mothers work outside the home.[20]

Today, Gen-X fathers are sticking around more, and they are making their presence known. Whether as a result of parental example, counterexample, or altogether different cultural and emotional influences, the number of children being raised in father-absent homes has leveled off in the past decade, [21] and one thing has become clear: Daddies don't "babysit" any more, and Gen-X men are playing active roles in their children's day-to-day lives. A recent Harris poll asked today's dads to compare their experiences as parents with their childhood memories of their own fathers. They said they spent more time helping with homework (69 percent), playing with their kids (68 percent), taking their kids to extracurricular activities (69 percent), and making decisions about their children's education (60 percent) and health care (57 percent).[22] Because childhood memories can get fuzzy, however, and sons and daughters are often unreliable family historians, we made it a point to take the Harris poll results one step further. We called the wives of each father we interviewed and asked them to play Truth Police about their husbands' involvement with the kids. Although we definitely tapped into some resentment over housework issues, the majority of the wives gave their husbands high marks as fathers and acknowledged their bona fide participation in the full spectrum of child care issues.

The Good Provider

While fathers' expected levels of emotional engagement in family life has changed, the parallel social expectations and internal pressure that men feel to be Good Providers has barely budged. The fact that 30 percent of working wives currently make more money than their working husbands has yet to completely deprogram men from their primal instinct that it's ultimately *their* responsibility to bring home the proverbial bacon. Rob, a 34-year-old bachelor with a BFA in painting and a lucrative career as an art director for a video game company, is one of many progressive young guys with traditional concerns. He says, "I am terrified by the idea of having a family and struggling to make ends meet."

Rodrigo, a Texas small-business owner, feels the same way. "Men feel they need to have arrived at a certain comfortable point in their careers before settling down," he says. "Another thing men think about is 'How can I support a wife and kids if I can barely support myself?' In spite of double-income/fewer-kid families, men like me still ask this question because, theoretically or biologically, it's all going to be on our shoulders."

Not surprisingly, the fathers we spoke with felt this pressure most acutely. One dad confessed, "I worry all the time about what would happen if I lost my job and how it would affect my growing family. I worry that the linchpin will come loose, and everything will come to pieces." This from a 32-year-old father whose wife works four days a week and makes nearly as much as he does.

To fully understand the male point of view, it's also important to remember that all of these Involved Fathers/Good Providers work in the same demanding workplaces that we do—workplaces that require so much of our time and, by extension, so much of our lives. All of these converging pressures are causing many Gen-X/Y fathers to wonder: How much of It All can *they* really have?

Brian lives in a split-level house a few miles away from a strip mall. He married his college sweetheart, and he drives a Jeep equipped with a DVD player to keep the kids entertained on road trips. This computer analyst looks more like Ray Romano than James Dean, but the truth is, he is more of a rebel with a cause than even he realizes.

● BRIAN, 34 YEARS OLD
COMPUTER ANALYST
Murraysville, Pennsylvania

Last month, our biggest client called out of the blue and hit us with a project that needed to be done immediately. There were rumors that they were talking with one of our competitors, so when Jack said, "Jump," my boss said, "How high, sir?" and told the rest of us to drop everything and focus 150 percent of our energy on this project so we could keep the business. It was a complicated assignment, so the entire staff was mobilized. We got it done on time and under budget.

Just before we sent that material off to the client, we had a full staff meeting to make sure we'd covered everything. There were probably 20 people in the conference room, and just as many on the phone dialed in from other branch offices. Someone's kid was making noise in the background and a few guys rolled their eyes because it was messing up the call, but it was no big deal.

Just before the meeting ended, my boss said, "I'd like to thank Stan for his work on this project. He has been at Disney World for the past week with his family. But when I called and said that we needed his help, he picked up his laptop and went right to work. So Stan, a special thanks to you and to your wife for taking care of the kids while you did great work. You are a real team player, and your level of commitment should be commended." Congratulations. Blah, blah, blah . . .

While everyone on the call was singing his praises, I couldn't help but think that Stan's family vacation must have really sucked. I'm sure he was working the entire time, and his wife was probably pissed. Who could blame her? She didn't sign up to be the single parent. Plus, he missed out on Disney. We took Jenna there a few years ago, and she still talks about it. Meanwhile, the powers-that-be congratulate him for being such a great guy, such a team player. It just doesn't make sense.

I have two terrific kids—Max is four, and Jenna is six. Jenna's a little princess—she's got my wife's blue eyes and curly blond hair. And Max is going to be a comedian when he grows up. (Honestly, the kid cracks me up. Who knew a 4-year-old could have such a sense of humor?) My wife and I have been married for eight years. She's an accountant at Deloitte and Touche. She likes her job, and between the two of us, we bring in good money. We just bought a house and a new car, and we put money away for the kids' college funds every month.

Max and Jenna need to be picked up from daycare at 5:30 P.M. every day. It's a long day for them, but they have great teachers, and we like the feel of the place. Since both my wife and I work full-time, every afternoon at 4:30, we have the same conversation. "Are you going to be able to leave to get the kids? What does your schedule look like? Can you get away?"

When it's my turn to pick them up, I literally sneak out the back door so no one gives me crap for leaving at 5:00. I've got some seniority here, I work hard, and my performance reviews are always excellent. But that doesn't seem to matter much. Every time my boss sees me leave before 6:30 or so, he looks at his watch and says, "Leaving early today?" He laughs like he's joking, but let me tell you, the man is serious. He's got three kids who are all my age, and a few grandkids. His wife never worked, and I just don't think he has any real understanding of the reality of my responsibilities outside the office.

I know I'm not the only one who feels this way, because sometimes I see other guys sneaking out "early" also. They have car seats in their SUVs, too.

Daddy-Tracked

Brian is right—he isn't the only guy out there feeling heat at the office for doing the right thing by his family. Catalyst recently surveyed hundreds of professional Gen-X men, asking them to rate their values and goals. The findings once again reinforced the fact that our male peers unequivocally value personal and family commitments more highly than work commitments, with 79 percent of men rating "to have a loving family" as extremely important; "to enjoy life" secured a close second place. Career-specific goals, including "to have a variety of responsibilities," "to earn a great deal of money," and "to become an influential leader" ranked at the bottom of the list.[23] For Brian, living a life aligned with his priorities has translated to a dual-career marriage (so his "loving family" has enough income to "enjoy life"), and its side effect is that he feels as stressed out as his wife does about juggling the practical realities of competing professional and family responsibilities. The remaining unanswered question is this: Will guys like Brian continue to handle their work-life balance issues by stealthily sneaking out the back door to pick up their kids at daycare a few days a week, or will they actually take a stand by taking advantage of family-friendly workplace policies that many companies currently offer to working *mothers*?

As they often do with men, actions speak louder than words. For now, the answer to that question is a resounding "not yet." Most companies still observe a great disparity between the numbers of men and women who choose to utilize flexible workplace policies. Looking at the issue through the singular lens of the ultimate working-father benefit— *paid paternity leave*—it's clear that even those New Age, Snugli-wearing dads who aced Lamaze class routinely take a pass on extra paid time off when companies are progressive enough to offer it. At Michigan-based Republic Bancorp, only 10 men opted to take more than a week or two of the *six weeks* of paid paternity leave available to more than 2,000 employees.[24] And at First Union Corporation (now Wachovia) in Charlotte, North Carolina, only 12 men took full advantage of a generous parental leave policy, although the human resources department offered it to 70,000 employees.[25] On a broader scale, the 1996 Family and Medical Leave Act (FMLA) requires all companies with more than 50 employees to offer some kind of paternity leave, yet a Columbia University study reported no increase in the number of fathers taking extra time off to make room for baby since the FMLA was enacted.[26]

Kerry's older brother, Josh, was president of his fraternity, played rhythm guitar in a rock band, and had a reputation for always knowing where to find the party. His priorities shifted after he met his wife, and his transformation into a respectable family man was complete after their son, Jack, was born a few years ago. At 35, he consistently puts his family's needs before his own; he is the most involved father Kerry knows.

A few weeks before his second child was born, Josh turned down a job offer with a raise because he felt the timing was wrong. They could have used the extra cash, but Josh knew that proving himself at a new company would require long hours and inevitably take him away from his baby, his three-year-old son, and his wife at a time when he was "truly needed at home."

Let's rewind the clock to 1968. If Kerry's father had been offered a new job and a raise weeks before Josh was born, he would have jumped at the offer, and he would have been as certain as Josh that he was making the right choice for his family. But even modern dads like Josh are willing to push the envelope only so far. When Kerry asked her brother if he was planning to take paternity leave or if he might ask for a compressed workweek after Zoe was born, he looked at her as if she were nuts. "I am a family man, and so are most of my friends," he said, "but I don't know any guys who would do that. It's just not done."

Although Gen-X men's personal priorities have shifted, by and large their professional realities have not—and most guys fear they'll find themselves unceremoniously Daddy-Tracked if they choose to use family-friendly policies. "Men want to know specifics," Rosalind Chait Barnett, Ph.D., director of Brandeis University's community, families, and work program, told *Working Mother* magazine. "Can they make partner if they work reduced hours, and how many more years will it take? They will need proof that it will be recognized as a legitimate option by their employer, and not something that will make them a marginalized second-class citizen."[27]

While there is some indication that the times are once again a-changin', men who demand flextime or elect to take full advantage of parental leave are still more likely to be perceived as slackers by their bosses than women are. David Stillman, a management consultant and co-author of *When Generations Collide: Who They Are. Why They Clash. How to Solve the Generational Puzzle at Work*, traces the problem back to a classic generation gap. "The Boomer men were in a rat race to the top," he says, "but if Gen-Xers leave work early to go to a school event, we are proud of that."[28] While Stillman's analysis certainly paints a clear-cut symmetrical and sympathetic picture, the Gen-X men we interviewed were not universally understanding or supportive when dads ducked out of work early either. Rob, the art director at a video game company, related that when the staff sound engineer recently became a father and began leaving

work at 7:00 P.M. and stopped showing up on weekends, his countercul-
ture colleagues openly speculated that perhaps he had "lost his edge" to
"baby world." We can only imagine the more colorful phrases that competitive young lawyers, traders, and account executives use to describe
male colleagues whose billable hours dip after becoming fathers, and we
seriously doubt that twenty-something dads who proudly announce they
are leaving work early to go to a school event are always cheered on by
their unmarried peers. The company-wide applause that Stan received
after working nonstop during his family trip to Disney World also tells a
different story.

Roland Warren, president of the National Fatherhood Initiative, says
that by and large, corporations have not done their part to support a male
work ethic that values family as much as it values work. "Every major social change that has ever happened, happens because there is grassroots
support for it in families, faith communities, government, and business.
The business community has been totally silent on supporting fatherhood," Warren says. However, the reason that many companies have not
stepped up to the plate is complicated, he continues. "On the corporate
level, it's just easier to do stuff for women. Many of the CEOs I speak
with say, 'If we do something specifically to support fathers, all the
women are going to be up in arms.' They must understand that if they
want to make things better for working mothers, they need to make
things better for working fathers, too. It's time for women to take up this
challenge and tell corporate America that it needs to better support
working fathers. Women need to say, 'If you don't support working fathers, you're not supporting me.'"[29]

Warren makes a very good point. The only way family-friendly policies will ever move from the pink ghetto to a ritzier address is if men and
women alike start to take advantage of them. If we're ever going to break
this vicious cycle and actually live the integrated lives we all say we want
in survey after survey and study after study, we need to make a little noise
together and at least seize existing opportunities to prove it is possible
to put family first and still get the job done. Only then will work-life

conflicts be recognized for what they really are, because 9 times out of 10, the clash is not a "life" problem, it's a "work" problem. Suzanne Braun Levine drives the point home in her book *Father Courage*:

> Yes, the understanding of fatherhood and its contribution to children's development is changing. Yes, the dynamic of marriage is changing. Yes, the priorities of a critical mass of people are changing. These changes pose hard questions about power, responsibility, leadership, and family structure; about what money can buy; about how we value time; about the state's responsibility to families and children. How are we going to address them: One by one or as a society? [30]

Where Do We Go from Here?

This examination of the interaction between young women and men makes it more obvious than ever to us that the only way out of this Midlife Crisis at 30 mess is to close the gap between our ideals and reality by working *together* to demand workplace changes that will allow us to honor the values we are expressing as a generation. That means it's the responsibility of Gen-X men and women alike to stop thinking so much about ourselves and how to make our individual situations work out and focus more on leaving our generational mark—by demanding political, social, and corporate changes that will allow us the time we need to develop the real equal partnerships and parenting opportunities we claim to want but are struggling to achieve.

When our parents' generation recognized the problems they faced as *flaws in the system instead of flaws in themselves,* they lobbied for new laws, crashed through glass ceilings, and changed that flawed system for the better. Now, it is our generation's responsibility to initiate a subtler wave of change that will allow us to seize the benefits of our parents' accomplishments without compromising the integrity of our personal relationships and family values. In practical terms, that means we need to get the dialogue started by more aggressively defining our shared needs and common goals. It means we have to take some calculated risks *together* by demanding more flexible professional arrangements and more generous vacation policies. It also means that with our encouragement, Gen-X/Y men are going to have to step up and use the family-friendly policies that many Fortune 500 companies currently offer but that few men currently consider using. Moreover, it means we need to learn how to take advantage of some of the technological advancements that are, by and large, used against us. (For instance, if remote computer access could require Stan to work through a family vacation, the flipside is that he could be rewarded with a week of working from home.) What we're suggesting is not a mass overhaul of the corporate structure but only fair revisions that address the evolving dynamics of the personal and professional lives we are living.

Without a clear plan for the future, society idealizes a flawed past. If we don't begin to create a new platform for a family-oriented political agenda from the *middle,* those on the far right—with a retro-feminist agenda that ultimately puts women back in the kitchen—will jump in to fill the void. With best-sellers that applaud female submission, such as *The Rules* and *The Surrendered Wife*, there is evidence that their message is already taking hold as the plausible panacea for an epidemic of private work-life–related angst. Yet, as Stephanie Coontz, who teaches family studies at Evergreen State College in Olympia, Washington, explains in her book *The Way We Never Were: American Families and the Nostalgia Trap* , even a tiny step backward to the rigid male breadwinner/female homemaker model—when alcoholism rates soared, 1 in 10 children did not live with either birth parent, and husbands and wives reported lives of quiet desperation—will buy us nothing but a "surrendering" of all that two generations worked to claim:

> Pessimists argue that the family is collapsing; optimists counter
> that is it merely diversifying. . . . Too often, both camps begin
> with a historical, static notion of what "the" family was like be-
> fore the contemporary period. . . . The actual complexity of
> our history—even of our own personal experience—gets

buried under the weight of an idealized image. Families have
always been in flux and often in crisis; they have never lived up
to nostalgic notions about "the way things used to be."[31]

It is up to our generation to avoid this careless slide back in family
dynamics and to build on the changes of the past two decades to create a
realistic work, life, and love model for a changed world. For every action
there is a reaction, but when there is silence amid individual struggle,
things remain the same. Our individual situations will not improve until
we recognize that it's our turn as a generation to continue a cultural
march forward, both literally and figuratively. If the revolution of the
1960s helped create a blueprint for gender equality, it is time for us to
initiate the evolution of that progress in the form of a new revolution—
one that leverages the strength of equal partnerships into balanced foun-
dations that will support our inevitably challenging and dynamic futures.

PART TWO

The New Girls' Club:

Your Dream Team of Mentors

BEYOND 30

MORE THAN A YEAR AFTER LIA AND KERRY started talking to Gen-X/Y women about shared problems, it became clear that the blueprints for shared solutions would come through conversations with Baby Boomer women. Our research led us to the conclusion that what was not working our lives—and those of the young women we interviewed—was intrinsically linked to the unfinished business of our mothers' and older sisters' feminism. But at some point over the past 30 years, the political had become so personal that women of our age no longer recognized the common thread running through our individual dilemmas. Although the acknowledgment of that shared struggle was empowering, we were still looking for some practical and immediate advice. We knew we'd have to turn to women who had lived life longer than we had to find those answers. As Maya Angelou eloquently stated: "Some of the things I know, I know only because older women have told me their secrets. I have lived and am living long so that I can tell my secrets to younger women. That's the reason we women go on improving." We were in search of some secrets.

Yet a good mentor is hard to find, and this lack of a support system continues to have real consequences for women of our age. A recent Catalyst survey of 25- to 35-year-old professional women reported that 66 percent of young women who recently changed jobs said that seeking a workplace "with greater mentoring opportunities" was an "extremely important" reason behind their decision to leave their former jobs.[1] Half of all women of our age group cite lack of mentoring as the number one barrier to women's advancement.[2]

Determined to do something about this, we sat down and compiled a list of many women we admired who seemed to have thriving lives as well as impressive résumés. We solicited interviews with physicians, lawyers, entrepreneurs, journalists, politicians, actors, and women who have "stopped out" of their respective fields to focus on their families. Just as patterns of universal conflict emerged during our interviews with the twenty- and thirty-something women profiled in part 1, we imagined that a parallel and inspiring prescriptive pattern would emerge during our interviews with the more seasoned and settled women of part 2—and it did.

What we discovered was that none of these women had smooth lives in which professional and personal successes came easily, yet each has managed to build a fulfilling, multidimensional reality guided by a similar process. That process is complex, and it involves a combination of self-analysis, honesty, and pragmatism. Not one among this group of power players found accelerated career success by becoming a more devoted corporate solider or a more aggressive political operator. Instead, they found professional fulfillment by following their passions and taking calculated risks. Similarly, women who were single did not find husbands by going on more dates; instead, they found love when they engaged in thoughtful realignments of their priorities and goals. No one found the "perfect" relationship, but many of these happily married women realized that embracing imperfection in partnerships is the key to sustaining them.

The lessons embedded in these stories is clear: The women of the New Girls' Club each feel they Have It All—largely because they purposefully reevaluated what "all" means to them. And they each did it at a critical moment, during their late twenties or early to mid-thirties. But perhaps the most important thing they have common is something quite simple—*They are women of action*. They never waited for, nor did they expect, wonderful lives to "just happen." When these women faced crossroads moments, they were not always certain they were making the right decisions or doing the right thing. But in the end, they each chose to live with purpose, optimism, and creativity. There is much to learn from their experiences.

The spirit of the New Girls' Club is embodied in the story of Deborah Rosado Shaw, an entrepreneur who grew up in the South Bronx, the poorest congressional district in the country. Shaw faced violence and fear at every corner—literally—as gangs dominated both her neighborhood and her school. But by the time she was in her thirties, she was a self-made millionaire, raising three sons in a magnificent home that surpassed her own childhood fantasies. In our interview, she described what it took to get there:

I think that a lot us walk of around desperately seeking clarity. We have this prayer that goes something like, "If I only knew exactly what the right thing was to do, and how to do it." And we say to ourselves, "When I get that moment of clarity, I'll take action." What I have learned is that prayer for the lightening moment when everything becomes totally clear is not actually a prayer for clarity—it's a prayer for an insurance policy to protect us from looking stupid or feeling dumb. And there is no such thing. Even if you are moving powerfully in a direction that you are clear is the right one for you, you'll still have plenty of moments of feeling stupid. I certainly have.

I've flopped in Macy's window big time. And believe me, I've been in that scary place where you are living week to week trying to figure out *How am I going to pay my mortgage and take care of my kids?* I know what that's like. But I've taken those risks for something that I feel strongly about, and that's what makes it all worthwhile.

Waiting for the clarity to strike and tell you exactly what

to do with your life is a guarantee that you will never get the right answer. It is always in action that life happens. It's the action that produces the clarity.[3]

So on one hand, when taken at face value the Anything Is Possible message of our youth may have been too good to be true, but on the other hand, it was right on target. Because *everything* is possible when we, as adults, shed the inhibitions and expectations we've outgrown and deliberately set out to build richer, more meaningful lives. What we know now, and what we did not know at 30, is that time to claim our dreams is not running out—it is only beginning.

Escaping the Sequential Success Trap

Finding Happiness, Maintaining Equal

Partnerships, and Redefining Family

MANY GEN-X/Y WOMEN HAVE ASSUMED their lives would play out in a specific, sequential order: Stage One: work. Stage Two: marriage. Stage Three: kids. Some of us have focused so much energy on conquering Stage One that we failed to recognize that unless each stage of life makes sense with the one that follows, work and marriage and kids can eventually become mutually exclusive categories. These members of the New Girls' Club figured out how to avoid falling into this trap either by learning to make choices that led to integrated lives or by recognizing that not all visions of happiness will come in traditional packages or on predictable timetables. Instead, these accomplished women have embraced new versions of a Happily Ever After that comes on their own terms and by their own design.

● JULIA REED
SENIOR WRITER, *VOGUE* MAGAZINE

AT 30 . . .
Julia Reed was a staff writer at *Vogue* magazine, and she was living in New York. She had also just called off a wedding.

TODAY . . .

Julia Reed is a senior writer at *Vogue*, where her profile subjects have ranged from Bill Clinton, George Bush, and Condoleezza Rice to Robert DeNiro, Barbara Walters, and Barbra Streisand. She is also a contributing editor to *Newsweek* and a contributor to the *New York Times Magazine*, for which she writes a food column. She is a regular guest on CNBC's *News with Brian Williams* and MSNBC's *Hardball with Chris Matthews*. In March 2004, Random House will publish a collection of her essays about the South, titled *Queen of the Turtle Derby and Other Southern Phenomena*. She divides her time between Manhattan and New Orleans.

Julia Reed is a member of the New Girls' Club because her wise choices reflect a new version of the Happily Ever After fairy tale for women.

WHEN I WAS IN SCHOOL, I used to sit around in algebra class, and because I was bored out of my mind, my best friend and I would make up our weddings—we'd figure out *everything*. We had a list of the bridesmaids and knew what kind of cake we would serve and what kind of flowers we would carry. But the groom was always the big question mark, because at 8 or 10 or 15, you don't have a clue *who* you are going to marry. And I think that's what gets a lot of women in trouble—when you're a young girl and imagining your wedding day, the least important thing is the groom, and the focus is on the pageantry. You keep imagining this thing— this big event—that is all about being pretty and being the girl, and you forget about visualizing the most important detail, which is, of course, the man you are going to marry. But when you wait as long as I did to head to the altar, your focus is finally, clearly, in the right place—on the marriage, not the wedding.

I almost did get married at 29—and even when I was 29, which is pretty old by some people's standards, it was going to be an "event." My parents had their list, I had my list, the groom had his list, and suddenly there were a thousand people invited to this wedding! My mother and I talked on the phone about 350 times a day, which kept me from having to think about what I was actually doing. Again, with these weddings, and especially if you live in the South as I do—and in the Mississippi Delta specifically, which is famous for huge wedding bashes—romantic unions become social events of extraordinary magnitude. The day I called it off—or told my mother I called it off—the champagne had been delivered to our house, and there must have been hundreds and hundreds and hundreds of cases there. We couldn't take it back, which was fine with me, because I got to celebrate not getting married to the wrong guy, which was sort of the point anyway.

By the time you are 42 and planning your wedding, everything is a little bit different. Even though you are never too old to stop fighting with your mother, your maturity accords you certain rights. You can say, "We are not having Cousin Jack or my father's great aunt, and we are not having everybody he has ever done business with in his whole life."

You even get to modify a few mainstay rituals. I've seen pictures of 50-year-old brides, and they have 40- and 50-year-old attendants in those ludicrous bridesmaid dresses that nobody ever looked good in, even when we were young. My rule was to not have anybody over 12 in my wedding party, for fear that it would look like the Mrs. America pageant. By this point in life, you really know who your close friends are, and they know it, too. It's not like you have to say, "Judy, I want you to know how much I love you—you get to walk down the aisle in front of me." My nieces had been after me to get married from the moment they met my future husband because, of course, they wanted to be in the wedding, so they became my perfect bridesmaids.

Some of the preparation leading to the wedding day is different, too. When you imagine yourself getting married as a child, you imagine yourself as this gorgeous, dewy-skinned knockout. I was the rice girl in all of these beautiful girls' weddings when I was growing up—weddings of gorgeous young debutantes. So, of course, I was thinking I was going to be the same kind of 22-year-old dewy-skinned bride. Well! Instead, I got Botox to get rid of the crevice between my eyes, and I had a million facials in the months leading up to the wedding. Let's just say the maintenance level is definitely a little higher! My mother dried her hair out the window of a car the day she married and wore no makeup except lipstick—and still looked absolutely gorgeous in her wedding picture. Well, baby, I had *two* hairdressers there!

When you are being bossed by Andre Leon Tally, editor-at-large at *Vogue*, your choice of a bridal gown is a little bit different, but the one thing I knew was that I couldn't be prancing around out there in a big white dress. At first, I was intent on having this silk print dress that I could wear over and over and over again. And everybody kept saying, "You're crazy." And then you get to the bridal salon—in my case, it was Carolina Herrera's studio, but I think it would have been the same if I had been at the department store in the mall in Birmingham or in Ann Arbor—and in that moment, you just become *a bride*, no matter what age you are. It's hard to resist, because that is the one thing that does stay with you from that little-girl fantasy. So I had the gorgeous dress, but it was a pale, pale green. I will say this, though—it stayed on my body for only about 30 minutes after the ceremony. Then, on went the sexy, short, polka-dotted Carolina Herrera—and spike-heeled shoes so I could feel like who I really was again.

That sense of clarity about who I am and what makes me happy is what stands out in my mind about that day. All my life I've heard of jittery brides. But when you know that you are doing the right thing, when you've thought about the decision—and especially when you have resisted it and overcome it—you are calm the whole time.

I remember when I was supposed to be getting married at the huge wedding that had been planned when I was 29. I kept trying to imagine myself there, and I almost never could. And when I did, it was like watching a movie of someone else's life. It never felt comfortable. People tell me they don't remember their weddings, or they were scared to death. For me, when I *did* get married the whole thing, from start to finish, just felt completely *right*. People flew in from literally all over the world for this wedding. It is not easy to get to Greenville, Mississippi, even if you are flying in from New York. But people made the effort because they cared about our happiness, and that made it about 50 million times as meaningful. So when I walked out—just walking out my door to my front yard, which was a much more intimate setting than a big church or a hotel—I was able to sort of look into the faces of people gathered on the lawn, and it all registered.

I remember thinking on my wedding day, "I am so glad this is happening *now*." I am so glad I didn't make a mistake earlier. In my late twenties and thirties, I saw a lot of women make ridiculous decisions, beneath their intelligence level, because they felt pressure. They were not making informed decisions about what their own needs were or what they were getting ready to do and the reality of this at all. One of my closest friends fell head over heels in a senseless kind of way when she was in her twenties and never stepped back. That marriage ended disastrously, and then she married a second time for all the wrong reasons. Another one of my closest friends living in New York at the same time I was there was doing really well at her job and having a great time, but she was about to turn 30, her older sister was already married and having children, and her mother was putting pressure on her to do the same. I think she was most scared of the age thing, and she was dating a nice guy, so she married him. But she didn't really find out who he was until about two years into it, at which point she got divorced.

Because I almost did this myself, I know how easy it is to get caught up in "Well, it is *time*." In my case, I had been with this guy for a really long time, and he had moved from England to be with me because I couldn't think about moving there. And at the time, his career was much further along than mine, so he was making sacrifices for me, and I felt guilty because he had made all of these life changes. The problem was that by the time he pulled them all off, I was no longer into the relationship. But then I thought, "I've got to do this for this guy because he has done all of this for me." And thank God, at the last minute, I saw the light, because I guarantee you we would have been divorced. I almost had what would have been a disastrous first marriage out of sheer guilt!

When I called off the wedding, which almost gave my mother a heart attack, mostly because she had to dismantle this juggernaut, I had to call one of my father's closest friends, a much older man who was coming in from Connecticut. Everyone else had looked at me like I was totally insane. It was as if I had leprosy. People were a little leery of being around me because they thought I might have lost my mind—"If you have a good chance to get married, why wouldn't you take it?" This was right after the *Newsweek* "terrorist" cover, saying that women had a better chance of getting attacked by a terrorist than of getting married if they were over a certain age, so that contributed to the drama. Anyway, people looked at me like I was nuts. But I called this one man, who was very smart, and all he said was, "Relief is a wonderful emotion, isn't it, Julia?"

The truth is, when I canceled my wedding at 29, I really did feel like I had been let out of jail. And I just watched all of my friends immediately go into this tailspin of misery when they married the wrong people at roughly that same time—and there I was, feeling terrific. Immediately after calling off the wedding, I got a book contract for a project on the South. Then I came down to New Orleans to cover a governor's race that I was going to write about as part of the book. Realizing how much I missed the South, I moved here. All of this coincided with changes in technology—even though laptops weighed about 100 pounds, I could fax things in. When I turned 30, my life opened up in ways that I didn't count on. If I had married at 30, my existence would have been a lot narrower. I would have been stuck in New York with my husband in a life I did not want. Instead, I got a place in New Orleans and started making decisions that were important to me.

That's not to say everything was perfect. I didn't make the most ingenious romantic choices at the time, but what the heck? I learned a lot about myself while I was screwing up. The guy that I fell madly in love with after I called off my wedding was definitely not a person I was supposed to marry, but it took me about a decade to figure that out. When you see a shrink, they tell you that you can't change the problem in your life unless you recognize the pattern. I think that's true with women and dating: The first people you fall in love with are usually punching all your wrong buttons. I don't think most people can figure that out by the time they are 23 or even 25—for most of us, it takes longer to discover who we are. The good news is that when you are in your late thirties or forties, you have had a while to figure it out. It's not like my mother's generation, where they thought, "What did we miss?"

When I turned 30, my life opened up because I was released from a really clear-cut path that didn't have a lot of flexibility. But when I turned 40, my life opened up even more. I was finishing up the book that had been hanging over my head for a decade, and I had I started writing a food column for the *New York Times Magazine*, which is a direction in which I never thought my career would go. My life was full, and I was more confident than I had ever been before. And it was around this time I started seriously dating my husband, John. When I came down here and started doing what I wanted, those choices eventually culminated in this marriage.

It was clear to me from the beginning that this relationship was different and much calmer than my other ones. Of course, in the beginning, I questioned that: "Well, I don't feel it; my heart isn't racing 30,000 miles an hour." I still have friends who say, "I don't know, it didn't *feel* like true love." And I feel like saying, "You have no idea what the hell true love is; you haven't ever had it. What you are having is more like a cocaine rush." All of these myths about falling in love lead us astray—not only are you supposed to wear the white dress, but you are supposed to have palpitations every time he looks your way. We have this sort of Danielle Steele, Judith Krantz ideal of what it's like to fall in love, which usually has nothing to do with everyday life.

Just looking at all of the women I know, I think 35 is the right time to think about getting married. You still have time to have children then. When I got out of college, the last thing on my mind was getting married. I had already worked for *Newsweek*, and I knew I could pretty much do whatever I wanted, one way or another. I felt like I had my whole twenties to get through before even thinking about marriage. If the guy I was previously engaged to had not completely rearranged his life, I wouldn't have even considered getting married then, I don't think. Happily Ever After for us cannot look like it did for our parents—many of them married for economic reasons. Not all of the women were able to go out and get fabulous jobs.

When I wrote about my wedding day for *Vogue*, I received many letters from women on this point of our many options. One of the letters I got was from a woman who is 22 years old. She said, "I just finished reading Julia Reed's article, 'Saying "I Do," at 42,' and it absolutely blew me away. I was in awe of her experience of falling in love but being still apprehensive about getting married. Even though I am only 22, I feel that same anxiety about marriage. What if something better comes along? Am I missing out on my one true love because I am already hitched? I dread that feeling, and I am scared of making a wrong decision." This girl ended the letter by saying, "Don't get me wrong, I am only 22 and won't be heading down the infamous aisle anytime soon, but thanks to the article, I will be able to realize what blessings I have and keep them close." A 35-year-old woman wrote that she was laminating the article and wearing it around her neck so she could whip it out for discussion when her perpetual singleness was questioned by critics.

The point is that we have new and wonderful lives to lead, so it's important to realize that your life is not empty because you are not married when your mother thinks you should be. Just get the good foundation going so that when you do make a choice, it is a right choice and a free choice, made for all the right reasons.

● MARCIA KILGORE
Founder of Blissworld

AT 30 . . .
Marcia Kilgore sold 70 percent of the company she began in her living room to LVMH (Moët Hennessy, Louis Vuitton) for an estimated $30 million.

TODAY . . .
Marcia Kilgore spends her days developing new products, writing catalog copy, giving a facial or two, and spending time with her husband.

Marcia Kilgore is a member of the New Girls' Club because she recognized that successful businesses and thriving marital partnerships have something in common: Both require maintenance.

THE BIGGEST PROFESSIONAL RISK I EVER TOOK was going from Let's Face It—my little 3-room skin care studio—to opening Bliss, an 11-room spa. I didn't create a business plan because I knew that once I saw all the numbers staring up at me, I'd be too intimidated to take the plunge.

So I just did it. I found a contractor and a space and spent $400,000 (that I didn't have) building our 5,000-square-foot loft from scratch. I remember picking out lighting, knowing that the fixtures I wanted would cost an extra $15,000, and just saying, "This is the kind of lighting I need, so it's the kind of lighting I'm going to have." I was broke, but I followed my instincts and hoped it would all work. Somehow I had to believe that I would come up with the cash to pay those bills on time. And I did.

I went from zero to 60 in a little less than a week. I had never really managed a staff, and suddenly I had 25 people who all needed job descriptions and directions. I interviewed massage therapists, nail techs, and estheticians; a bunch of kids to meet, greet, and answer the phone; and a manager who had worked as an assistant on the front desk at an upscale hotel. None of us had any real experience in starting a big business, but we were incredibly enthusiastic and excited. Most important for me was that everyone knew how to do the treatments properly. We figured out "structure" along the way. These days, when people come to work at Bliss, they have a more formal orientation to learn about expectations, goals, our company culture, and basics like benefits, but in the beginning, it was sink or swim.

Working so many hours over the past seven years could have become a really big personal problem. I think that a lot of ambitious women spend too much time on their careers at the risk of losing sight of any kind of balance. When you work constantly, you can start to think, "If I'm not spending my time doing something that is productive, it's not time well spent." It's easy to slide into a rut where you do lose touch with the small pleasures of life. If you can't come out of it, you can end up really lonely.

These days, I try to limit my working from Monday through Friday and average about 10 hours a day. (I've tried working weekend days, thinking that I'd take a day off during the week, but it never works out.) I stay very focused while I work—I don't chat, I don't take personal calls, and I don't daydream. My workday might be intense, but it's a little shorter, and when I go home, I don't feel that gravitational pull back to my computer. As with any Type A person, I still feel a little guilty every day if I don't complete what I set out to accomplish. I do try to quiet that nagging voice in my head—and I try not to take work calls or get distracted when I'm spending time with my husband. I try to remember how important it is to our marriage that I am present when we are together.

My husband, Thierry, also worked for Bliss up until a few months ago. Because there was always something happening at the office, we never lacked dinner conversation. Our relationship used to be an extension of work, which—because it was very entrepreneurial and spontaneous—was easy to discuss and debate. Now that he's not working with Bliss, it's a completely different story. He's not particularly interested in chatting about my career challenges, and I don't blame him.

I often see couples eating dinner together without speaking a word, and I made a pact with myself to keep things interesting so we would never be strapped for something to talk about. Now, when my workday is over, I spend 20 minutes scanning some news Web sites so we always have something fresh to discuss at dinner. People often wonder why their relationships don't work, but they don't realize that it takes effort to keep it interesting. If I'm going to spend 10 hours a day making an effort to improve my capabilities at work, why wouldn't I spend at least half an hour making an effort to improve my relationship? You can't be interesting unless you're interested, and if your relationship is more important to you than your job, you shouldn't take it for granted.

Apparently, Jackie Kennedy used to study up on her guests' interests before hosting a dinner so she could keep the conversation lively. While being social was her career (and granted, most people do not have the time for hours of socializing study), if everyone tried a little bit harder to be interesting to his or her partner, we'd see a drastic decline in divorce rates.

● PAULA ZAHN
CNN ANCHOR

AT 30 . . .
Paula Zahn was unemployed—by choice.

TODAY . . .
Paula Zahn is the Emmy-winning anchor of CNN's weeknight primetime program *Paula Zahn Now*. She also hosts *People in the News*, the network's feature program with *People* magazine, profiling newsmakers from politics, sports, business, medicine, and entertainment. On her first day with CNN, Zahn began continuous on-scene coverage of the September 11 terrorist attacks on the World Trade Center. Before joining CNN, she was host of *The Edge with Paula Zahn*, a daily news program on the Fox News Channel. She also spent 10 years at CBS News, cohosting the *CBS Morning News* and anchoring the *CBS Evening News* Saturday edition. Earlier, Zahn was coanchor of ABC's *World News This Morning* and anchored news segments of *Good Morning America*. She joined ABC in November 1987 as anchor of *The Health Show*.

Paula Zahn is a member of the New Girls' Club because she is not afraid to admit that Having It All looks a lot different in real life than it does in the glossy images presented in magazines and on TV.

WHEN I WAS 30 YEARS OLD, I reached a major crossroad. Having worked hard throughout my twenties paying my dues in various local markets—the Midwest, Texas, Boston—I had a clear sense of my professional aspirations. I was thrilled that by age 30, I had landed my absolute dream job: I was an anchor and reporter in Los Angeles, a top-5 market.

Just as I hit my stride professionally, I was thrown a curve ball in my personal life. My job was in L.A., but to get married and live in the same city as my husband, I would need to move to Boston.

It was a crossroad that I knew I would get through, but as in all life decisions, it was one that challenged me to look at the totality of my life. There were days when I wondered, "Should I be giving up one of the best jobs in the country?" Even my friends were conflicted. Some were supportive, but others who had just as deep a commitment to their work as I did said, "You're going back to Boston without a job? What are you going to do, read the newspaper out loud alone in your living room?"

While I was passionate about journalism, I knew that it could be a singular existence. There were times when I'd be out covering a natural disaster and would think, "Am I going to be the last person standing on Galveston Island after it's been evacuated for a hurricane, with a mike in my hand?" I decided to take the leap and head for Boston.

It was perhaps my first adult choice in balancing work and family. However, I had looked to my own family as a guide. When I was in my late twenties and feeling pretty invincible, both my parents were diagnosed with cancer within six months of each other. Watching my parents suffer and making the critical decisions about their care shook things up for me. As they fought their battles, it became even more obvious to me just how important family was. I don't think either one of them would have endured if they hadn't had the support of our wonderful family around them. That experience really centered me.

So I quit my dream job, packed up the very few worldly possessions I had, and moved to Boston.

Of course, it was unsettling not to have any specific plans, particularly when the reality set in that for the first time in my adult life, I did not have a paycheck or a sense of financial independence. However, there was no doubt in my mind that I was going to work again one day, because I believed that if I was committed to a career in journalism, I would find a way to continue.

As luck would have it, shortly after I began my job search, I got a call from ABC News with an offer to anchor a one-day-a-week health show based in Washington, D.C. Spending a few days a week out of town seemed like a reasonable challenge that we could endure, so I took the job. A few months after that, they asked me to sub on *Good Morning America*. And it was during that week—my first weekday national television exposure—that a plane was hijacked. It was a huge story that caught the attention of ABC's top management.

It was a Friday afternoon, and I was in Reagan National Airport heading back to Boston when I was paged by Roone Arledge's office. He said to me, "Look, we are going to make some changes in the morning. Is this something you can do on a full-time basis?"

I remember thinking to myself, "The king of the television industry is asking me if I want this terrific job!" So on the one hand, I was thrilled, while on the other hand, I had just made the decision to quit my job to live in the same city as my husband, and now we had to make the same decision all over again. I told him, "I am absolutely flattered. But as you know, I have just gotten married and moved to Boston. I need to think about it."

After some important heart-to-heart conversations with my husband, we decided that the offer was too good to pass up. So basically, we started our lives over again, together, in New York City.

It was not an easy life that we signed up for. Our transition to New York caused my husband tremendous wear and tear, not only at a time when he was trying to grow his business but also at a time we were trying to start a family. Richard commuted every single day between Boston and New York for nearly three years. We lived in a hotel. And working on a network morning show meant I went to work at 2:30 A.M. every day.

It was a stressful time, but it was also a great adventure. It allowed us to grow up together in many ways, as a couple. The lesson we learned from our odyssey through those first years is that flexibility and patience are essential in marriage. I had relocated once to Boston, and he had relocated once to New York. We had no hard-and-fast rules to play by, but it did give us a good start in making decisions together when either one of us hit a crossroad, large or small.

Three children later, my life is very different today than it was when I was 30. But what hasn't changed is that there is still no such thing as the perfect balance. Are there days when things feel totally out of whack? Absolutely. It's not possible to have everything fall into place in the perfect order every day. But the best lesson for me was to focus not only on the short term but also on the long term. In doing that, big decisions are clearer. You're more able to look back at your life as a whole and see that you have enjoyed your family and your career, and—dare I say—achieved some peace of mind in the process.

● SUSAN LOVE, M.D.
Oncologist and author

AT 30 . . .

Dr. Susan Love was on the verge of being able to stop moonlighting and start making a living as a surgeon.

TODAY . . .

Dr. Susan Love is president and medical director of the Susan Love M.D. Breast Cancer Research Foundation, a nonprofit organization in Santa Barbara, California, that is dedicated to the eradication of breast cancer. She is clinical professor of surgery at UCLA's David Geffen School of Medicine and founder and senior partner in LLuminari, a multimedia women's health company. She is one of the "founding mothers" of the breast cancer advocacy movement and continues this work by serving on the boards of the National Breast Cancer Coalition and the Y-ME National Breast Cancer Organization. She was appointed by President Clinton to the National Cancer Advisory Board in 1998. Her book, *Dr. Susan Love's Breast Book*, has been termed "the bible for women with breast cancer" by the *New York Times*.

Dr. Susan Love is a member of the New Girls' Club because she figured out how to have both the family and career she wanted—even when neither came on conventional terms.

MY LIFE IS A LOT LIKE THAT OLD JOKE—you know, be careful what you wish for. . . . When I was 30, all I was wishing for was a partner and a white picket fence and kids. When I came out as a lesbian, I thought I would never have that dream. But in the end, I got exactly what I wished for—just differently, because here I am today with a partner of 21 years and a teenage daughter, two dogs, two cats, two goldfish—the whole white picket fence package.

I got pregnant at 40, and kids came later in my life for a few specific reasons. First of all, if I had gotten pregnant during surgical training, I would have been fired. Outright. As it was, they were pissed that women were there in the first place. I remember someone saying to me, "I hate operating with women residents because I feel like they're going to cry if I yell at them." So I said, "Well, maybe the guys might appreciate it if you didn't yell also." He was like, "Funny, I haven't thought of that." Still, one of the questions in my interviews for surgical training absolutely was "What kind of birth control are you using?" This was not that long ago! So getting pregnant in my twenties or early thirties was not an option.

Then, when I came out at 32, I figured "that's the end of that." I am the oldest of five, so I was not as invested in having kids, but my partner really wanted children. She tried to get pregnant for a year, then we switched, and it worked with me. We used donor insemination; my daughter's biological father is my partner's cousin.

My family is very ordinary. Our lives are much closer to those of other straight parents than to most of the gay community in Los Angeles. You know—you run your life around your kids' school schedule and around work. Truthfully, the only real perceptible difference for anyone is when I roll over in bed, I see another woman instead of a man. Of course, we've talked to Kate since she was very young about how there are homophobic people in the world. We tell her, there is nothing wrong with you, but isn't it too bad that there are people who are so intolerant? She is a very solid kid and has not had any problems at all. She even likes us still—and she is 15 now, so that's no small accomplishment!

I recently did one of my famous five-year plans that never go quite exactly as scripted and decided to stop traveling as much until Kate goes off to college. What I see now is that you don't always see when kids are younger that they need you more when they are teenagers than when they are toddlers. The teenage years are the time when you are really getting your values in. Sometimes I overhear Kate spouting things that I have told her—so although she'd never admit she is listening, she is. With toddlers, it's much easier to negotiate quality time because they will play with you whenever you want. When Kate was little, I would call from New York and tell her a bedtime story over the phone. She loved that. Little kids are always excited to see you, and they are up for playing all the time. But when girls become teenagers, you never know when they are going to want to talk to you, so you need to be around more. I think it's more important to be physically home more now than it was early on.

The key to balancing work and kids is all about tight scheduling. You know how you sit down with a calendar at the beginning of the year and pick vacation time? That time then gets crossed out—nothing else gets slotted in those weeks except vacation. It's the same thing with juggling career and family. You really have to be deliberate. When Kate was younger, I took her to school every day, so that time was just crossed out for work. I was not available for appointments during those times unless it was a real emergency, and that was just my schedule for a lot of years. If people don't want to hire you because of your scheduling needs, you are creating an uphill battle for yourself. It's so important to find a place that matches your life.

You have to live your life how you want to live it. So much of the lesson I learned by coming out is really one that applies to anyone's life, straight or gay. Because every time you lie or go against what you think is right for you—whether it's pretending you are straight or pretending you don't mind working a million hours a week and missing time with your kid—it makes a little nick on your soul. Those nicks add up. But when you live true to yourself, even though it seems like you may be giving up certain opportunities, you live so much better. And then different opportunities come that turn out to be better because they match the way you are. Fitting a round peg in a square hole never feels right.

● IRIS KRASNOW

AUTHOR AND JOURNALIST

AT 30 . . .

Iris Krasnow was the national feature writer for United Press International in Washington, D.C., where she specialized in celebrity profiles. On the surface, her life was very glamorous—but she felt something was profoundly missing.

TODAY . . .

Iris Krasnow is the mother of four sons, ages 13 on down, and the author of two best-sellers, *Surrendering to Motherhood* and *Surrendering to Marriage*, as well as the recently released *Surrendering to Yourself*. Her work has been featured in many national publications, including *Parade* magazine, the *Wall Street Journal*, and the *Washington Post*. An assistant professor of journalism at American University in Washington, D.C., Krasnow lives with her husband and children in Maryland and speaks on marriage, childrearing, and all aspects of personal growth to groups across the country.

Iris Krasnow is a member of the New Girls' Club because she made changes in her life to accommodate her evolving priorities.

I WAS 30 AND SINGLE when I interviewed the Queen of Jordan. There I was, at her gorgeous palace in Amman, being served icy orange juice and almonds from a silver tray, and I was thinking: "Oh, my God, I have really arrived." Then, a week later, I was by myself, standing alone at the kitchen counter in my tiny Georgetown apartment eating cold Chinese food. Chewing in total silence, no phone ringing, I remember thinking, "But where did I arrive to?"

When I graduated from Stanford in 1976, in the thick of the feminist movement, I was determined to make my mark in journalism, the career of my dreams. At 28, I landed the position of national feature writer for United Press International. My beat was to interview celebrities. As a female on the rise in print journalism, I felt proud to flex every single tentacle and muscle that women used to not be able to flex. I had a real sense of power and a real sense of loyalty to the sisterhood.

But there was something gnawing in my gut. I began to realize, "So what if I met all of these famous people. It wasn't like they were calling me to go have coffee." They weren't my friends. My profession was in full gear, but I was empty deep within. What was twanging in my heart was a deep desire to get married and have babies.

One night, when I was about 31, I was curled up on the couch talking on the phone to my father in Chicago, and he was asking, "How's your job?" And I said, "It's great, Dad!"

After a pause, he said, "You know, maybe you'll want to get married soon and have babies."

I knew he was right, but defensively I shot back, "What would I want to do that for? I am traveling all over the world. Who would want to give this up?"

This father of three responded softly, "Because family is the essence of life, that's why." It took me a while to admit how right he was.

God, I've been so lucky, I realize this now. I got married at 33 and right away, we started trying to get pregnant because we had seen so many friends suffering through fertility problems. Chuck and I had baby after baby, something we both wanted and articulated right away when we met. We were at a restaurant in DuPont Circle, drinking Rolling Rock beer from the bottle; I think it was our third date. And this adorable, adoring man told me that he wanted four children by the time he was 40. I said, "Sounds good to me; we better start moving on this." Our motto became "Four before Forty," and we made the deadline when I delivered twins Jack and Zane two months after my thirty-ninth birthday.

I know women who are clear that they don't want children. And I say, "God bless you for knowing that," and not trying to have babies just because you think you should. But for those of us driven by a profound urge to reproduce, we need to surrender to motherhood, and that often means downsizing our careers.

In retrospect, I see that leaving daily journalism was the best deci- sion I've ever made. By extracting myself from a profession that can eat the heart out of your family life, I had extracted myself from a seesaw of stress and guilt. When you're a mother of young children in an office all day, too often while at work you are consumed with the children back home. And while you're at home, you are consumed with unfinished business at the office. This is a wrenching tug of war no person can win; something's got to give, or else your sanity goes.

Letting go of a full-time profession was not easy for a driven woman like me. But after doing it all, graduating from a great college, ascending in a great career, I realized that "it all" is just too damn much. Yes, there were times I did wince—seeing Diane Sawyer on the air interviewing some celebrity I'd like to be interviewing. Reading a riveting profile in *Vanity Fair* that I wished I had written. But when our four babies started turning into kind and compassionate and respectful little boys, never once did I look back and say, "Wow, I wish I hadn't given up the fast track." The slow track had been the right path to go on at that point in my life. After all, no matter how powerful or prestigious is your job, work is just work. Family is everything. Don't worry that unstoppable working women will think you're copping out.

The most important point I can express is to tell young women not to want anyone else's life. It's a myth to think that anyone has it more together than you do or that someone is far happier than you are. What you see on the surface is never really what's going on in someone else's life. I am 48 years old, and what I've learned as I mature is that the more I dare to be myself, the more I get to have a life built on joy and adventure and peace. And if people don't like it, it's their problem, not mine. All that matters is that you are living your truth—that's where real power lies.

● LT. GENERAL CLAUDIA KENNEDY
U.S. ARMY (RETIRED)

AT 30 . . .
Lt. General Claudia Kennedy was training to become an intelligence officer at the National Security Agency.

TODAY . . .
When Lt. General Claudia Kennedy retired from the U.S. Army in June 2000, she had made history by becoming its first woman three-

star general. The highest-ranking female officer of her time, she was deputy chief of staff for intelligence, overseeing 45,000 soldiers worldwide.

Lt. General Claudia Kennedy is a member of the New Girls' Club because she has learned that some women can feel that they Have It All without having children.

A WOMAN'S EMOTIONAL RESILIENCE and self-esteem have to be found internally. If you are looking for support from outside, you're wasting your time, because whether or not you get it will only be a random result. You need to interpret both the negative and the positive as merely interesting but not definitive. If you see it as definitive, you will spend your whole life reacting.

I got married in November of 1974, and by August 1975, I was in the advanced course for military intelligence. That was a huge turning point in my career—and it was more than a little daunting because male peers in the course had been in intelligence for years, and up until that point, those assignments had not been an option for me. I had to make up for a lot of lost time.

Though I did not have a real clear concept of what was ahead, I did gather that going to Korea would be a good thing for my career, but I was married, and I also wanted to be with my husband. We had to decide whether he should follow me to my next assignment and be at loose ends professionally or whether he should move separately to someplace that we could guess would be my next assignment. The question of "How are we going to make a life together?" loomed large—I can vividly remember thinking about it and mulling it over for a long time. Yet I also wondered if there would ever be a time when this was going to be easy, and I was pretty sure that time would never come. Every single assignment was going to be a bit of a struggle, because he would have to start over in his career or find work some way, over and over again. He was already unhappy that he was not fulfilling any major work ambitions at the time, and he was not going to play Army wife.

For all of these reasons, it felt particularly crucial to have clear thoughts about a potential game plan for making my career work with my marriage when the time came for me to meet with the assignment officer, toward the end of the military intelligence officer advanced course. The assignment officer is like a career counselor, but when I explained my situation, he said, "You women are never going to make any progress in the Army until male chauvinist pigs like me are out." He was just that obvious and direct. And by the way, he was the guy who was supposed to be encouraging all of us! He was the career counselor!

Still, I knew that there was a level of support as well as a level of resistance, and I knew other officers felt differently than he did. But the main reason that I stuck with it was that I loved being in the army more than I cared about what the guys thought of me. Sure, I wanted to know who was on my side and who was not, but by the time I met with that assignment officer, I already realized that it was not up to them decide if I would stay in the army or not—it was up to me. That was a very important factor in my resilience.

Ultimately, my husband and I ended up getting divorced. It wasn't the Army's fault; we just really were not meant to be with each other. He was not the right choice for me. That was really hard, because I also knew getting divorced meant that I was at risk of not having time to have children. If you rewind and do the math, I was about 28 when I realized this marriage was not working and it was only a matter of time before it would collapse. I knew I wasn't going to have children with this person. And then, it would be a few years to recover and a few years to figure out what's coming next. At that time, the thinking was that 35 was the oldest you could be to get pregnant. By the time I got to 35, I thought I still had until I was 40. By the time I was 40, I thought *maybe* 45. My friends listened to me agonize about this for 15 years. The issue of children and motherhood was alive all the time for me. Yet I think I stayed in the Army because I just found the work so compelling. I knew for sure I could make it work there, that it was just up to me, and if I worked hard, it would come out right. I had already seen that working hard would not necessarily make a marriage work out right. And maybe I needed to grow up a lot more before I could really be happily married.

I ultimately realized that even if I did not have children of my own, there were children substitutes everywhere. There were nieces and nephews and children of friends, and there are lots of ways to participate in society to help support other parents who have not been able to do some of their job. There are ways that you can do part of it for them, and that is both for the young soldiers and for the soldiers who have children of their own. In the Army, it's part of leadership to make sure that your people are well cared for at all times. I took it on to try to do concrete things to make life easier for the soldiers who were also parents. I'd look around and see if it was a reasonable thing to ask soldiers to work rotating shifts 24/7 and not provide child care. Does that make any sense? Nope. I worked really hard to remedy that when I was a battalion commander, without success, and then later as a brigade commander, I found a very innovative way to provide child care on the base. I was very pleased with that.

I retired as the first woman three-star general in the history of the U.S. Army, and I am proud of that, but I feel most successful when I meet my own expectations—when I think about my priorities and when I live up to those priorities. So I would not declare myself a failure for not having a successful marriage and children in my first 30 years as an adult. I finally realized, over a lengthy course of 10 or 12 years, that my life was just not going to happen that way. Today, I am married. I have been married since September 2002. And though there won't be any children, I've got his children and his grandchildren, and I feel really good about that. If these relationships remain healthy and functional and happy from every viewpoint, that will feel like a huge success to me.

Any number of times in my life I've thought, "Well, okay, it's over for me." This or that was never going to happen because of some particular milestone that I had missed, that I thought signified the end of whatever it was that I was working to achieve at the time. But what those missed milestones almost always did was give me more time to develop internally, to get more depth and more profound experience at something that later proved to be the reason I accomplished the next big thing, the next big step.

It's important to understand that time is fluid. I think that women go through a crisis at 30, or whenever, when they feel their youth is over.

But you know what? Your youth may be over in terms of chronology, but you might just be about to become free of all the silly high school things that were holding you back from being experimental and innovative and creative. There are times in your future when you will be more beautiful than you are today; you need to get old enough to be that beautiful. What I do with flowers is a metaphor for this. When I get cut flowers, do I throw them away after the third day or after a week? Never. I keep changing the water, then after a certain point, I don't put any water in there at all and let them get dried and beautiful. They are often more beautiful dried than they were before. You're just wasting that beauty if you prematurely throw the flowers away. You don't ever see what their peak could be. When they get too old to stay on the stems, take the petals and put them in a ginger jar. There's no end to it. But truthfully, what is the point of saying they are more beautiful dried than they are fresh? It's just another kind of beauty—that is really the point.

CHAPTER SEVEN

Navigating the New Glass Ceiling
Finding the Right Fit in the Work-Family Puzzle

IN MANY WAYS, working out the work-life/kids-family puzzle is the most painful manifestation of the Midlife Crisis at 30 because it's not just about us—it's about the people we love, our promises to them, and the means we devise to honor those promises. When we're up against the New Glass Ceiling, the first things we're tempted to sacrifice to make it work are our promises to ourselves. These members of the New Girls' Club have found a way to keep both promises, and in the process, they've identified a new middle path between the black-and-white choices their mothers faced. Their hard-won revelations provide road maps for the rest of us as we collectively traverse new work-motherhood territory.

● MARY MATALIN
POLITICAL STRATEGIST

AT 30 . . .
Mary Matalin was a first-year law student. She dropped out before her 31st birthday.

TODAY . . .

Mary Matalin has served as assistant to President George W. Bush and counselor to Vice President Dick Cheney and was the first White House official to hold a double title. Before joining the Bush/Cheney White House, Matalin hosted CNN's critically acclaimed debate show *Crossfire*. She has written for various periodicals, including *Newsweek* and the *Los Angeles Times*, and is coauthor of the best-selling political campaign book *All's Fair: Love, War, and Running for President* with her husband, James Carville, who was the chief campaign strategist for Clinton/Gore in 1992.

Mary Matalin is a member of the New Girls' Club because she was not afraid to step away from her esteemed position at the White House when she recognized her family needed her more.

BY THE TIME I WAS 30, I knew I wanted to work on campaigns. But I didn't want to be a phone-bank or mail person, I wanted to really be with the big boys in THE campaign. I wanted to work on a presidential election.

Life on the campaign trail is nomadic, and it is juvenile—and I loved it. As sophisticated and strategic as the issues are, the actual daily life of the people who are solving problems in the field feels a lot like being in grad school. You live in hotels, and your family is the campaign. No matter whether it was at the Republican National Convention or the presidential campaign, my room would always become the place where everyone gathered at the end of the day to drink wine, eat pretzels, and smoke cigarettes. It was much more than a job—it was a lifestyle.

Then we lost in '92, and not only did my whole social and professional structure collapse, but I was so high profile in the campaign that I became radioactive in the business. Nobody wanted to hire me. It was extremely disorienting, but I couldn't sit around and wallow, because I was supporting myself. I couldn't afford to be myopic in pursuit of a single goal because my actual options in the political world were suddenly extremely limited.

Luckily, someone called me and asked me if I wanted to do a TV show, and that launched me off in a completely different direction—one not of my own making. Before I knew it, I was doing 3 hours of radio every day and a half-hour of TV every night. I never would've thought to do that on my own; the opportunity just kind of fell in my lap. Then I got married and had kids, and the rest is history.

The only time I ever stopped and actively reevaluated my career was after George W. Bush won. He was changing the trajectory of the party, and it was thrilling. I wanted to contribute, to give back, to be in public service again. My evaluation process was, "I'll never have another chance to do this; I'll never be as devoted to anybody as I am to George W. Bush." And that changed everything.

Before I took the job at the White House, another working mom gave me some very good advice. She said to me, "You need to understand in your heart why you want to do this, because for the next however-long-you-do-this-job, people are going to be telling you that you made a stupid decision." I knew it wasn't going to be fun at all—it was a really hard job. And it got even harder after 9/11. But even when the stress was overwhelming—those days when I'd cry in the car on the way to work, asking myself, "Why am I doing this??"—I always knew the answer to that question: I believe in this president.

The job was very tough on my family. Let's start with the practical—I cut my income by 90 percent by working for government again. We had babies, we had committed financially to a certain lifestyle, and my husband thought money was important, as it should be at my age. And the hours were awful. It was an abrupt change, and it was a big one.

I told James everything would work out with the girls, and for the most part, it did. Other mothers will recognize that your kids can handle pretty much anything, because it's not necessarily the being-there, it's the being-present that matters most. And unless there was a huge catastrophe or I was at an undisclosed secure location, I'd shut the work part of my life down when I got home and was focused and present in a way that I almost can't do now. So the kids were fine.

The real difficulty was James. Let's put the cards on the table—he is not a twenty-first century man. He left off at Beaver Cleaver. His mother was tough and smart and did a hundred times more stuff than I did, but you had this impression that she was June Cleaver. A critical difference with women of your age is that your men grew up with serious working mothers, so they seemed to be more attuned to the juggle. James is from the South, and he was 49 when we got married. He expected things would be a certain way, and it was very disorienting to him when it was not Norman Rockwell. His emotional support was absent for a long time, though I doubt he was aware of that. What's most important is that he put up with it at all; that he took it on blind faith that I would make it all work is truly the highest form of support that could be gotten from this.

James and I worked a very careful balance, but there is a certain amount of life that you cannot plan ahead for, and some very big things went wrong. Like, our nanny [who'd watched the kids since birth] died— which was horrible, painful, and very sudden. She was so much more than just a nanny; she was like my wife and their other mother. She calibrated everything, and losing her was terrible. We all loved her.

My extended absences upset the balance, too. When I went to the Middle East for 10 days, I had everything so pre-wired before I left it was almost Stepford-esque. But what I didn't anticipate was that the hamsters would die, Matty would lose her first tooth, and James would feel inadequate as a father because a school project he helped with did not go over as well as he would have liked (though Matty was just fine with it).

After a while, the question became not whether I could Do It All or Have It All but rather "How can long can I do it all well?" If I had had a job where I could perform at 80 percent, it probably would have worked out fine, but that was not the case. I had a very important job for a man I adore, revere, and respect. Dick Cheney is brilliant, and he has certain standards. I felt oftentimes more inadequate at the office than I did at home. That's not a good place to be. And on top of it all, I was perpetually exhausted.

Ultimately, I had a Real Woman Revelation (one that had nothing to do with June Cleaver). I finally asked myself, "Who needs me more?" And that's when I realized, it's somebody else's turn to do this job. I'm indispensable to my kids, but I'm not close to indispensable to the White House. I love my husband to the bottom of my feet, and I felt he deserved better. And I really missed my kids—they are just so much fun to be around. As hard as I tried, quality time did not always happen, because my kids don't always run on my clock. I wanted to be around more.

I am 50 years old—I had my kids when I was 42 and 45—so the stakes were completely different. I wanted to provide a service for the Cheneys, and it was extraordinarily fulfilling for me, but I was not trying to build a career with the administration—it was an anti-career move, as a matter of fact. I don't know what I would do if I was in this situation at your age, because I think the emotional quotient of not already being 100 percent established would have been very pulling on me.

If you want to know the solution, this is it: Having control over your schedule is the only way that women who want to have a career and a family can make it work. You've got to look for ways to create options for yourself that don't necessarily fall on a linear career path. All that stuff about goal setting and career trajectories is oversold and distracting.

My absolute favorite statistic is the phenomenal rate of growth of women-owned businesses—the entrepreneurial path is emerging as the practical solution to the impossible juggling act. Smart women have a low tolerance for institutional B.S. Working mothers have an immense capacity to multi-task, but you can't multi-task if someone else is yanking your chain. I love that women everywhere are asking themselves, "Why is this meeting taking so damn long? I can do this better, faster, in some other environment." Every time I walk down the street in my neighborhood, there's a new linen shop or antique shop or flower shop—and that is the sign of happy women saying, "Been there, done that, and now I'm doing my own thing. I'm proving myself to myself."

The pace of feminism is so accelerated that by the time we internalize and act on changes, they're changing again. The search for Having It All in a way that's sustainable for an endless period of time is causing younger women to be more creative. I think that's very cool—it's better for families, it's better for you, and it's completely new terrain. What is still lingering, unfortunately, is the notion that when things don't go as planned, it always feels like it's our fault. I'm incredibly excited about where women in their twenties and thirties can and will go—but we really have to get beyond that guilt to keep things moving forward.

● TEYA RYAN
CNN EXECUTIVE VICE PRESIDENT AND GENERAL MANAGER

AT 30 . . .

Teya Ryan was producing magazine stories for local news in California.

TODAY . . .

Teya Ryan is responsible for CNN's day-to-day news operation, encompassing all aspects of programming and production. Named to this position in 2002, she previously served as executive vice president and general manager of CNN Headline News. Ryan was the creator and architect of the redesigned Headline News, which launched in August 2001. She's received numerous awards for her work, including an Emmy, a CableACE, and several American Women in Radio and Television awards, Houston awards, and Environmental Media awards.

Teya Ryan is a member of the New Girls' Club because she mastered what so many Gen-X women are struggling with—how to manage a new baby and a big job at the same time.

MY DAUGHTER ALEXA WAS BORN exactly one week before we relaunched CNN Headline News. I remember looking at my husband and saying, "I have no idea how I am going to get through this." But I was there for the launch of the network, and I was in the delivery room when my daughter was born. Truthfully, it felt like I gave birth twice in once week.

We connected with a birth mother when she was about seven months' pregnant. That's always a very tense time, because you never really know what's going to happen—the birth mother can change her mind at any time. So it's a very nerve-racking experience, and my way of dealing with all that uncertainty was simply not to talk about it until I knew the adoption was definitely happening. My direct boss, Jim Walton, was the only person at work who knew what was going on. Most people found out the day she was born.

My daughter was actually was born in San Diego. I flew out with my husband on Sunday, and she was born Monday morning. I stayed with her Monday, Tuesday, Wednesday, and Thursday, then flew back to Atlanta on the red-eye on Thursday night and went to work Friday, Saturday, and Sunday. We launched the new Headline News on Monday, and I stayed in Atlanta until Wednesday night. I flew out Wednesday night, was with her on Thursday, and we brought her home Friday. My husband was with her the whole time. That was the last time I have been separated from her for more than two nights—and very rarely that long—since that first week.

It was an exhausting and exhilarating week in my life. I barely caught my breath. I suppose the way I got through it was that all the groundwork for the launch was done, and I worked with a lot of very talented people who kept things going for me. I very much believed I was doing the right thing and was confident that what we were going to see on the air would reflect the picture I had in my mind. Was the technology going to work? That I did not know. Were there going to be things I could not control? Probably. But I knew at the end of the day we were going to do okay with the relaunch of the network.

One of the things you learn how to do very well in this business is to be where you are in that moment with laser attention. When you are in a control room, you can't think about anything else. If there is breaking news, you have to focus on that entirely and deal with everything else when it's over. So part of it is just the way I am wired. This ability to bifurcate helps me a lot. I can remember a few minutes after Alexa was born, she was a little blue. We went over to the nursery, and the nurses put her under the heat lamps—she was doing fine, but we ended up staying there for about 4 hours while they raised her body temperature. I was with her the entire time, and I promise you, I did not think of anything but her for those 4 hours and beyond that into the night.

The minute you have a child, your work gets riskier. Before kids, your husband has his work, and you have your work, and you come together when it's possible—but the whole equation changes when you have children. Because the thing that really matters is your family. You want to be able to support your family, and it's important to have a sense of pride in your work, but when a six-month-old baby needs you—there is just no comparison. It's not a fair fight. The child wins. The incredible, unspeakable power of the love you can feel for another human being just brings you to your knees. It's just that wonderful. The biological, emotional, and cultural pull of wanting to be with your children is real. It's extremely difficult to balance these feelings and the demands of your work. It's a daily struggle for most working mothers, including me.

There are some bad days, and I do not think I should sugar-coat it. But I also happen to love my work. I love the physical building of television, I love edit bays, I love the process of the control room, I think breaking news is exciting, and I love doing long-form documentaries. I have a real passion for that creative expression—it's like being a painter. And I also believe passionately in the power of a free press; it's a crucial part of democracy. So for me, it's exciting to come to work.

My career has been a series of one big risk after another, of doing projects that people said would never work, of doing projects that were controversial and very visible. The Headline News relaunch was extremely risky—I was taking a relatively lucrative business that needed an upgrade in a very well known company and doing something so radical, so visually obvious. You can't go hide; it's right there—laid out for everyone to see. But in my mind, the minute you stop taking risks is the minute you are no longer creative. And if you trust your creativity, you are going to fail sometimes and succeed sometimes, but you are always going to feel alive.

Now that I am a mother, I take different kinds of professional risks, too. I walk out of work as early as I can and leave work on my desk. I walk away. And you have to trust that no matter how much you do that night, there's always going to be more. So don't blow your brains out on it—

walk away from it, go home, see your family, be with them. Again, it's focus. When I go home, I am with my family. But would I be entirely honest to say that work never impedes on my family time? Quite the opposite—it never goes away. Not in the 24/7 news business.

What makes me feel successful? It's not awards, promotions, or job titles. What makes me feel really successful is that I did what I wanted to do and what I believed in. I kept proposing things in my career that excited me, and I managed to convince others that it was to their benefit to do them also. Does that happen all the time? No. There are a lot of things that I want to do that I can't convince a boss or a company to do. But I've done enough that I am happy.

● BERNADINE HEALY, M.D.
SENIOR WRITER, *U.S. NEWS AND WORLD REPORT*

AT 30 . . .
Dr. Bernadine Healy was an assistant professor at Johns Hopkins University in Baltimore.

TODAY . . .
Dr. Bernadine Healy has led the National Institutes of Health (NIH), the Research Institute at the Cleveland Clinic, the College of Medicine and Public Health at Ohio State University, and the American Red Cross. She led the Red Cross response to the events of 9/11, mobilizing volunteers, blood, and financial support for the range of services triggered by the president's activation of the Federal Response Plan. At NIH, she conceived of and launched the NIH Women's Health Initiative (WHI), a $625 million effort to study causes, prevention, and cures for diseases that affect women at midlife and beyond. The WHI was the largest clinical research study ever established and will continue to provide information on the full range of women's health and disease well into this century. She is now a medicine, health, and science columnist and senior writer for *U.S. News and World Report* and serves on the President's Advisory Committee for Science and Technology.

Dr. Bernadine Healy is a member of the New Girls' Club because she managed to sustain a long-term balance between the demands of her career and the demands of her family—whether she was married or single.

I HAVE ALWAYS BELIEVED THAT I could be passionately committed to my career and still be passionately committed to my family. To me, developing and using your God-given talents—man or woman, mom or dad—brings something positive to any relationship, provided that the career endeavor is positive. When I was starting out many years ago, it was common to say that a woman's career would inevitably detract from her family. I have always resisted that tyrannical, sure-to-lay-a-guilt-trip kind of view, always believing my career in medicine would be the opposite. A nurturing, humanitarian profession which challenges one to keep up with science and society makes for a pretty interesting if not important perspective. Looking at the close relationship I share with my daughters and my husband today, it's worked for us.

I had my first child when I was 34 and my second at 41, so my kids came along when I was well into my career. (My preference would have been sooner, by the way.) Sadly, right after my first daughter was born, I was divorced, becoming a single mother and head of household. Suddenly there was no question that I needed my career—I was the breadwinner. But the logistics of balancing career and motherhood as a single mother proved to be not much different than they were with my next child, who I had in the embrace of a wonderful, happy second marriage. Whether you are doing it alone or with a partner, you can have a strong family life and a rich career at the same time—as long as you recognize that it's going to involve some sacrifice and a lot of focus. You are not going to have much time for some of the things you used to do. There are certain things you'll have to give up, such as those weekly theater tickets, and there are other things that you'll have to decide that you are not going to worry about—perhaps window washing.

Some years ago, there was a story in one of the medical journals about the desperation of the doctor mom. It described her hectic day generally in these terms: Getting the kids ready for school, fixing breakfast, throwing in the laundry, running off to work. Then, after a heavy day of medical work, her life became schlepping off to pick up groceries and dry cleaning, running home to cook, clean up, supervise homework, and have a guilt trip about her son's stuttering. A daunting double shift.

The key to being a working mother is to learn how to be an executive as well. You are not going to be able to do everything. Being a good wife or mother does not mean you have to cook every meal, wash every bit of laundry, do all the grocery shopping, or, for that matter, suffer guilt trips for all that you are not able to do. You have to plan ahead and do your best, but no one really does it all. It's not realistic. The details you have to figure out for yourself, but getting help is crucial. There is no Superwoman.

My kids are 24 and 17, and they are both girls who can stand on their own two feet. And I am extremely close to both of my daughters even if I am not there physically with them all the time. Actually, they do not want me to be there with them all the time. But they sure know that those chains of communication are always open. You have to be on the same wavelength and make sure you don't let too many hours go by without touching base in some way. With phone, fax, e-mail, communication is easier than ever before, and communication in every possible way is really what relationships are about. Of course, it's the talking face-to-face and hugging and loving time together, too—and the utter commitment that you will drop anything and everything if they need you. The glue that keeps families together even after the young fly from the nest is the pattern of communication that has largely been defined during their growing-up years.

Everyone needs to set boundaries to allow a personal life as well as a marketplace life. That applies whether you have kids or not. My boundaries have never been a 30-hour week; it's been more like a 60-plus-hour week. But I also have as compensation what I call my Weekend Rule, which I very rarely violate: I do not allow work to intrude on my family time on the weekends. (And in every job, I have always respected my staff's weekend time as well.) As a doctor, there are on-call schedules, and that's fine, but you have to make sure you compensate for that time, too. I once gave up an honorary degree at an Ivy League university because it meant being away over a long weekend. The president of the university was utterly shocked, and he was certain I was turning him down because I was accepting a similar honor at a competing Ivy League institution. It was hard for him to believe it was really because it violated my family Weekend Rule.

The other key to balance is creativity. When my first daughter was about four years old, I was asked to accept a 10-day lectureship in Australia and New Zealand. I called them up and said the only way I could do it was if my daughter came along, too. Asking to bring your little munchkin on a serious business trip was totally unheard of in those days, but I must say, my hosts were great about it. My daughter was a good sport, too, making me instantly famous for having my closest kin fall asleep the moment I got up to speak. That trip reminds me of a tender moment we had way back then. One very early morning, I was preparing a lecture as my little one crept in and started working on her "letters" nearby. Barely disturbing me, she slipped me a little note adorned by pretty crayon art: "I love you, mom. You're a mush." I guess I've always been a mush, for my family—and for my career. And it's mostly worked out just fine.

● JUDY BLUME

Author

At 30 . . .

Judy Blume was a stay-at-home mother.

Today . . .

Judy Blume's work has been translated into more than 20 languages, and more than 75 million copies of her books have been sold worldwide. Adults as well as children recognize such Blume classics as *Are You There God? It's Me, Margaret*, *Superfudge*, *Blubber*, *Deenie*, and *Forever,* as well as her latest, *Summer Sisters*, the *New York Times* number one best-seller. Blume is the founder and trustee of the Kids Fund, a charitable and educational foundation, and she serves on the board of the National Coalition against Censorship, working to protect intellectual freedom.

Judy Blume is a member of the New Girls' Club because she figured out that it was all right to have kids first and a career that comes later—and that everyone must eventually choose the work/life/family path that is right for them.

I GAVE THE COMMENCEMENT ADDRESS at Mount Holyoke College this year. While I was writing my talk, I thought about a young woman who'd graduated from there 20 years ago. She's had a fantastic career, so I e-mailed her and asked, "Laura . . . what do you wish you had been told at your graduation?" Her response was immediate and strong. She said that women of her generation were told not only could they have everything, but also that they *must*, or else they were failures. She begged me to tell the graduates that you can't necessarily Have It All, and you shouldn't feel guilty about it. I think she's right.

Women can have serial lives (so can men if they choose to). There's a time to have babies if you want them, and it's important to allow yourself that time. Some women can pull off having a thriving career and a family simultaneously, but don't beat yourself up if you can't. The whole thing about freedom is to have the choice to decide what works for you, on your own, and not to feel pressured to prove to everyone "I can do all of this!" and then to consider yourself a failure if you can't.

My kids believed that my career came easily. For better or for worse, I think I protected them from both my disappointments and my successes. I don't think they gave much thought to my work when they were growing up. I was the only mom on the block who worked then, and I think I must not have wanted them to see me as being different. Or maybe I played down my writing because my then-husband tolerated it only as long as it didn't interfere with his life. If I were doing it all over again, I would make my work a more integral part of our lives. In the '70s, everyone on my suburban block, including my own family, considered writing my hobby. It's funny that I get still get letters from kids asking,

"Do you have any other hobbies besides writing?" That always cracks me up because writing is definitely not my hobby. It's neither easy nor fun. Most writers would tell you that.

I realize now that determination is every bit as important as talent. You can have all the talent in the world, but unless you're determined, you won't make it through the inevitable rejections. I must have been really determined, because I got plenty of rejections! I wasn't driven by a need for success—rather, it was about my need for creative expression. Were I coming of age today, I'm not sure what I'd be doing. I know it would be in the creative arts, but would it be writing? For me, writing was something I could do at home, and there was no financial investment involved. All I needed was my college typewriter and the stories that had always been in my head.

Women can look at my life and say, "Yeah, but you had a husband to support you while you were trying to get started," and that's certainly true. My story is different from those who have to worry about how to get food on the table while having a burning need to do something else.

Creating structure when you're working at home is always a challenge. When you have little kids, it comes down to being really focused. If you have 2 hours to write when they're with a babysitter or at preschool or napping, that's when you need to get it done. You can't afford to answer your e-mail or pay your bills during those hours. But just because you're not actively writing doesn't mean you're not thinking. I get my best ideas when I'm away from my computer. A really successful day can be one where I think of a line that might turn into a story idea, or the voice of a character pops into my head. The trick for me is to write that line down, get that voice on the page—even on the side of a Kleenex box or the back of a grocery list. Otherwise, it may fly right out of my head.

The worlds of men and women will be different as long as we're the ones having the babies and ultimately making the changes in our lives to accommodate them. I know women who have very nurturing partners. I know men who stay at home with the kids. I know gay and lesbian couples who seem to have worked out how to have dual careers and raise children at the same time. I don't think I could have handled a demanding career when my children were young. It would have been too stressful for me.

I've learned that when I feel overwhelmed or stressed, I need to back off and remind myself that I can't do everything at once. Then I get away from my computer, get out of the house, and go for a walk. If it's family life that's stressing me out, I run to my computer, close the door behind me, and lose myself in work. Every woman has her own rhythm, and the key is to find your own and then listen to it.

● SUZANNE VEGA
Singer/songwriter

At 30 . . .

Suzanne Vega had earned three Grammy nominations, including Record of the Year. Her song "Luka," written from the perspective of an abused boy, hit number three on the charts—after her demo tape had been rejected by every major label.

Today . . .

Suzanne Vega has released eight critically acclaimed albums and continues to perform to sold-out crowds. She is author of *The Passionate Eye: The Collected Writings of Suzanne Vega*, a volume of poems, lyrics, essays, journalistic pieces, and more.

Suzanne Vega is a member of the New Girls' Club because she is honest enough to admit that the reality of motherhood can be as overwhelming as the biological desire to have children.

Thirty was a very strange time for me. I had gotten my first record deal at 24 and had the biggest success of my life at 27. At 30, my third album, which was more artistically expansive, had just come out, and the timing of the release was terrible. It was 1991, and we were on the verge of going to war with Iraq. The economy was in bad shape, and the tour was not going as well as the last one had. Also, there was a lot of new competition. Before "Luka," everyone told me, "We can't sign you. You are just a girl with a guitar." Then, after "Luka," every record label was like, "Oh, wow! We need a girl with a guitar!" I was bewildered.

I also wanted to have a baby. I remember walking down the street, and when I'd see a pregnant woman, this feeling would well up inside of me. I was so jealous of what they had. When that biological desire to have a baby hits, it's a physical reaction, almost like an appetite. The intensity of that feeling took me by surprise.

The physical demands of touring made me really skinny, run down, and anemic. So I was going to the doctor a lot, and the nurses would always tease me, saying, "When are you going to have a baby?" And "If you haven't married him by now, you're not going to." And "Listen honey, you have got to have a child now, because after you get to be 35, it's no fun. Go get busy." The way they laid it out was just so practical: So this is how it is.

My mother had four children before she was 24. I was born when she was 18, and I remember always feeling that I somehow interrupted the flow of her life. And I thought, "I am not going to have a bunch of kids early on like my mother did." So you wait, and wait, and wait—until panic sets in and it becomes, "Oh, my God, I waited too long! Now I won't be able to have children at all!"

Then I met Mitchell. I was 32 years old, and he was my producer. We had this great working relationship and an uncanny chemistry. We fell very much in love, but he was married. I did not want to get involved with someone else's husband, so I stayed away from him until he separated from his wife—which I think was wise.

I wanted a baby, but Mitchell had just broken away from his family and his child, and he felt a lot of guilt about that. I don't think he would have leaped into another relationship so quickly if he had a choice in the matter. He would have preferred to wait a few years, but I was afraid that I might not be able to get pregnant if we didn't start trying right away. I was under the impression I would be very delicate like Audrey Hepburn and need a lot of bed rest. But that isn't what happened. I became pregnant immediately—I was as big as a house, as strong as an ox, and not at all delicate. In retrospect, I pushed things along faster than I should have.

So we met. Had a baby. Got married. Everyone says babies change your life, and they really do. First of all, the creative process went right out the window. All I could think about was, "Is the baby eating? Is she not eating? What can I do to make her eat?" And feeding doesn't solve all of it. Sometimes they're coming down with something, sometimes they're bored, and sometimes you have no idea why they're crying for 4 hours straight. Figuring out the baby's demands was often puzzling, overwhelming, and really hard. I was shocked by how completely unprepared I was for the reality of motherhood.

After we had Ruby, Mitchell moved to my house in New York from California, so that was an adjustment, too. He maintained his own house in California as well; we were always running back and forth. We had this great equal partnership at work, but after he moved in, it was clear the household-running came down to me. You see, Mitchell came from a very traditional family. So he would come home at 6 o'clock, look at me, and say, "Where's dinner?" He was never accusatory, like, "Where is my dinner, woman!" Rather, it was more like, "How will it appear? Where might it be, Suzanne?"

Then I would freak out. "How the hell am I supposed to know?" Crying baby, ringing phone, leaky roof, burned food . . . and oh, yes, there was a contract to negotiate because I was a recording artist. Our life was kind of like *The Lucy Show*—but it wasn't funny.

Mitchell's response was to withdraw into his work. It would be midnight and Sheryl Crow would call on the phone. "Hi, is Mitchell still up?"

"Hang on a second . . . Sheryl."

?!?!?!?!?!?!

Now, I have nothing bad to say about Sheryl Crow. I think she's a great musician and a lovely person. But now she got to be the Cool Chick in the studio with my husband while I was at home, 20 pounds heavier, trying to unlock the mystery of the crying baby all day. I was jealous. I wanted my Cool Chick role back!

It was really hard to make those worlds merge. The best times were when we were on tour together. Mitchell was my musical director with the band, and that lent an element of peace to everything because everyone was earning money, we were all together as a family, and our roles were clear. We had a lot of great moments just hanging out and playing with Ruby on the tour bus. But when I would pack up the baby and follow him to a studio somewhere, it didn't work. I felt like a weight, yet I didn't want to stay home without him. It put a big strain on our marriage.

Finally, I realized I couldn't keep dragging Ruby around the world. She had to start socializing and going to school. It was very hard being the artist, the mother, and the wife. And wife was the thing that had to go. Mother could not. Artist could not. We made the decision to separate, and he went back to California.

My fantasy was that if you really loved someone, they would tune in and know what you felt all the time. You'd anticipate each other's needs. You'd never have to explain things, like how you were exhausted from feeding the baby all night. Or that this other person was driving you nuts. Or could you go around the corner and get stuff for dinner? Relationships take a lot more talking and a lot less intuition than I ever imagined. The more you know what the expectations are, the better off you will be.

Today, I spend a lot of time writing love notes. I find myself telling my daughter, "Sweetie, Mommy loves you. I promise you we can spend time together and play with the lizards as soon as I come home from the tour." Then I find myself saying to my audience, "Hey, I am coming out with new stuff soon. Sorry it's taken a while. I have been a little busy playing with the lizards with my kid." There are days when I feel I am failing at both jobs. But then there are other times when I think I am really managing to do it all well. I have a great career and a beautiful daughter, and I am in a good long-term relationship. And those are the moments that make it all worthwhile.

The one piece of practical advice that I can share is this: When you have a baby, it really helps to have experienced people around. My sister lives around the corner, and my mother lives three blocks away. That is so incredibly helpful. They both work, so they understand the juggling, the reality of everyone's life who works and has kids. So stay close to your family if you can, if you get along with them, or just be sure to have a community of women around you who have children and know what you're going through. It makes a world of difference.

● A'LELIA BUNDLES
AUTHOR, JOURNALIST, AND EXECUTIVE

AT 30 . . .
A'Lelia Bundles had just begun a nine-month leave of absence from her job at NBC News to begin the research that ultimately resulted in her best-selling biography of her great-great-great grandmother, Madam C. J. Walker—America's first black female millionaire.

TODAY . . .
A'Lelia Bundles is director of talent development for ABC News in Washington, D.C., and New York. She was deputy bureau chief of ABC News in Washington from 1996 to 1999, after 20 years as a network television producer with ABC and NBC News. Her critically acclaimed book, *On Her Own Ground: The Life and Times of Madam C. J. Walker*, was named a 2001 *New York Times* Notable Book. Among her journalism awards are a du Pont Gold Baton and an Emmy.

A'Lelia Bundles is a member of the New Girls' Club because she recognized the importance of setting boundaries to maintain a work/life balance.

AFTER SPENDING MOST OF MY TWENTIES and a good deal of my thirties working so much that I had very little personal life, I became very adamant about setting boundaries. I accepted that I wasn't going to be CEO, that work was a *part* of my life but not the center of my life. But just because you make the decision once to establish limits, that doesn't mean you don't have to keep making the decision again and again as new opportunities and challenges arise. I know that if I were willing to move to New York, there would be many more opportunities for me at ABC. But at least for now, I've been able to work out an arrangement where I can split my time between New York and Washington, where I prefer to live. The reason: After years—decades!—of hoping to find the right guy, I finally found my wonderful significant other when I was 44. At this point in my life, I'm very clear on what I need for my sanity and happiness. And once you're clear on what you want and need, you know what to do.

As for balance—ha-ha! I don't think I'll ever really figure out the balance. I've always been—and probably always will be—on too many boards, in the middle of too many projects, willing to take on too many more projects, etc. For the past three years, I've been commuting from my home in D.C. to New York two days a week for my work at ABC News, while also traveling at least a couple of times a month (more in February during Black History Month and in March during Women's History Month) to other cities to give speeches and do book signings. I'm juggling lots of balls and feel as if I'm always behind on just about every aspect of work and life. The life I live now would be impossible if I had children.

What does make it possible and workable is a significant other who is understanding, supportive, and willing to tolerate my paltry contribution to cooking and other household duties. My favorite cartoon, which I saw in the *Wall Street Journal* a year or so ago, shows a man at his desk looking at a stack of papers and saying to his assistant, "And that's the pile of things I'm never, ever going to get to." At 51, I've come to accept that there are some things I'm never, ever going to get to.

Ultimately, I think each woman has to create her own definition of success, of Having It All. I'd like to have so much money that I could spend as freely as I wished, but unless I hit the lottery (which I don't play), that's not likely to happen. I'd like to have limitless time off to read books, to write, to travel, and to sit on my porch and watch the sunset every night, but unless a trust fund materializes out of the blue, that's not likely to happen. Life is a series of tradeoffs. If I had had children, I probably would not have written my book, or at least not the kind of comprehensive, heavily researched book that I wrote. If I had been married in my twenties or thirties, I probably would not have lived in as many cities as I did and done as well in the early years of my career. If I had not been adamant about creating some balance in my life, I might have missed meeting my significant other.

It's clear to me that during the times when I am working full-time, I absolutely enjoy the salary and the things it allows me to do. But the tradeoff is that I don't have enough free time. During the year and a half when I was writing my book and when I've taken leaves of absence, my time was totally my own, and I reveled in marching to my own rhythm. But the tradeoff was that I was on a very strict budget. Both scenarios have worked for me at different times. And I suspect I'll always bounce back and forth between the two.

On the subject of children: While I went through a phase when I was frustrated and sad both about not being married and not having children, I got over that. In hindsight, I think if having a child had really been as critical to me as it was to many of my friends, I would have had one or adopted one. It's not so much that I made a decision but rather that the circumstances just never were quite right. Still, I don't feel deprived or regretful about the way things worked out. I enjoy my friends' children and grandchildren. And my books and my work at ABC continue to provide many opportunities that allow me to mentor younger people. And maybe that's exactly as it was supposed to be.

CHAPTER EIGHT

Tactical Maneuvers

Strategies, Pragmatism, and the Power of Perseverance

SOMETIMES SUCCEEDING IS ALL ABOUT STRATEGY or thinking about challenges in a new way. These members of the New Girls' Club have learned that often, the way you approach a problem makes all the difference when it comes to launching a career or sustaining it. Whether that means following your passion instead of a corporate path, understanding how to raise capital to join the growing ranks of women starting their own companies, or recognizing the value of persistence and the importance of "showing up," these women have set new standards for success and have cultivated longevity in competitive industries. Good mentors are hard to find, but these women—including business and creative visionaries and leaders from Hollywood, Wall Street, and the nation's capital—share their own inspiring stories of perseverance and words of personal guidance. In many cases, their tactical maneuvers have created the very opportunities that we now enjoy.

● GERALDINE LAYBOURNE

PIONEERING CABLE EXECUTIVE AND FOUNDER
AND CEO OF OXYGEN MEDIA

AT 30 . . .

Geraldine Laybourne was working at the EPIE Institute, a nonprofit
organization for teachers.

TODAY . . .

Geraldine Laybourne founded Oxygen Media in 1998 and has
served as its chairman and chief executive officer since its inception.
Oxygen is currently in 43 million cable households. She was ranked
number one among the 50 most influential women in the enter-
tainment industry by the *Hollywood Reporter* in 1996 and named one
of the 25 most influential people in America by *Time* magazine. She
spent 16 years at Nickelodeon, and under her leadership, it became
the top-rated 24-hour cable programming service and won repeated
notable honors, including Emmys, Peabodys, and CableACE and
Parent's Choice awards, among numerous others. In 1995, she was
inducted into the Broadcasting and Cable Hall of Fame. She and her
husband, Kit, are the parents of two children.

*Geraldine Laybourne is a member of the New Girls' Club because she rev-
olutionized children's television programming by following her passion instead of a traditional corporate career path.*

I HAD A PASSION TO DO SOMETHING GREAT for kids, and that
became my overriding mission. I didn't go into television because I was
in love with television. I went into television because I was in love with
kids, and that helped my career enormously. I would put forth the case
that this is the way women have a much greater chance of succeeding than
if they take a traditional hierarchical approach to their careers.

Early in my career, I had someone working for me—a very bright
young woman. I was at director level, she was at manager level, and she
asked me if I wanted to become a vice president and inquired as to how
long I thought it would take for me to get the job. I just looked at her and

said, "I couldn't really give a hoot about that. I am concerned with creating something great for kids that can never be taken away from them, and I think that if I just focus on that, other things will fall into place."

She looked at me and said, "If you are that lacking in ambition, I'm going to have to find another job, because I can't report to somebody who doesn't have any ambition." I replied that I had enormous ambition to do something great for kids, but that I just didn't care so much about defining my career trajectory.

So, she actually left and has had a pretty average career. I tell that story often to groups because she was completely focusing on the wrong thing. I think for women, what motivates us even more than our male counterparts is when we do something that has a positive, productive result. Often that is a result of collaboration and focus, not competition.

For me, the greatest thing about Nickelodeon was that I had a *team* of winners. My pact with every one of them was "if you come and bring your full brains to the table and don't think about your narrow division and your narrow career, I promise you that you will be in the presidents-in-training program (we called it the PIT program)." Consequently, Anne Sweeney went off to be a president, Debby Beece went off to be a president, Geoffrey Darby went off to be a president, Rich Cronin went off to be a president, Mark Rosenthal went off to be a president. They all ended up as presidents—sometimes presidents of divisions, sometimes presidents of companies, but that was the pact. It was more about how we all worked together for the greater good, and I think that is where women feel more comfortable because it is ultimately a win/win situation for everyone.

I know that I was in an incredibly lucky spot—that I got to Nickelodeon at the right time. But understand that I was a manager and just kept my eyes open. When things needed to be done—whether they were in my job description or not—I just made sure they were done. I think we all have a lot more power than we give ourselves, and we spend way too much time bemoaning the fact that we "can't do this" or "can't do that." I think that we actually can do a lot of things that we tend to self-limit ourselves on. If you are truly focused on the greater good—and not just on yourself—you can get by with murder, and in the end that will always propel you forward.

● NANCY PERETSMAN
EXECUTIVE VICE PRESIDENT AND MANAGING
DIRECTOR, ALLEN AND COMPANY

AT 30 . . .

Nancy Peretsman was a vice president at Salomon Brothers. She was single.

TODAY . . .

Nancy Peretsman has been named one of *Fortune*'s "50 Most Powerful Women in American Business," *Money*'s "50 Smartest Women in the Money Business," and the Financial Women's Association "Woman of the Year, 2001." She has led the transactions for major media and new media corporations and is regarded as one of the top investment bankers on Wall Street. Peretsman is a trustee emerita of Princeton University and a vice chairman of the board of the New School. She lives with her husband and daughter in New York.

Nancy Peretsman is a member of the New Girls' Club because she is willing to share practical business advice with women who may wish to join the growing ranks of female entrepreneurs.

MOST OF THE GREAT BUSINESSES that were run by women were built by women. When you look at the cosmetics industry, you have Estée Lauder and Bobbi Brown. In the financial area, you have Muriel Siebert, and in retail, you have Donna Karan and Lillian Vernon. There have always been women whose businesses attracted capital, so there is nothing new there. What is new is that we have now reached critical mass when it comes to accomplished women. When I first showed up on Wall Street, I was an anomaly; my problem was more that I was weird, that I was different, than that I was female. It wasn't about women's issues; it was simply that "you" were not "them," and it was the same issue that any other minority encountered because the world was so homogeneous.

Fast-forward 25 years, and you have a totally different story. You can have Carly Fiorina—meaning a very successful, very prototypical, tough, hard-charging CEO who happens to be female. You can have Condoleezza Rice as national security advisor. You can have Shelly Lazarus, the powerful CEO of Ogilvy and Mather, who has always had a spectacular career and has also managed to have several kids. The point is, these women are all successful females, but they are not alike—you now have diversity within the category. Once that happens, interestingly enough, then you actually have some level of acceptance, because it doesn't mean that because you are female, all assessments will be derivative. You've got a whole broad spectrum—you have women who have succeeded, women who have failed. You've got the whole map, and that is very liberating for the next generation of women.

So now is a good time to not be afraid to do what the guys do—which is, if you are accomplished and have a track record within a certain area, consider the alternative of building and running your own business. Women need to understand that capital is not prejudiced against gender. In fact, it is gender neutral and looking for accomplishment.

There are some things to consider before you make that move. If you're going out on your own, you have to have a good reason for doing so. Going out on your own is not a sufficient reason—meaning it is not about *you*, it is about the product. I say this all the time—Oprah Winfrey did not set out to be a successful billionaire, she just did what she loved and what she was good at. The notion of, "I don't want to work for a big corporation, I want to go out on my own" is not a route to success from what I've seen. A route to success is, "I have something I want to do, and it is best accomplished independent of a large organization." Most entrepreneurs recognize that they want to make something happen on their own terms, so they have to do it independently.

The second thing you need is a reality check: Are you and the market really at one here? You have to consider, "Just because I have a passion for gingerbread houses, is there really a market for this?" Sometimes you can *invent* a market if the idea is good enough. For instance, Starbucks showed us there was a market for the $4 cup of coffee. But sometimes, guess what? No one cares. To ultimately get out there and be successful, you need either an idea and a product that is compelling or an ability to convince people that you have a better product to fill the market need— Pampers is the best example of that.

The third thing is that you absolutely need to have a sense of humor and perseverance, because there will be a lot of failures. Not everything goes right, so a lot of it is just about not giving up. I can't think of a single successful entrepreneur's story that started at Point A and went straight up. I tell people all the time, "Great baseball players only bat 300." Obviously, in business, your odds have to be a little higher than that, but it isn't 1,000, and it's never going to be 1,000. You have to be right more than you are wrong, and you can't give up. The key is taking what doesn't work, repositioning, and moving forward.

● MARIE BRENNER
AUTHOR AND JOURNALIST

AT 30 . . .
Marie Brenner was the first female baseball columnist in the American League, traveling with the Boston Red Sox.

TODAY . . .
Marie Brenner is a writer-at-large for *Vanity Fair*. Her investigation into the Enron scandals made national news when Senator Peter Fitzgerald quoted her story as he questioned witnesses testifying before a Senate committee. Her explosive article on Jeffrey Wigand and the tobacco wars became the basis of the 1999 film *The Insider*, starring Al Pacino and Russell Crowe, which was nominated for seven Academy Awards, including Best Picture. Brenner is the author of five books, including the best-seller *Great Dames: What I Learned from Older Women,* and is adjunct professor at Columbia University's Graduate School of Journalism.

Marie Brenner is a member of the New Girls' Club because she helps other women better envision and realize their goals. She shares with us a valuable lesson about striking the balance between courage and class.

I HIT A WALL AT 29. It happened in London in the spring of 1979. For two years, I struggled as a freelance writer and was barely able to support myself living abroad. I worked for editors at the *Washington Post*, the *New York Times Magazine*, and most for Don Forst, the canny editor of the *Los Angeles Herald Examiner*. April that year was particularly dreary. It seemed as if it rained all the time—that cold, dank English weather. My then-boyfriend and I came to a parting of the ways. I missed my friends from home. I was in London—glorious London—and the British Museum had lost its charm.

And then the telephone rang. It was Don Forst calling from Los Angeles. "You are beginning to sound weird—like an expatriate. I'm on my way to Boston. A new job. Boston. The *Herald-American*. It's a tabloid that has seen better days." And there it was, via Don Forst—a miracle.

I was assigned an exotic beat—to travel with the Red Sox for a column. Why exotic? Here's why: It was 1979, the first year women were allowed in the clubhouses of major league sports. Forst thought "a skirt" could boost the circulation of a paper that was losing ground in New England, the home territory of Red Sox Nation, the zone of obsessive fans whose heart-breaking passion for this particular team is part of literary history.

I was woefully naïve, a baseball idiot. I showed up at Fenway in high heels, pearls, and a blazer. Who wears heels to Fenway Park? I am sorry to say, I did. And I had a faux-Brit sound—those two years in London did wonders for my pretensions. I was the picture of European elegance—in my mind. I tottered up the ramps at Fenway.

And then my life began.

I traveled with the team for the season. It was the most difficult assignment I had ever taken on. I did not have a baseball molecule in my body, and I was suddenly surrounded by world-class athletes—and the most conservative team in baseball.

I filed two columns a week; somehow it worked out. A third baseman had an injury and the first player to integrate the Red Sox showed up in California; I talked to Red Sox wives; the team captain Carl Yastrzemski struggled to make his 3,000th hit and 400th home run. One day I noticed that I was sitting in a ballpark that did not seem to have one black fan. That became a column, too. "Why Are There No Blacks at Fenway?" The paper received a bag of hate mail. Don Forst was happy.

In late June—in the Yankee Stadium press box—I met and fell in love with Jonathan Schwartz, a New York radio personality and writer. Jonathan was a Red Sox expert of almost eccentric dimensions—passionate about the team since the age of seven.

Jonathan guided me and inspired me to think like an anthropologist about the team. I allowed myself to learn. We married at the end of the baseball season in 1979. Our marriage didn't last, but our friendship and devotion to each other and our daughter Casey—now 21—certainly did. We both remarried, and our combined families are uncommonly close.

In our twenties, women of the 1970s felt the need to say everything and anything. This was praised as truth-telling, or "being real," as we called it. We burned our bras, had consciousness-raising sessions, attended rallies, and changed history for generations of women. Now one hears more and more another point of view—acquired in later years. The history of the women's movement is that of one step forward, two steps backward. You can see it through the decades of the twentieth century—each time women progressed, from voting rights to job advancement, the tidal wave of legislators and moral scolds arrived to stop the progress.

We are living in such a retro time. You hear accomplished women actually talk about the need for scaling back and listening more, saying less. Playing a courtesan. Power dynamics to survive in the male pantheon. Is it 2003 or 1925?

Somehow at 30, I knew to be guided by that old cliché that 90 percent of life is accomplished by just showing up. I showed up, and it changed my life. The composer Cole Porter once said, "Say yes to everything." In my opinion, the man who gave us "Night and Day"—and scores of other glorious songs—had it right.

● CATHERINE HARDWICKE
AWARD-WINNING DIRECTOR OF *THIRTEEN*

AT 30. . . .

Catherine Hardwicke was struggling along on low-budget films in Los Angeles. She was working on a Roger Corman movie and was the set decorator, second-unit director, and did all the motorcycle stunts, wearing a black wig and a flowered dress.

TODAY . . .

Catherine Hardwicke has been honored with the 2003 Sundance Film Festival Director's Award for her feature-film directorial and screenwriting debut, *Thirteen*. An accomplished production designer and architect, Hardwicke developed *Thirteen*'s bold visual style in part by pulling from her experience working on such critically acclaimed films as Cameron Crowe's *Vanilla Sky*, Costa Gavras's *Mad City*, and Richard Linklater's *Suburbia*, as well as being responsible for the visual intensity of David O. Rusell's *Three Kings*. (Her vision for the film was influenced in part by *Three Kings*, which embodied a high level of deeply felt kinetic intensity.) Co-screenwriter for *Thirteen* was 13-year-old Nikki Reed, the daughter of Hardwicke's ex-boyfriend, with whom she maintains a close relationship.

Catherine Hardwicke is a member of the New Girls' Club because she pulled off a transition from accomplished production designer to award-winning director of Thirteen *by never taking no for an answer.*

AS A PRODUCTION DESIGNER, I worked on tons of projects of various budgets and scope. I worked with Cameron Crowe on *Vanilla Sky*, a big-budget movie where I had 150 people working under me in my art department. *Three Kings* with David O. Russell was another really big, fun project I was proud of. But I also worked on smaller films like *Laurel Canyon*, which was an artistic, cool little movie, and a small movie for Richard Linklater called *Suburbia*. All of these different directors are outstanding, and it was great to be around them, in the front seat with them collaborating on the projects from the very beginning. But when you do that as a production designer, everyone sees you as a production designer, not a director. It isn't necessarily intentional, but they see that as your skill, and they can't really imagine that you would be able to do something else. They think, "You are good at this; we can't lose another production designer!"

I talked to Rick [Linklater], and his producer, Anne Walker, when I decided I wanted to make my own movie. I said, "I really, really want to make my own movie—can you guys help me?" I truly thought that because we were all like a family—a bunch of Texans and everything—that they would help me. And Rick's big way of helping me was saying, "You want to make a movie, then just do it, Catherine. You've just got to do it." I was so shocked!

Later, I thought David Russell, a major talent, would at least read my script for *Thirteen* and give me notes. But basically they were all doing their own thing, and they were way too busy to help with a career transition. Yet, in a real way, they did help, because it made me realize that doing it on their own was exactly how they started, too. Both Richard and David made these low-budget movies like *Slacker* and *Spanking the Monkey*. Nobody helped them.

I was starting to get it. Blood, sweat, tears, on your own—that is how you owned it, without anybody really helping you. And so that is what I did.

Getting a movie made is almost like starting your own business. The first thing you decide is that you are going to make tremendous financial sacrifices in the short term as a long-term investment in your plan. I was actually offered a huge-budget movie with a really great director right before Nikki and I started writing *Thirteen*. But I thought, "No. I'm going to keep getting offers for nice, cool jobs like that, post *Vanilla Sky* and *Three Kings*. I will have those opportunities as a production designer, but I might not ever have the same kind of opportunity to make my own movie." So I just had to say no to everything, live on my savings, and launch this idea, even though I knew it was a risk. I had no idea whether it was going to happen or not. It's terrifying. But I just believed in this project so much,

I thought, "I have to try!"

And it wasn't the first time I tried to get a movie made. After I worked on *The Newton Boys* with Rick and Anne, I realized that I had to work in movies that I believed in, movies that offered something good to the world or had something important to say. So I started going to the library and researching stories about strong women. I found a true story set during the Civil War era about a girl who disguised herself as a boy for two years so she could fight for the North and a cause she believed in. I found out that the book was checked out of the library all the time because there are so few female heroes that we ever study. Cleopatra, Joan of Arc—then it's all downhill after that. I thought it would be great to put some more choices out there for girls.

I wrote the script and was convinced that I came up with a very economical plan about how to shoot it. It was budgeted at about $9 million, and it would have great scope. I did drawings and some really cool renderings, and I story-boarded locations. I shot little scenes and built a Civil War tent in my living room. I put together costumes and pieced period music together. I had it all planned out. I had done all of these big movies before, and this one was cheap and compelling. I just really thought, "This is a slam dunk!"

But nobody would finance it.

So then I decided to write something even less expensive to produce. I decided I would take a job and do a big movie, and then, in between shoots, I would take screenwriting classes and acting classes and start doing presentations and drawings for my own movie, even when I didn't know what it was yet.

Eventually I wrote another script, one that was budgeted at around $5 to $7 million. But people would still say to me, "You are never going to get that much money to make your own movie." I was discouraged, but I kept remembering that Richard and David made their own very low budget movies before they made the bigger ones. I thought, "I can't cry over this; I just have to come up with the right low-budget idea." One that gels. One with a message. One that is totally right.

Who knew a crisis in Nikki's personal life would lead me there? I noticed when I was working on *Laurel Canyon* that something was very wrong. This was a kid that I loved. I needed to be there for her and wanted to help her, help her parents, and play some small role in getting her out of whatever she was going through. I wanted her to do positive, creative things instead of destructive things, and that is why I started working with her. We tried everything from surfing and drawing to acting classes and visiting museums—anything to get her interested in something artistic and meaningful. One thing led to the next, and we just started to write *Thirteen*. It was one of those situations where things just all came together fast.

Bizarrely enough, in six days we had a draft that was already tight and good. After our initial period together, she went back to eighth grade, middle school, winter quarter. I read that draft and thought, "Holy shit! This is something radioactive!" There is stuff going on in the culture that I had been observing with Nikki and her mom and her friends. I thought, "I've got to make this!"

I refinanced my house and decided I would not work for a year. I didn't take any money personally for the film—any financing available was put right back into the movie. I passed up on many jobs. My agent would continually call me and say, "So-and-so called, such-and-such big director you've always wanted to work with called," and I would say, "Well, Paul, I don't want to be mean, but I don't know if you get this—I am making my own movie." And he would say, "Well, couldn't you do this, too?" And I would say, "No, you cannot do two things at once."

And that focus has everything to do with how the movie was made. *Thirteen* was made within the span of one year. From the moment we started writing it, on January 3, 2002, to January 2003, one year later, it was in the can—casting, prepping, shooting, editing, everything. This is an incredibly compressed production schedule for a movie you can actually see in a theater. It is almost a record. But I worked on it 24/7. Absolute tunnel vision, absolute focus. I did everything I could think of—not the conventional things you do, but just any idea I could come up with to get the movie made: "I am going to shoot a scene," "I am going to make a presentation," "I am going to learn how to edit with Final Cut Pro and present this thing." Anything and everything I could think of, and I never took no for an answer.

It all reminded me of a little made-up game that I played with myself when I was about five or six. I would stand at one end of my house and just start walking and crashing through anything—furniture, pets, food, or my sister, my brother, my parents—whatever was in the way, just smashing through it to get to the other side of the house. The whole time I would chant, "NOTHING CAN STOP ME, NOTHING CAN STOP ME, NOTHING CAN STOP ME." I realize now that I did the same thing to get the movie made—nothing could stop me. I just kept preparing and working toward the goal. I was ready for any challenge.

But I was also confronting a steady steam of obstacles along the way. First there were casting issues, especially with respect to the critical lead role of Tracy, eventually played by Evan Rachel Wood. Initially, we were having a very hard time attracting anybody who had any acting experience. Their agents, their managers, and their parents did not want them to be in this movie for obvious and legitimate reasons. There was no distribution, it was the lowest budget ever, they would barely get paid, I was a first-time director, and the material looked risky. Evan's agent would not let her come in and audition.

We tried to get Holly Hunter attached to the film but met the same problems: no distribution, a project that did not look good on paper. Then Michael London, one of the producers, actually convinced her manager to meet with me. So I went in there all enthusiastic, gangbusters, and got the manager excited enough to convince Holly to at least take a look at the script. She read it, and she was fascinated by what she saw as this other world that she knew nothing about, and she agreed to meet me. I found out at 4:00 P.M. on a Thursday in L.A. that she wanted to meet me at 3:00 P.M. the next day—in New York. I was literally in a casting session, and I said, "I've gotta go," grabbed my little video camera from the casting meeting, and drove to Nikki's house.

Luckily, Nikki was home, and I filmed her walking through her bedroom, her living room, and the kitchen, as she was saying, "Hi, Holly, I'm Nikki. We love you! Please be in our movie." I went straight to the airport, jumped on the red-eye, and went to see Holly the next afternoon in New York. I pulled out the video camera, opened the little viewing screen, and said, "Hey, this is the teenager I wrote the movie with. This is her house, and these are the sorts of things we described in the movie." Holly's jaw just dropped. I don't think she realized it was a real 13-year-old girl, a real teenager who had inspired the film, but she was immediately responsive to the idea of something that came from an authentic place.

She was very enthusiastic, but she still did not say yes. She said, "I've been burned by first-time directors before. I want some more shadings and nuances to my character, and I am not going to say yes until I see that on the page." I wrote on my laptop on the plane on the way home, and she got the new pages Monday morning. And she said yes.

Once Holly signed on, we went back to Evan's agent and said, "Are you sure you don't want her to play . . . Holly Hunter's daughter?" Evan was then allowed to read the script. She came in to meet with me, and we hit it off instantly; I hoped that she and Nikki would, too. They came over to my house and shook hands, and about 3 minutes later, I had them film a scene. They were like firecrackers. They instantly bonded, and the chemistry was just alive and crazy and great. I was so excited, and I thought, "I can make the movie now!" I knew it was going to come alive.

But there were still problems, including money. Jeff Levy-Hinte, one of our producers, had come up with about a million dollars, but we needed more. Even as we were about to go into shooting—and even with Holly on board—it was hard. I had worked with Working Title [an independent film production company], as had Michael, another of our producers, so we decided we would ask them for a discrete, small amount—the least we could get away with to pull off the film. We asked them for a half-million dollars of equity financing, and miraculously, just before we started shooting, they agreed.

Even then, I still cried 20 minutes every day, at least. I don't know why, and I am not even ashamed about it. I would just burst into tears; you know, you still feel incredible pressure and don't know whether or not you are being an idiot. I have so many friends who have made movies that didn't go anywhere, that were never released. You know from experience that anything can happen and that there are a lot of ways that set meltdowns can occur while shooting that aren't your fault. Somebody can get sick. The star can break a leg—anything can happen. It is a miracle when a movie gets made and it comes out good. I knew it was a big risk, but I just really believed in it. I also believed that if I worked hard and tried to think of everything, it would work.

I also tried to listen to other people, which was a big thing for me. I learned how to do this by taking a comedy improv class, a class that literally changed my life. I started listening to other people more instead of just focusing on my own train of thought. I knew that people would say, "I know Catherine has the production side down, the look of the film, but how is she going to know how to work with actors?" So I started taking random stealth acting classes with strangers and would force myself to get up there on stage and go through the painful things. Even though I didn't want to be an actor, I forced myself to do it, and that changed everything for me. For instance, the Meisner technique is all about listening to someone and seeing how the other person is responding to what you are saying. For some weird reason, that had never occurred to me. Like my game, NOTHING CAN STOP ME, I would have a great idea and just assume it was going to happen because my heart and soul were in the right place.

There is another exercise you learn that's called, "Yes, and . . ." If somebody walks up to you in improv and says, "Hey, I love your blue hair," and you say, "I don't have blue hair—what are you, stupid? Do you need to get your glasses fixed?" you are negating what they said. The skit goes nowhere; it just leads to an argument or a dead end. But if you say, "Yes, and . . . I like that green hair that you've sculpted into the shape of a swimming pool," then suddenly, the blue hair and the green hair start turning into these magical creations—it goes somewhere. It turns into a great kind of creation by agreement and collaboration.

I took that, "Yes, and . . ." thinking and applied it to the movie. Many times when making the movie, people would come up to me and say that things would be impossible. They would say things like, "You are losing the kids in 7 minutes. You have 7 more minutes today to get this scene, we don't have a permit for this street, and the car doesn't run. I'm sorry, but that's how it is." To take those 7 minutes and say, "Why doesn't the car run?" or stop and question why we didn't have a permit, or ask why the girls had to leave early could take up to 5 of the critical 7 minutes. And then you wouldn't have the scene at all. So I just said, "Okay. Yes, and . . . I have 7 minutes, the car doesn't run, and I am going to make it the best 7 minutes you have ever seen!" And somehow, that's what I had to do on a daily basis, on an hourly basis, on the movie.

You can dwell on the negative, and you can talk yourself out of everything, or you can say, "I am going to make something good out of it." This was the spirit of the movie. On *Vanilla Sky*, there was one point on the movie when I stood and watched the coffee barista getting a massage from the full-time masseuse. I probably had four or five times the budget on that movie—just for the art department—as I had for the entire budget of every department on *Thirteen*. So we tried to make the most of every second and every opportunity, and that energy is what you feel when you watch it. You ride with it, you are in it. The actors did not have time to sit around in their trailers. And I think that energy and urgency are what helped make the film reach people.

● A'LELIA BUNDLES
AUTHOR, JOURNALIST, AND EXECUTIVE

See page 183 for her profile.

A'Lelia Bundles is a member of the New Girls' Club for her track record of helping women develop their careers and for having the wisdom to see the key to her future lay in discovering her family's past. She is also noteworthy because she reminds us that perseverance is a key ingredient for success along a path that is often long and winding.

I WISH I HAD KNOWN AT 30 something that Martin Luther King Jr. once said: "The arc of the universe is long, but it bends towards justice." If we live long enough and take enough risks, we all hit obstacles in our personal and professional lives, but experience has shown me that right usually triumphs over might. Not always, but often enough that I can look back at the situations where the actions of an incompetent or adversarial boss or colleague made my life momentarily difficult and see that I survived, moved on, and accomplished what I had set out to do. It really is true that adversity makes us stronger. Not that suffering is fun or desirable, but over time you figure out how to navigate and negotiate your way around the obstacles. And when you win the battles, the satisfaction is very sweet.

As a young producer in NBC's Houston bureau in the late 1970s (when I was in my late twenties), I spent my first two years with a great group of people: a bureau chief, correspondent, producer, camera crews, and editors who all were talented people willing to mentor me and help me learn the business. To this day, I credit them with preparing me to be a competitive network news producer. And thank goodness my experience with them was so positive, because during my last year in Houston, when they all had been assigned to other bureaus, I was miserable. The bureau chief was replaced by another person who had been demoted from the bureau chief's job in the large Chicago office to the bureau chief's job in the much smaller Houston office. To make matters worse, the new boss, who was white, had been replaced in Chicago by NBC's first black woman bureau chief—a move that must have been a blow to his ego.

From the moment he arrived, we clashed. I had never experienced such severe work-related stress. I started grinding my teeth in my sleep at night. I was a smoker at the time and went from smoking a pack of cigarettes a day to smoking a pack and a half. Fortunately, my father, who was a businessman, coached me through the situation, reminding me to just keep doing the best job I could. Meanwhile, I also was doing everything I could to get transferred. And I smoked my last cigarette with the resolve that I would not let a jerk make me kill myself! Finally, an opportunity came to move to the Atlanta bureau, where I happily spent the next five years. I have not looked back. The Houston bureau chief faded into oblivion with a less-than-distinguished career, and I kept on stepping. At the time it was no fun, but I often use this story to tell younger people who are frustrated in their careers that they can survive and overcome. As they say, "One monkey don't stop no show."

● LINDA CHAVEZ

SYNDICATED COLUMNIST AND PRESIDENT OF THE
CENTER FOR EQUAL OPPORTUNITY

AT 30 . . .

Linda Chavez had just given birth to her second child and had gone
back to work (after a four-week leave) as a political appointee in the
Department of Health, Education, and Welfare in the new Carter
administration.

TODAY . . .

Linda Chavez is president of the Center for Equal Opportunity, a
nonprofit public policy research organization in Washington, D.C.
She writes a weekly syndicated column that appears in newspapers
across the country and is a political analyst for the Fox News
Channel. She has held a number of appointed positions, including
chairman of the National Commission on Migrant Education, White
House director of public liaison, and staff director of the U.S. Com-
mission on Civil Rights. Chavez was the Republican nominee for
U.S. Senator from Maryland in 1986. She is also a member of the
Council on Foreign Relations and author of *Out of the Barrio: Toward
a New Politics of Hispanic Assimilation* and *An Unlikely Conservative: The
Transformation of an Ex-Liberal*. In 2000, Chavez was honored by the
Library of Congress as a "Living Legend" for her contributions to
America's cultural and historical legacy, and in January 2001, she
was President George W. Bush's nominee for secretary of labor until
she withdrew her name from consideration.

*Linda Chavez is a member of the New Girls' Club because she is willing to
share her political survival strategies—lessons that apply to politics in the
office as well as on Capitol Hill.*

ONE OF THE MOST IMPORTANT THINGS that I've learned in
Washington—and it is a lesson too few people do learn—is that you
should never confuse what your job is with who you are. So often, people

try to fuse their identity with their job, particularly as they gain more and more powerful positions. Eventually, it becomes tempting to assume that you are treated well because of who you are instead of what job you happen to occupy. I saw that particularly when I worked as director of public liaison in the White House.

When you work in the White House, your phone calls are instantly returned. When you make a hotel or restaurant reservation, you get the best treatment. You live in a kind of bubble. I think a lot of people have difficulty dealing with that—it goes to their heads, and they really begin to believe that they are powerful rather than understanding that they simply hold powerful jobs. This is a tremendous problem because, in the world of politics, jobs change. They change frequently, and often in unpleasant ways. You lose your job when an administration goes out of power. Or, if you are running for office, you may lose an election. If your whole sense of self-worth is wrapped up in what your particular job is, these moments are going to be devastating.

The second key to succeeding over the long term in Washington is to "remember the little people"—certainly remember them on the way up, because they will be very helpful to you on the way down. I have always believed that it is important to have respect for people who do a good job, no matter what that job is. If that job is emptying out the trashcans and dusting the furniture, and they do it diligently and well and reliably and cheerfully, that deserves respect. I think that some of my clarity on this point has to do with my background as the daughter of a house painter who was often out of work. I grew up in less than ideal circumstances. But the way you treat the people around you is also important strategically, because sometimes people who work for you in various positions go on to do very important things and may even one day become important allies.

In my life, John Miller was one of those people. I was basically his first employer. He had an internship at *The New Republic*, and then he came to work as my research assistant. He was just terrific, so when I decided to go off and form my own think tank, I formed it with John, and he became the vice president. Years later, when I had all of my labor nomination woes, John was out there defending me—he wrote a wonderful piece in *The National Review* about his experience. His public observations corroborated what I had said—that the woman from Guatemala who was the subject of all the allegations about my employing an illegal alien wasn't an employee but someone I had given shelter to during difficult times.

This was one of the most devastating incidents in my career, and what was interesting and important to me was that when I stepped aside, I didn't do it alone. I was able to pull around me a group of people that I had helped personally, including a couple of immigrants—one of whom I had taken in and provided shelter for when he was a refugee from Vietnam, and another woman who had actually worked for me as a housekeeper and babysitter for my two children and later worked for me at the Civil Rights Commission. They were all there at my side when I was withdrawing and told their stories about my helping them. So I have always felt it isn't just altruistic to be good to other people— particularly to the people who are less fortunate or who work for you—it is also good insurance, because you may need their help at some point in the future. If you have treated people well, they tend to remember it, and they tend to be there for you in ways that you have no way of anticipating at the time.

The third key to success in Washington is resilience. It is very interesting that if you look around Washington, there are a lot of people who have become stars in some way or another, and then something goes wrong, and they basically disappear. One of the things I think has been more unusual about me is that I keep coming back. I've had a lot of lives in this town, and it's because I've been able to take failures and turn them into opportunities and have not been willing to let a failure define me. What happened after my loss in the U.S. Senate race is a good example of this.

When I entered the Senate race in 1986, I knew I was running in the second most liberal state in the country. Just a tiny fraction of the electorate were Republicans: The voter registration figures were something like 2½ Democrats for every Republican, and it was even higher for some cities like Baltimore, where it was more like 7 or 8 to 1. It was an uphill battle, and I knew that running for the U.S. Senate my first time out, I was not likely to succeed.

There is almost no failure more public than losing an election. You are really out there, exposed in many ways. And I didn't just lose—I got trounced, winning just 39 percent of the vote. That was certainly a low point in my career. I will never forget that weeks before the election (particularly because I entered the race having just come from the White House), people were always banging down my doors with invitations and opportunities. Everybody wanted to be my friend. But when I lost the election, suddenly phone calls weren't being returned. You are yesterday's news, and nobody wants to be helpful.

I had difficulty finding a job. I had sort of anticipated that if I lost the race, I could go back into the administration. As it happened, right after my defeat, the Iran-Contra scandal broke, and the White House was totally preoccupied. Meanwhile, a lot of the people who I assumed would leave the administration at that time did not, so there were no job openings. And I didn't want to be a lobbyist, so it was really tough to bounce back.

Nonetheless, my failed Senate race opened up new opportunities for me. I had become well known nationally because I ran against another woman, Barbara Mikulski. This was the first time in modern history that two women had run against each for a Senate seat, which generated a great deal of local and national media attention. After the campaign, I started doing regular commentaries for National Public Radio. I also started writing my own column, which was published in the *Chicago Sun Times* and several other newspapers. It is clear to me that had I not taken the opportunity to run for the Senate, editors might not have given me the time of day. So even though I lost the race and suffered a very public failure, I took advantage of the visibility, and that opened doors for me. Ironically, from that failure I was able to end up doing what I always wanted to do, which was to write.

● SUSAN SARANDON

ACADEMY AWARD—WINNING ACTOR

AT 30 . . .

Susan Sarandon accompanied her then-husband, actor Chris
Sarandon, to an audition and landed a role in the feature film *Joe*.
That job led to more work and soap opera roles, and by 1975,
Sarandon was starring as Janet Weiss in *Rocky Horror Picture Show*.

TODAY . . .

Susan Sarandon has appeared in dozens of acclaimed movies and portrayed strong women in numerous films. She hit her stride in the late
1980s with a string of Oscar nominations for her roles in *Thelma and
Louise*, *Lorenzo's Oil*, and *The Client*. She won her first Academy
Award for her portrayal of Sister Helen Prejean in the death penalty
drama, *Dead Man Walking*, adapted and directed by her long-time
partner, Tim Robbins, with whom she remains an outspoken activist
for free speech and human rights around the world.

*Susan Sarandon is a member of the New Girls' Club because she turned
a compromised role into a pivotal performance opportunity.*

My experience on *The Witches of Eastwick*—showing up for work to
learn my role had been given to Cher—was initially daunting and humil-
iating. I needed to work to support my daughter financially, but I was also
aware that she was very sensitive to my unhappiness. At one point during
the filming, I realized I either had to find a way to turn the situation
around, or I had to figure out a way to leave. So I decided to turn straw
into gold.

I had been cast opposite Jack Nicholson, in the part that was the
strongest of the women, the most confrontational. During the summer,
just before flying from Italy where I was living, I received a call from
George Miller asking me if I would consider playing another part, which
was almost nonexistent in the script—the woman who played the cello.
I said no. I was committed to Alex, my part, and looking forward to the
filming.

Upon arriving, I learned I had indeed been switched. Even though I had some minor work obligations, I was now sitting in rehearsals listening to Cher read my part. They claimed they would write my character more fully, but no pages were coming. And I began learning to play the cello—an intimidating experience for someone who didn't play an instrument and was expected to fake a complicated piece three weeks later! For some reason, I also ended up shortchanged in the costume department, and I had to borrow gowns from Cher's *Sonny and Cher* vaults. If I quit, the studio said they would sue, so that was not really an option. But one day I came home from rehearsal—where I was required to just sit and listen to the other two actors—and I was in tears. My 18-month-old daughter looked at me with such empathy and shock I knew I had to do *something*.

So I decided to rewrite my character myself; I would do that by the way I chose to play the part. I decided the great thing about a small part that doesn't connect to anything is that it leaves you free to *do* anything. I decided that my character—since she had no children to pull her—would be the one to love Daryl (Jack) the most. I got a red wig, lots of props, and did not read the script again until the morning I showed up to play the role. I actually ended up having more fun than anyone else, since the shoot was twice as long as expected, and the set was a battleground between the other elements. My situation improved once I decided to take control of it myself. It turned out to be an important role for me, and the cast members are still good friends to this day.

● DENISE AUSTIN
Fitness guru

At 30 . . .

Denise Austin was host of a fitness show on a startup television network that no one had ever heard of—ESPN.

Today . . .

Denise Austin has sold millions of exercise videos and has hosted two daily workout shows, *Denise Austin's Daily Workout* and *Denise Austin's*

Fit and Lite, on Lifetime Television for Women, for more than seven years. The author of seven books, her column "Shape Up" appears every month in *Prevention* magazine. Austin is a member of the President's Council on Physical Fitness, and in 2003, she was inducted into the Video Hall of Fame—the first fitness expert to be so honored. She's the wife of Jeff and the mother of two girls, Katie and Kelly.

Denise Austin is a member of the New Girls' Club because her individual story of strategic persistence reveals the universal value of continuing to ask—until you get to "yes."

I MOVED TO WASHINGTON, D.C., FROM LOS ANGELES right after I got married, because that was where my husband was based for business. I was bicoastal for about a year, but I knew that I would eventually need to give up my L.A.-based show, *Daybreak with Denise*, which aired on KABC. Yet, I wanted to maintain a television presence because I knew I had something good to tell people. I was really the only fitness expert out there who had a degree in the business, so I was determined to figure out another way to get on television that would allow me to stay on the East Coast with my husband.

One day I saw the *Today Show* credits identified the show's executive producer as Steve Friedman. So I called him—about 35 times! I would leave a message with the secretary, and he would never call back. But I kept trying. One day I called him at a funky hour, like 6:30 at night, and he answered the phone. After the conversation, he gave me a chance for a meeting, and I flew up practically the next day and made a presentation to him in his office. So there he was, sitting there holding a baseball bat in his hands while I was on the floor demonstrating the best way to tighten your tummy! And that's how I got my opportunity for an on-air audition.

I continued to think strategically about the opportunity, and the first time I went on the *Today Show*, I received over 8,000 letters because I built my own focus group into that appearance. I wrote a little free pamphlet, titled "Tone Up at the Terminals—An Exercise Guide for

Computer Operators," which was very relevant in 1984. When people requested the pamphlet, the executives had a way of calculating how many viewers I was reaching. And because there was evidence that I was capturing an audience via so much immediate feedback, I got a four-year contract for monthly appearances on the *Today Show*. That contract led to many other opportunities and marked the beginning of my career on national television.

CHAPTER NINE

Changing Direction

Deliberate Action, Definitive Results

WHEN DEVELOPING HIS THEORY OF INERTIA, Galileo found that an object in motion must stop—however briefly—before it can change direction. We are no different. Many women feel that they are stuck, charging along in the wrong jobs or relationships, or are frustrated that their personal or professional lives are not moving forward as they had planned. These members of the New Girls' Club have mastered the art of deliberate living by hitting "pause" and taking the time to identify areas of their lives they would like to change. Their inspiring stories prove that personal or professional reinvention is easier than you might imagine and that engaging in strategic thought about change can produce swift, clear results.

● ALI WENTWORTH

TALK SHOW HOST, ACTOR, AND COMEDIAN

AT 30 . . .

Ali Wentworth was working in sitcoms and living with a comedy writer in Los Angeles.

TODAY . . .

Ali Wentworth is cohost of a nationally syndicated talk show, *Living it Up! with Ali and Jack* and lives in New York and Washington, D.C., with her husband, George Stephanopoulos, and their daughter. In 2002, Wentworth appeared in the film *Office Space* and recently starred in Disney's remake of the classic film *The Love Bug*. She also finished production on the independent film *Live Virgin* as well as the Michael Moore/CBS television pilot, *Better Days*. Additionally, Wentworth has a feature film in development—*A Model World*, based on her own original treatment. Her other movie credits include *Trial and Error*, *Jerry Maguire*, and *The Real Blonde*. Her first book, published in October 2002, is *The WASP Cookbook*, a collection of 90 recipes (including 11 cocktails). Wentworth appeared on *In Living Color* and developed a recurring role for herself on *The Tonight Show with Jay Leno*.

Ali Wentworth is a member of the New Girls' Club because she took control of her life when it was time to move in a new direction. As a result of her strategic decision-making, she found personal and professional success.

EVERYTHING STARTED TO CHANGE IN MY LIFE about a year before I met my husband, George. I believe it is no coincidence that this happened at exactly the moment I made a conscious effort to take control of my life. I made a deliberate choice to start going after what I wanted, and I stopped looking to other people to feed that, or to a relationship or a job to fulfill that need.

I took the two biggest risks of my life at this time. I ended an eight-year relationship with a man to whom I was engaged and was living with. He was a lot more successful than I was and had been a source of emotional and financial security for a long time. After we broke up, I did what everyone thought was a *really* crazy thing. I bought a big house that I knew I could not afford and hoped that I would find enough work to make the mortgage payments. My parents were very upset, but it was the best thing I ever did. I started working harder to pay the bills, and it felt great.

At the same time, I became very focused and realistic about my professional strengths and goals—it was time for me to be honest about my creative path. Yes, I would love to be Meryl Streep, but at some point I had to admit that wasn't happening for me. That was tough because I had convinced myself there was more integrity in dramatic roles than in comedic ones. And of course, my mother would love to see me doing Gilbert and Sullivan on Broadway. But it was time for me to focus. Comedy was what I enjoyed and what I was good at—it was where I had fun. So I finally embraced it. I started writing screenplays and made an effort to go after jobs and opportunities that I enjoyed and seemed right for me. In my personal life, I was changing, too. I became far more open to dating and meeting new people than I had been before.

By the time I met George, about a year later, I had made a million changes in my life, and I was happier and more independent than I had ever been before. I'm sure that is what allowed me to recognize immediately that he was "the one." I knew who he was before I met him, of course, but I was not much interested in his accomplishments or politics. Yet, when he walked into the restaurant, I liked him immediately and was attracted to him right away. It is clichéd to say "spark," but I guess that's what it was between us. We found out right away that we had a million things to talk about that had absolutely nothing to do with what we did for a living. We were mutually smitten and excited—we were like teenagers looking at each other, pushing our food around on our plates. It was obvious immediately that this relationship was going to go somewhere.

Of course, it did. Right after meeting George, my life took off, and everything started moving about 100 miles an hour—we were engaged in three months, married in six, and I got pregnant on my honeymoon, which was not even planned! Then, while I was pregnant, King World called about the show, and we must have moved about six times in the past year. If someone had told me three years ago that this was what my life would look like now, I would have laughed in his face. But I am certain that if I had not made all of the difficult choices and changes several years ago, none of it would have happened—and it certainly wouldn't have happened so quickly. I really do believe that.

I am very grateful for everything I have in my life right now, so I do try to set boundaries to protect it and to make sure that I balance the demands of my job and my personal life in a way that works for everyone. On the weekends, I don't take business calls, and I only check e-mail once a day. I am in sweatpants, spending time with the baby, going to the grocery store, and my husband is asking me if I'm making chicken for dinner. During the week, both George and I get up very early, so that's another time that we spend together with our daughter. The other thing we do is say no to about 99 percent of the invitations we get—definitely during the weekends, but even during the week. We don't go anywhere unless it is really important and special; we both feel fortunate that we get enough excitement from our jobs and from our time with each other that we don't need to be out every night.

● KAREN HILYARD

ENTREPENEUR

AT 30 . . .
Karen Hilyard was divorced, in debt, overweight, and stuck in a job she hated.

TODAY . . .
Karen Hilyard is a happily married mother and a marathon runner, and she has a job she loves. She is vice president of the Idea Farm, a marketing and public relations firm based in Danville, Kentucky. When she was a vice president of the New York advertising agency Spring O'Brien, her accounts included Hewlett-Packard, Global Crossing, and the Welsh Development Agency. She enjoyed an 8-year tenure with CNN, where she served as an assignment editor, overseeing editorial content of live interviews for CNN, CNN International, and CNN Spanish, and as a senior producer/booker for CNN and Company. She has been awarded an Emmy, a CableACE, and a National Headliner Award for her coverage of the Oklahoma City bombing.

Karen Hilyard is a member of the New Girls' Club because her choices are the embodiment of what it means to live deliberately.

I TURNED 30 IN 1995, and I have to say the year really sucked. At the sudden end of an unhappy long-term relationship, I was emotionally wounded and financially struggling, and I felt I was at a dead end in a job that just a few years earlier had seemed great. Everybody I knew seemed to be driving a better car, taking a more exciting vacation, and having more fun with their free time. A lot of my single friends were in relationships, and most of my married friends were having babies. Against the backdrop of my loudly ticking biological clock, I was unhappy, unsure of myself, and, at least for a time, unable to see the light at the end of the tunnel.

To say things have turned around for me would be a huge understatement: My life after 30 bears virtually no resemblance to my life before. Five years ago, I went from lifelong couch potato to completing my first marathon. Three years ago, after several unsatisfying relationships and some lonely single years, I married the most wonderful, attractive, and considerate man I have ever known. Two years ago, we made a decision to step out of the rat race, leave the big city, and find a place where we could achieve work-life balance. A year ago, living in the idyllic Norman Rockwell small town we had chosen, I gave birth at age 36 to a beautiful, healthy baby girl. Since then, things have fallen into place professionally for me, and I am part owner of an international strategic marketing firm a block and a half from my house. When I turned 30, back during the Year That Sucked, I had no idea that birthday would be the milestone when life really began for me.

A lot of my friends and acquaintances would like to believe I live a charmed life, and luck may indeed have something to do with it. But finding my place in the world has been the result of a lot of work on my part and a de facto philosophy that has guided my life since right around the time I hit the three-decade mark: I consciously stopped being buffeted by events and the actions of others and started taking deliberate action designed to put me closer to what I identified as my life's priorities. Looking back, I realize that the way I'd gotten to the Year That Sucked was a process of a decade or more of not taking control of my own destiny but of just rolling with whatever life brought my way. Life is too short to simply take whatever comes.

Several epiphanies over time have led me where I am now, but if I had to trace things back to a pivotal moment, it would be a weekend I spent with one of my best friends, just after we both turned 31. Both of us were feeling adrift, in need of direction, so we took up the offer of a beachfront condo in November, when we knew the cold and blustery weather would keep us focused on our task of figuring out our lives.

Before you mistake me for one of those people who are really achievement oriented and always setting goals and objectives, I hasten to say that I have always been a list maker but not a goal setter. That is, I was great at accomplishing daily tasks, but I had never sat down and written a list of big-picture goals before, except when I was required to as part of some extracurricular enrichment exercise that I promptly forgot all about. But at age 31, I felt so strongly that my life was on the wrong track—or worse yet, maybe not even on any track—that sitting down with a pen and paper was the only thing I felt I could do to get some degree of control over it.

Truth be told, the goals that were most important to me were probably more focused on dating than anything else, but the process was the same one I followed as I examined every facet of my life, so it's a useful example.

For a long time, my focus had been on meeting as many men as possible, as though finding the right mate was a numbers game and nothing more. Instead, I now wrote down on paper all of the many qualities I was looking for in a relationship. I reexamined old relationships—what had worked and what hadn't. I wrote down the positive attributes I was seeking as well as the negatives that would be red flags for me. It wasn't just the surface stuff, like finding someone who was handsome, kind, funny, and smart. I visualized what he would read, what foods he would like, and how he would spend his weekends. I imagined the type of relationship he had with his mom, his dog, and his car. What emerged was an image so solid and well formed that I could almost—though not quite—*see* what my soul mate was going to look like when I met him. And I definitely knew I would *recognize* him—or his behavior, at least—when he appeared. That last word is a little of a misnomer, though, because I didn't just wait for him to "appear."

Instead, I approached finding a relationship the way a police detective would solve a mystery. I had a sketch of my "suspect"; it was my job now to figure out his habits and his hangouts and put myself in the place he would most likely be. I asked myself questions like, "If I am a guy who enjoys a party but doesn't drink excessively, who is athletic but doesn't like sports on television, who is intellectual but not an intellectual snob . . . where would I be on a Saturday afternoon?"

I knew finding Mr. Right would take effort—he wasn't going to just come knocking on my door, unless of course Mr. Right happened to work for FedEx. I hadn't dated a lot and felt pretty inept at it, but I barreled ahead and focused on putting my effort where it would pay off. I joined the groups and took part in the activities where I thought my dream guy would be. Where groups didn't exist, I started them. Expanding my networking circle challenged me to do things I had always wanted to do but had never tried wholeheartedly, such as running, hiking, camping, and playing pool, among other things.

Of course, I also had a contingency plan, and I think that was key to helping me take the risks inherent in my search. I never had to be scared of failure, because if one plan didn't work, it didn't mean failure, it just meant to move on to Plan B. In the case of "soul mate search," I contemplated what would happen if by age 35 or 40, I was still on my own. My contingency plan was to be economically self-sufficient enough and in a sane-enough job to raise a baby on my own. I'm glad I didn't go to Plan B, but my point is that it wouldn't have been a defeat if I had.

It took a year and a half for me to meet my husband, but I am convinced that the level of detail I went into in visualizing the man I wanted to meet—and the actions I took to put myself in a place where luck and happenstance would bring us together—were essential to making it happen.

On that chilly beach weekend in 1996, I took the same approach to sorting out and visualizing my career situation and my finances. It worked. I decided the tradeoff for my "glamour job" in television news wasn't worth the low pay and the long hours, so I made a list of plans for changing my situation and broke it down into easy-to-complete tasks, each with their own deadline. In less than two years, I had launched in a different career direction in a new industry with better pay and better hours than my old job. On the financial side of things, I determined to pay off my debts, establish contingency funds, and create significant retirement savings, and I tried to think as creatively as possible about how to make it happen. In less than two years, I had paid off all my student loans, refurbished my house, and learned to manage my own investments. Making the list of goals was the easy part; accomplishing the tasks took an enormous personal commitment.

Just because you focus on goals and fix your life once, that doesn't mean it stays that way. Fast-forward a few years to my new husband and me, working 80-hour weeks and living in New York City. Our move to Manhattan just after we got married had always been a gamble, and we found the long hours, the noise, and the anonymity too much to handle and too high a price to pay for the culture, excitement, and sophistication that many people love about the Big Apple. We were trying to have a baby, and it just wasn't the place we wanted to raise our kids. Fueled by my positive experience a few years before, we decided to put our priorities in writing and find a way to pursue them. After hours of introspection and Internet research and many weekend trips, our search led us to a small college town in Kentucky where we felt sure we could achieve the lifestyle we were looking for. Once again, we reduced the risk by having a contingency plan for finding jobs here or elsewhere or for pulling up stakes and moving if we realized we'd made a mistake.

We're now in a place where neighbors know each other and people leave work at 5 o'clock in order to be home for a family dinner. We have time for our hobbies, our daughter, and each other. We're living in a big historic house two blocks from Main Street in a region so lovely the phrase

"God's country" must have been invented to describe it. A lot of people thought it was a big risk to move to a place like this without jobs or connections, but to me, the only risk would have been staying in what was, for us, an unhappy situation. Of course, things both good and bad that we didn't plan for have happened along the way. It hasn't been so much planning as *positioning* that has put us in the right place at the right time for good things to happen.

Several of my friends refer to my career and geographic moves as me reinventing myself over time, but I think I've really just been finding the real me and the right environment by process of elimination. The bottom line, though, is that I took action. The older I get, the more I realize that most of the unhappy people I know feel that way because they have failed to take responsibility for their lives. They complain about what's wrong, but they don't take steps to correct it. They blame other people and events for their circumstances, then use those circumstances as an excuse not to make a success of their family, career, or emotional or financial situation.

Life deals all of us temporary setbacks, and it's only human to occasionally get in ruts. But there's nothing superhuman about getting out of them. You can either control your life or let it control you. I've chosen the former, and for that decision, there is no contingency plan!

● SUSAN LOVE, M.D.

ONCOLOGIST AND AUTHOR

See page 154 for her profile.

Dr. Susan Love is a member of the New Girls' Club because she never stopped being professionally guided by her passion—breast cancer research—even when it meant making professional sacrifices and unexpected career changes.

WHEN I WAS 30, I wish I had known that there was no rush. In your twenties and thirties, you really think you are choosing how you are going to live the rest of your life—but the script you write for yourself rarely works out the way you imagined it would, whether you want it to or not. The flipside of that is you are never really stuck in something, even it feels that way.

They say what doesn't kill you makes you stronger, and that really applies to my career. When I went to medical school, there were few other women in my class, and I was the first woman surgeon on staff at Boston's Beth Israel Hospital. Early on, I got recruited to set up a breast cancer center at another hospital, and when I told my bosses at Beth Israel, they matched the offer. I agonized and agonized and ultimately decided to stay. A week later, they called me and said that they changed their minds. They said it was because my fellow surgeons didn't think that I was enough of a leader, which really meant that they didn't want a woman running the show. So I left. The irony was that when I ultimately left Boston, they put women surgeons in every hospital in town in hopes of finding the next Dr. Susan Love.

But the big revelation to me came a little later. I went to UCLA in 1992 for my dream job—to be a professor and start a breast cancer center there. When you are in medical school, a professorship connected to a research center is what is held up as The Best. I always thought it was exactly what I wanted, but after doing that job for four years, I realized I was not happy. I knew I could do it and be successful, but it wasn't matching my interests anymore.

I went through a little bit of counseling at the time, not because I was feeling crazy but to help sort through why I felt so stuck. That's how I realized that my path was going to be different from the average academic surgeon's career path, because my power really came from women—not from colleagues or institutions or the guy who hired me or the people who promoted me. Therefore, I realized it would go wherever I went, and it was fine to leave the alleged dream job. It was very freeing.

I left UCLA in 1997, went to business school, and started a company based on my research. We got a lot done, but companies want to make money, and I want to eradicate breast cancer. Sometimes those goals match, and sometimes they don't. So I sold the company and decided to start a foundation because fundamental research is better done in that setting.

My career has been a zigzag in many ways, but I've always circled back to the same goal: trying to find a way to eradicate breast cancer. That is what drives me. The lesson I've learned is that you can reinvent yourself a lot of times as long as you are clear about what your real skill set is and what your real goals are. Once you know that about yourself, you can find lots of different ways to achieve those goals because what you're changing doesn't make you a chameleon that no one can recognize. Reinvention works when it grows from questions like, "Should I take the freeway or go the scenic route, or should we drive by the ocean this time?" The key is that you are still driving. You are not suddenly skydiving. You are going to the same destination, using lots of different roads.

What I see all the time with younger women in medicine is that instead of changing the way the jobs work—essentially, reinventing them—they struggle to do their jobs just like the boys do it and still have the rest of their lives as women. I don't think that works. Women of my generation worked like the guys because there was no other option. Now that there are enough women in the workforce, it's exactly the right moment for a new round of change. Young women can say, "We do not want to structure our careers like the guys do. We want to invent our own way of doing it." It's time to look at other models and routes to success—and to understand that careers are fluid, and opportunities come and go many times over the years. We should never, ever, ever give up the idea that we can Have It All, but we have to understand that Having It All happens over time.

● LISA GERSH HALL
COFOUNDER AND COO OF OXYGEN MEDIA

AT 30 . . .
Lisa Gersh Hall was a newly married founding partner at Friedman Kaplan and Seiler, a New York law firm.

TODAY . . .

Lisa Gersh Hall is cofounder and chief operating officer of the Oxygen network. Prior to joining Oxygen, she served as a founding partner of Friedman Kaplan and Seiler from 1986 to 1998. During this time, the firm grew from 6 lawyers to more than 40, serving a wide range of corporate clients in complex corporate transactions and commercial litigation. She lives in New York with her husband and two daughters.

Lisa Gersh Hall is a member of the New Girls' Club because despite her concerns, she left a secure, family-friendly professional environment for a more challenging and gratifying opportunity—and learned how to make the new life/work equation work for her.

PROFESSIONAL REINVENTION FOR ME is a little bit different than for most because my career change was dramatic—I went from being a lawyer to becoming a partner at a creative company. The lesson in it for me is that I should have done it sooner. But when you have kids and you are in a routine as I was—because I had my first child at 33 and my second at 38—it's easy to say, "I am doing a job I know how to do, and I shouldn't change it because I have so much going on with my kids that I won't be able to handle the change."

When I was thinking about what I wanted to do when I graduated from college, I really did want to go to business school, but I was afraid of the GMATS. When it came time after college to take the GMATS or LSATS, I took the LSATS and went to law school instead of business school. But I remained a business-school wannabe, so when the opportunity to do something different in business came along, it was exactly what I had been really wanting to do for a very long time. I had already been through startups—I started my own law practice, which had grown to 50 lawyers. I loved it, and I loved the business end of it. So when Gerry Laybourne, whom I had assisted as a lawyer in contract negotiations at her last two jobs, said, "Hey, I'm going to start this new company, and I want you to come be my partner," I knew I had to make the change despite my concerns about how changes in my schedule might affect my kids.

I was worried about whether people would accept my parenting needs in a new professional situation. I was in an environment at my own firm where everyone respected me and my scheduling needs. I could choose to leave at 6:30 P.M., but remain available all night from home if something needed to be done. But you don't know if that's going to be accepted in a new business environment.

It first hit me when Gerry left Nickelodeon and went to Disney— when we became so involved as partners working from that transition, and I had the opportunity to meet many people at Disney and ABC through the course of negotiating contracts—that I wanted to leave and try something new. But I hesitated, thinking maybe it is not the right time; it might be time to have another kid. But based on my experience at Oxygen, I've learned that you just have to go for it—just take the jump. Your kids are going to be challenging at every age, and the truth is that they are actually more challenging *later on*.

I always say that a nanny can go to the playground, and that's okay because while you may be disappointed about missing the first swing or the first slide, it's when they get to be older—preteens and teenagers— that being around is even more important, because they don't communicate as much. I have a 6-year-old and a 12-year-old, and I see the difference. With my 6-year-old, I don't have to ask for time—whatever time I have, she is willing to be with me. That's not always the case with my 12-year-old anymore. And what I always tell people about little kids is that planning things too far down the road is a waste of time because kids change so much! If you *are* trying to plan the perfect nanny or the perfect schedule, try to limit it to a year at a time. I think if I had listened to myself about this, I would have made my career change sooner. I always hear people say, "I am going to go back to work when my kid is X years old." I say if you want to go back to work, go back to work. It will never be the right time.

I have never regretted my decision to change careers or stopped appreciating the new and different challenges presented by my current role. When you work as a lawyer, you compete in a very structured environment—you bill by the hour and get paid for your time. I moved into a situation where it's not about your time, it's about your ideas and your ability to get things done. I remember one day we were going down to Washington, D.C., for a meeting at AOL. And we were taking that flight to Dulles that was always delayed. Besides myself, there were three or four people from the company, waiting for the plane, and I remember sitting there thinking that I should have never have brought all those people, that it was such a waste of money! Then I realized that I wasn't paying them by the hour, that I wasn't going to have to charge clients by the hour—we were just going to get something *done,* and it was important that everyone be there so that they would understand the deal. I loved that big change, and for me, getting to be the decision-maker instead of the advisor to the decision-maker was a big change that felt right. I knew that I could never go back.

What I learned about changing careers and managing small children is that kids are adaptable, and if you commit yourself to them, any choice you make is okay. You might as well be pursuing the professional opportunities that will really make you happy and challenge you to grow!

● SENATOR KAY BAILEY HUTCHISON
REPUBLICAN SENATOR FROM TEXAS

AT 30 . . .
Senator Kay Bailey Hutchison had just won her first political campaign—a race for a seat in the Texas House of Representatives.

TODAY . . .
Senator Kay Bailey Hutchison is the first woman elected to represent Texas in the U.S. Senate. In 2001, she was elected vice chairman of the Senate Republican Conference, becoming one of the top five leaders of Senate Republicans and the only woman. As chairman of the Military Construction Subcommittee and a member of the Defense Subcommittee of the Senate Appropriations Committee, she plays a vital role in shaping America's defense policies. Senator Hutchison was also the chief Senate sponsor of the marriage penalty tax relief bill, a key provision of the tax reform package

signed into law in 2001. She is author of the Homemaker IRA legislation, which significantly expanded retirement opportunities for
stay-at-home spouses, and she wrote and passed the federal anti-
stalking statute, which makes stalking across state lines a crime. Senator Hutchison lives in Dallas with her husband, Ray, an attorney,
and their son and daughter. The Hutchisons adopted both children
when the senator was 58 and her husband was 68.

*Senator Kay Bailey Hutchison is a member of the New Girls' Club because
she has spent her entire career breaking glass ceilings, even when that
meant turning unexpected professional detours into professional advancement.*

THERE HAVE DEFINITELY BEEN TIMES in my life when I thought I
was going to be a failure, and I think I became a better person because I
had those experiences.

When I graduated from law school and started looking for a job, I
thought I'd get the same kinds of offers my fellow law students got, but
instead I hit my first brick wall in life. None of the law firms wanted to
hire women at the time, and they were not shy about telling me why.
They said up front that they were concerned if they made an investment
in a young female associate, she'd just get married and leave town or drop
out of the workforce.

Before that, I was always able to do whatever I wanted. I was successful in high school, successful in college, and successful in law
school. I was active on campus and had a loving family. I hit some
bumps on the road, but this was my first real rejection. I was very
down and frustrated. It was the first time I truly wondered, "Am I
going to make it in life?"

On the way home from yet another bad interview with a law
firm, I started to think of other ways to use my law degree. On an im-
pulse, I stopped by a television station, went in, and said to the recep-
tionist, "I would like to talk to someone about a job." She said, "What
kind of job?" Figuring out the answer to her question as the words came
out of my mouth, I replied, "A news reporter." She said "Oh, so you

want to talk to the news director." I had no idea what a news director was at the time, but I said, "Yes. That's right. I want to talk to the news director."

Considering my background, I thought becoming a TV reporter was an off-the-wall idea. But the news director actually came out and talked to me, and he thought it would be great to have a lawyer covering the courts and the state legislature. I ultimately got the job, and it was the opportunity of a lifetime. I learned things I would have never learned otherwise, and it opened the door to run for the state legislature. I won that first race when I was 29, and it started me in a whole new direction.

The lesson I learned from that experience was that if you hit a brick wall, look for a way to climb over it, get through it, or go another route. You might find something better than what you originally wanted. Sometimes the closed doors open ones that you never anticipated, because being tested is a very important part of success.

● LORI NELSON
PRODUCTION EXECUTIVE

AT 30 . . .
Lori Nelson was at the tiller of a 40-foot ketch fighting a pelting gale while steering around Cape Horn.

TODAY . . .
Lori Nelson is a founding partner of Kaleidoscope Productions, a minority-owned, Birmingham, Alabama–based firm specializing in diversity-oriented and multicultural content development.

After graduating from UCLA in 1977 and spending three years on the fast track of the Hollywood film industry, Nelson left for an intended short sabbatical and spent the next decade traveling the world while writing for sailing, adventure, and environmental magazines such as *Outside*, *Sail*, *Cruising World*, *Road and Track*, and *Sea Frontiers*. In 1988, she settled in New York, where, with partners, she launched N*Vision Productions, a documentary production company that wrote and/or produced projects for Discovery, A&E, Disney, the Learning Channel, *Newsweek*, and *U.S. News and World Report*. Almost a decade later, she moved to Birmingham to marry a longtime friend, whom she had met at a car race in South America. In 2002, she merged N*Vision Productions with the new Kaleidoscope Productions.

Lori Nelson is a member of the New Girls' Club because she stayed true to her goal of "telling stories that make a difference," even when the journey took her to unexpected destinations.

IF YOU HAD SAID TO ME SIX YEARS AGO that I, a world-traveling adventurer and big-city addict by way of decades spent in New York and Los Angeles, would one day be living and thriving in Birmingham, Alabama, I would have said you were out of your mind. Yet here in the Deep South, in a state whose motto is, "Thank God for Mississippi," I have found a contentment and fulfillment that would be unimaginable in New York or L.A. I was brought here by trusting my heart and instincts enough to take a huge risk, which I can see now in hindsight has been the basis for every right decision I have made in my life's journey. It has only been when I've used my head and tried to do the practical, logical thing that I've run headlong into obstacles and dead ends.

As a child, I was always curious and outgoing, but the trauma of moving to different cities every few years as my dad climbed the corporate ladder must have toughened me up. I can't think of any worse experience than that first day in a new school, walking into the lunchroom and trying to figure out where to sit, wondering if you will ever find a friend. You learn the tricks of connecting with people and not being scared of something new.

My destiny was sealed at 14, though, when my dad gave me a copy of Will Durant's *Story of Philosophy* while I was struggling with my feelings about God. Amazed by that book's accounting of all the deep thinking that had gone on through time, I entered the world of dangerous ideas just as I realized I was conscious and could actually think them by myself. In short order, I became an atheist, agnostic, pantheist, and, by the end of high school, an existentialist—which meant, by my grasp of the concept, a rebel who took on every cause, whether it was the Vietnam War, my school's dress code, or the rape of the rainforest.

The existentialist motto, "Essence precedes existence," that you are the you that you create, not some hapless creature shaped by external forces and circumstance, made me challenge every convention in my philistine world. My parents prayed desperately that I just would make it to my diploma without disgracing them. When I headed to UCLA to study filmmaking, the one medium I knew had the power to change the world, they despaired, certain I would be a drug-addled Hollywood hedonist in no time. To their astonishment, after graduation, I won a plum job in a film production company—the same job Sherry Lansing had just been given at another company across town.

Nobody had prepared me for the reality of work at a film production company; it was not as glamorous as we are led to believe. For every 60 seconds of on-set excitement, there were 12 hours of tedious waiting around, bookkeeping, deal managing, and administrative chores. I was paying my dues, learning the business, and had a progressive boss mentoring me for success, but I felt I was losing my way, becoming a cog in some vast, misty L.A. movie fantasy world. Stressed out, unable to sleep, all I could see before me was clawing my way ahead inch by inch in a business that was as treacherous then as it is now, except then everybody was high on cocaine and twice as dangerous. At 27, I was having a bona fide midlife crisis. When a company reshuffling created my chance for a six-month sabbatical, my friend Jake Epstein (then a successful novelist who went on to become a producer for *NYPD Blue* and *LA Law*) challenged me to take a stab at writing the book I kept idly talking about. I opened up an atlas, picked a spot, and headed to Ibiza, Spain, to write.

Stepping alone off a plane in a strange land with nothing but a suitcase full of books and a typewriter under my arm was my life's defining moment. This was no school lunchroom. I was terrified but could only blame myself for such a rash move. I had abandoned the dream job, my brilliant film career, all financial security, and my friends. Secretly, I was overwhelmed by the idea of writing a book and knew it could only expose me as a fraud.

Yet, from this bog of dread, an intense exhilaration emerged. From that moment forward, I was totally free to invent every moment of my future, devoid of any context but what I created next . . . the existentialist dream. Whatever happened, I concluded, it would be a great adventure because I would make it that. I took a bus into a village, had coffee in a café, and surrendered my fear. Within hours, I had bumped into an American couple, the husband a well-known novelist, no less, who needed a house-sitter for the winter. I found myself ensconced in a rent-free villa equipped with a car and an offer of a literary agent if my work panned out. Nobody back home could believe my astonishing luck. I never looked back.

Since then, my life has taken a deliberately unconventional path. Once in Europe, I began to write for adventure magazines and travel around the world. I sailed in the Antarctic, lived with the dolphins in Australia, and spent giant chunks of solitude in remote natural places. At times, I have performed every lowly odd job in existence in order to keep writing and traveling. I was glad, and grateful, to have them. And of course, there have been passionate, and tragic, love affairs along the way. After four years abroad, I finished my novel, *Faking It*, a coming-of-age satire of a woman in the film business. This 700-page opus still sits in my mother's attic. Once I was no longer living my novel, publishing it didn't seem all that urgent.

Within a few months after I turned 30, my father died, and I began to realize that the quest I'd been on was not so much self-focused as it was a spiritual journey that he had, ironically, set me upon when, at 14, I tearfully told him I feared I no longer believed in God. My American girlfriends used to say in those days that I was "flying by the seat of my pants" through life, but there was a method to its quirkiness. My goal was to open myself to all experience and to love and embrace it without fear, no matter how hard, lonely, impoverished, or isolated circumstances might make me. In some sense, no matter what kind of lives we are living, I think we all test and train ourselves over and over, through every experience, to trust, have faith, and eliminate our fear. That's how we find our wisdom and our truth, and that, to me, is God.

Probably because I was the oldest of eight children and, having raised most of my siblings, had no illusions about childrearing, it never occurred to me to check my biological clock or make marriage a priority. All that could wait. Finally, though, I knew it was time to go home and get back in the game. I'd had enough perfect tropical sunsets to last a lifetime.

In my mid- to late thirties, I finally settled down in New York and decided to start a new career. This time, instead of film, I pursued writing and producing documentaries for television, where I am today. I love TV—it's faster paced, more immediate, and varied. I also knew I could never be happy in the corporate world and formed my own company with two women in Montreal with whom I had worked on a project and greatly admired. It took a while for us build a name for ourselves, but we were lucky to work in large part on projects we all passionately believed in. It doesn't get any better than that, professionally.

When I was 44, due to my screaming biological clock, I suddenly really wanted a family. I connected again with an old friend I'd met years ago at a car race in South America. Bill's life-changing moment had been reading Hemingway's *The Short Happy Life of Francis Macomber* in college. He had lived a wayward, adventurous life almost identical to mine—his in Africa, Pakistan, Afghanistan, and Honduras—and finally settled down in Birmingham, where he had family, to become a high-profile politico in the state. We'd been best friends for over a decade, so it seemed fitting, in our midforties, to get married and try to have a baby. The baby didn't work out—we don't know what we were thinking!—and, after five years, neither did the marriage. In some strange way that only the two of us can understand, marriage was ruining our relationship. We're still best friends, though, and always will be.

What did work out in a surprisingly gratifying way was moving to Birmingham, which I chose to do because Bill had to be here for his work, and I could essentially work anywhere. My New York friends were aghast that I could even consider living in the racist South—all any of us knew about Birmingham were the police dog and fire hose images from the six-ties. What I found was a city that has been so stigmatized by its racial his-tory that the community is far more sensitive to and working harder on improving race relations than any place I've ever known. Birmingham is a vibrant city full of hugely committed civic boosters and with a small-town-within-a-big-city quality of life that has been a welcome change from New York. It's such a great place, and everyone here tries so hard to make it better, that all my save-the-world instincts feel as if they have finally arrived at the *real* mission. And, this may be a matter of age or trav-eling exhaustion, but I discovered I *love* the South. Its eccentricities, com-plex issues and traditions, shabby elegance, and atmosphere suit me perfectly. I haunt the mailbox looking for my next issue of *Southern Living*. I eat grits.

In Birmingham, I've become immersed in race relations work, made deep and meaningful friendships, and joined a terrific group of citizens who are devoted to moving the city forward and creating a *new* Birm-ingham. This is a city, and even a state, where one person can make a huge difference. I've merged my company with a group of diverse, like-minded friends I've worked with here. All of us love the challenge, and the po-tential, of helping to create the future of a whole city—our city, Birm-ingham. Who could have known?

● CHAKA KHAN
Musician

AT 30 . . .
Chaka Khan was locked into a bad record deal. Her records were going gold, but she was barely making ends meet.

TODAY . . .
Chaka Khan has launched her own record label, Earth Song Enter-tainment. Her younger sister is her manager, and her mother is her accountant. She made more money from the proceeds of her first independently produced album than she did in her entire 20 years with Warner Brothers. Khan first arrived on the music scene in 1973

as the lead singer for Rufus, one of the first multiracial bands of its time. Since then, she has had a record-breaking solo career, performed with many of the most influential artists of our time, and been awarded eight Grammy Awards. She recently published her memoir, *Chaka! Through the Fire*.

Chaka Khan is a member of the New Girls' Club for staying true to herself during a life of extreme highs and extreme lows.

I HAVE THIS MECHANISM IN ME where I have been able to pull out of situations just in the nick of time before the shit really went down. I have learned to trust my instincts. Let me tell you—I have been in situations where I would not have come out at all if I did not listen to my intuition and follow it.

When I was living in New York in the 1980s, I was doing drugs heavily. I was going to all the hot spots, hanging out and getting high with people I didn't know. I remember one time I was hanging out in this rundown hotel in Harlem, getting high and all messed up. Maybe there was one person I knew in the entire room. It was a recipe for major disaster. But I was flippant, and I wasn't thinking much about the consequences because I was high—which is exactly why bad things happen to people on drugs. We were all having a good time, laughing and talking. Then all of a sudden something tells me, "It's time to go, now!" I got up, found my friend who I came with and said, "We have to go, NOW." She thought I was just trippin'—but we left. And you know what happened? Five minutes later, people came in and shot up the place. Someone was killed.

When my first grandbaby was born, that instinct kicked in again, but it played out differently this time. I'll be honest with you: At first, I was very reluctant to be a grandmother. I was 39 years old—I had my daughter when was 21, and she got pregnant at 18, and I was not ready for grandmotherhood. I even took my daughter to get some counseling about possibly terminating the pregnancy, which I just feel so terrible about now because I am totally against that, and I love my granddaughter so much. But at the time, I was much more interested in partying and being a rock star than being a grandmother. I wasn't using as much any-more, but I would often take a weekend and just go for it, then act right for a while. (They call that "chippin'.")

But when that baby came home, I looked at her, and something clicked inside of me. I got into her right away, and I said to myself, "Oh, hell, no! Hell, no!" I was going to be a different type of role model for this child than I was for my own children. I know my kids used to live with a lot of fear about me. They were not reacting to my behavior, because I was very careful to have it together around them when they were little. I never partied in the house or anything. But I was on the road a lot, and when I wasn't around, my mother instilled a lot of her worry into my chil-dren. She was really concerned about my well-being—about my life—and she drilled that into my kids, so they were always afraid about me. But when I saw my grandbaby, I thought to myself, "There is no way this child is ever going to have to worry about me. Not this one." And that was it—I stopped doing drugs.

I had a powerful realization that I could do something right away to make real change in my life. And I did. I think we all have that power—that power of instinct and self-control—but I think most people are re-luctant to flex it because once you start using that aspect of yourself, there are no more excuses. Once you start trusting your intuition and your in-stincts, you have to do it all the time, don't you? You can't live this way one day and not the rest. Lots of people are reluctant to practice that shit because it's for keeps. It's deep. It is my mantra.

My grandbaby is 11 now. I have always been honest and forthcoming with her. We talk about how I used to be and how I am now. Her mother always asks me to get the real information from her, because she tells me more about what is going on in her life. She calls me her best buddy, and I love it.

CHAPTER TEN

Letting Go of Perfect

Getting over Yourself to Get the Life You Want

WE ARE A GENERATION OF WOMEN who were raised to believe in futures without limits. However, the positive "you can have anything" cultural message that defined our youth can also shift in our minds to a "you *should* have *everything*" brand of guilt at 30 and beyond. This Expectation Gap leads many of the Gen-X/Y women we interviewed to question their choices if they're not well on their way to having the perfect career, the perfect body, the perfect husband, and the perfect kids. But perfect is, at worst, a myth and, at best, a distraction—having the ability to Have It All does *not* mean you have to have everything. These members of the New Girls' Club claimed futures without limitation by letting go of perfect and focusing on their true priorities.

● SUZE ORMAN

FINANCIAL STRATEGIST AND AUTHOR

AT 30 . . .

Months prior to her thirtieth birthday, Suze Orman was making $400 a month working as a waitress at the Buttercup Bakery in Berkeley, California.

TODAY . . .

Suze Orman is the author of four consecutive *New York Times* best-sellers—*The Laws of Money, The Lessons of Life*; *The Road to Wealth*; *The Courage to Be Rich*; and *The 9 Steps to Financial Freedom*. The personal finance editor on CNBC, Suze hosts her own national CNBC TV show, which airs each weekend. She is a contributing editor to *O: The Oprah Magazine* and appears regularly on QVC as host of her own "Financial Freedom" hour. She has written, coproduced, and hosted four PBS specials based on her best-selling books. The most recent, *The Lessons of Life* (which was inspired by *The Laws of Money*), premiered nationwide in March 2003 and instantly joined the previous three as among the most successful fundraisers in the history of public television. A sought-after speaker, Suze has lectured widely throughout the United States and South Africa, helping people change the way they think about money.

Suze Orman is a member of the New Girls' Club because she achieved success and personal happiness by remaining very clear and focused about her goals and desires instead of becoming distracted by the quest for "more." She sees every roadblock as an opportunity, and by doing so, she feels she truly Has It All.

I FEEL LIKE I HAVE IT ALL so much that I can't even stand it at times. But you have to understand that my "all" probably isn't the "all" most people would want. For instance, I only have one home now, and it's 900 square feet. Period. It's in New York City at this point. I sold the one I had in California, and that was only 900 square feet, too.

It might be that if I had many large homes, to everyone else it would look as if I Had It All. But the truth is that I wouldn't have anything because I'd be mortgaged to the hilt. But I am very clear about what Having It All means to me; it means that I love my life, I love my friends, I love every person around me that I work with. Everything I have is mine—I don't owe anybody a penny, and I have all the money I could ever want in the bank and in investments. Because I didn't go for *everything*—those multi-, multi-million-dollar deals and this and that, I really do Have It All as I've defined and desired it. My "all" is a very simplistic life.

People need to define "happiness" and "all" for themselves, but I'm also going to tell you it's not easy to Have It All, no matter how you define it. On the road to "all," there are all kinds of distractions that are put there to keep you from having it. And the problem is that most of us step on those minefields. We want to live in a bigger, fancier house so that everybody looks at us and can see how much we have. So most of us spend our lives spending money we don't have on people we don't even like or know. To work for the money means you have to spend your time and energy to get that money. When you are spending money you don't even have on people you don't even like or know, it is a self-worth issue. You are literally throwing your own life down the drain—for what? Instead of ending up with it "all," you end up with nothing. So you have to be very clear on what is Having It All—what it means to you and why. Why are you doing that which you are doing? Are you doing it for yourself, or are you doing it to impress others?

You also have to see every potential roadblock as an opportunity and a benefit. I had a radio show that was syndicated nationally, and Clear Channel cut it. Canceled it—BAM! Now, I might be really upset about it since today, I still don't understand why—it had strong advertising and ratings. Most people would have been devastated. But I was ecstatic because rather than looking at it as a rejection, I was like, "Okay, now I have five days a week free. What can I do to make something else work?" So then I put all of my energy into my television show, and now we are taking that television show to an international audience. Because of that one closing of a door, I had time to focus on another important part of my life. We learned how to tape five days a week and tape almost two months of shows, so I then can travel and do anything I want. It freed up an incredible part of my life to *create* more, when the radio show was keeping me where I had to be five days a week and keeping me from being what I really could become. Rather than being freaked about it when it was canceled, I decided, "This is the best thing that ever happened to me."

● PEGGY ORENSTEIN
AUTHOR AND JOURNALIST

AT 30 . . .

Peggy Orenstein quit her job as managing editor of *Mother Jones* magazine, got a book contract, and became engaged to marry her husband, Steven, within three weeks of turning 30. She says, "I spent the next year somewhat in shock."

TODAY . . .

Peggy Orenstein is an award-winning writer, editor, and speaker about issues affecting girls and women. She is the author of *Flux: Women on Sex, Work, Kids, Love, and Life in a Half-Changed World*, an examination of the politics and psychology of women's life choices from their midtwenties through their midforties, as well as the best-selling *Schoolgirls: Young Women, Self-Esteem, and the Confidence Gap*, an in-depth study of educational inequity and self-image conflicts among teenage girls in two diverse communities. A contributing writer for the *New York Times Magazine*, Orenstein has also written for such publications as *Vogue*, *Glamour*, *Discover*, *Elle*, the *Los Angeles Times*, *USA Today*, *Mother Jones*, *Salon*, and the *New Yorker*.

Peggy Orenstein is a member of the New Girls' Club because she recognized the necessity of accepting the value of appreciating that which we can't control and long-term happiness over short-term wins.

I REMEMBER BEING 34 YEARS OLD, sitting in an Amtrak train from New York to D.C. and wrestling with my confusion over whether or not I wanted to become a mother. At the time, I was not seeing my friends break new ground as they put the puzzle pieces of their lives together. It seemed that once they had children—in fact, almost immediately after their babies were born—their marriages changed, and they fell into these very traditional roles. Or new traditional roles—like ones where the woman worked part-time *and* did everything around the house. Or the woman worked part-time and did at least 90 percent around the house, and the man worked full-time and did a little bit. I don't think that everyone is destined to, or should have, a perfect 50-50 split in their household arrangements, but what was troubling me was that the women I knew were not feeling really satisfied and happy.

I did not want to live that way. I wanted to have my independent life, which was not just about career but about other things, too, including my marriage. My relationship with my husband was and is incredibly important to me, and what I was seeing happen to the dynamics of many friends' marriages scared me—a distance and resentment crept in after the kids. And all of these dumb little things flashed through my head, like how my husband and I love to snorkel together. We swim holding hands as we head out to the sea, and it's very romantic. I would start to think, "Hey, we won't be able to do that anymore! Someone would have to sit on the beach with a baby!" I was having a hard time envisioning how much our lives would change with children.

At the same time, I was going around the country and giving talks about self-esteem. It began to strike me that there was this big gap in messages between what we were telling teenage girls and what we were telling women when they came to be around 30. For girls and teens, we say, "You can do anything," and then for women, we turn around and say, "You can't Have It All." There was such a disconnect between what those two messages meant. I think it was, and still is, really confusing to deal with that disconnect when attempting to put together a satisfying life.

So I was very confused about how I felt about motherhood, and I wasn't sure if I wanted kids or not, but as I was rounding the bend around 35, I realized it was the time to make that decision. Then, my husband's father died. That was really a life-changing moment for us. Just after the funeral, when we were flying home from Los Angeles, we decided then that we did want to start trying to have kids. So I went off the Pill. Two months later, I was diagnosed with breast cancer; life began to go really off-track, and it stayed off-track for years. It was awful.

The kind of breast cancer I had was less typical for young women—

it was invasive, but it was a less aggressive type. One of the first things my surgeon said to me when she called was, "You are a lucky woman," and I felt like saying back to her, "Are you out of your mind?" But I see in retrospect that I was and am very lucky in the nature of my cancer. Still, I felt like my youth got pulled out from under my feet that day. People are not supposed to face their mortality at 35, and it was really profound.

The cancer made me think more about my life, but it also made me feel pissed off. It was *not* going to keep me from having my life. I thought, "If I can't have a kid because of this cancer, I am going to be really mad." And even though the time it took me to conceive was not directly related to the cancer, it felt like it was the fault of the cancer. I felt cheated.

Up until then, I had always been a high-achieving, very goal oriented person who got what I wanted because I just would not accept *not* getting what I wanted. I was a person who could make things happen in my life, and then suddenly, there was this big thing I could not make happen. It was beyond my control, and it was hard.

My body kept screwing up on me—I felt like I was constantly being told I was defective in some way. Most people say, "Hey, let's have kids," and then three months later, they're pregnant. If it takes you five years to get pregnant and you have miscarriages, each time you try again to conceive, you have to have a conversation with your spouse and with yourself and say, "Do we want to go through this again?" We had to make the decision over and over and over again.

During that time, my goal-oriented nature—which before had been my friend—became a very, very bad thing. It got in the way of living my life and seeing the things I had that were really good. The things that I did *not* have took control. The missing baby took center stage, and as time went on it, really began to overshadow everything else. It's hard to talk about it because I am still in the middle of it in many ways. Yet I think what I have learned is that you have to live the life that you have. You can have goals, but if you don't hit the marks, it can't be the defining thing determining whether or not you believe your life is successful. The ends don't always justify the means, either. What you push through and ignore to get to that goal may be as important or more important than the goal itself.

Truthfully, I am not sure how I would have come to terms with it if things turned out differently for me. Sitting here nine months pregnant, I have a different perspective now about all of these questions. I hope that I would have eventually come to the same set of conclusions, but it would have taken me longer.

Gosh, all of this makes me sound so beat up! It's been hard, and I wouldn't wish it on anyone, and I am not glad it happened. But at the same time, to a certain extent, I guess I have been pummeled into being a better person and certainly a more compassionate person. I've let go of some of my goal orientation and think less about what's going to give me an A in life as opposed to what's going to be sustaining to me across my whole life. And the things that sustained me during the dark times were all the things *besides* kids that, at least for me, make for a rich life: my marriage, my friends, my work, traveling, reading, going to movies.

It irritates me to no end that the discussion about women's lives keeps pitting career against family, women's independence against traditional roles—as if the two are mutually exclusive, as if they are the only components of our lives. Because for all the bashing women *still* take for working (like it's an option!), if I didn't have work that engaged me and was important to me during this period, I don't know how I would've gotten through it. My perspective is: Thank goodness for my career. Thank goodness for the opportunities I have built for myself through years of hard work and perseverance. Work gave me a place to feel valuable and competent, a way to create meaning and, not incidentally, to earn the money to do the fun things that gave me pleasure while going through all of this. That was so important to me. It still is.

● IRIS KRASNOW

AUTHOR AND JOURNALIST

See page 156 for her profile.

Iris Krasnow is a member of the New Girls' Club because she learned that embracing the imperfection in partnerships is the key to sustaining them.

A HAPPY AND FULFILLING MARRIAGE has little to do with sustained bliss and everything to do with surrendering to the grind. Learning to live and love in the grind of the ordinary is the ticket to happiness because that grind is actually the soothing, daily rhythm of life. That is what I learned when I was alone in the kitchen with four yelping sons under the age of the three—made possible by the birth of twins.

I had left my adrenaline-pumping job as a feature writer at United Press International to stay at home with the children. When I was single and unencumbered, I remember walking into my Washington office one day and my editor saying to me, "You are interviewing Yoko Ono today. You need to be there by noon and home by 5:00." That was not an unusual day on the job. And now here I was, wearing a gray bathrobe splotched with excrement, trying to breastfeed two babies at once—this with a three-year-old and a one-year-old simultaneously trying to hop onto my lap. Chuck had gone back to work, all clean and spiffy-looking in his pressed shirt and bolo tie, hopping into his shiny red car, leaving me behind. I was pissed.

Then, on one crazy morning, with four little boys heaped onto me, I just started to laugh. I realized for the first time in my whole life that I knew exactly what was expected of me. I was the spoke of this family, and it was up to me to keep the wheels turning. I felt totally stuck—but being stuck was sweet.

The real rub in life is when the extraordinary becomes ordinary, which it inevitably does time and time again, especially in relationships. I'm not saying that marriage is destined to be dull, but if you want the honest truth, here it is: Marriage can be hell. And the grass is not greener on the other side. So you may as well love the one you're with, especially if you have children.

Women have been programmed for decades to have unrealistic expectations about marriage. We go into it thinking, "Now I will find happiness." But the truth is, you need to be a whole and happy person going down the aisle toward matrimony, and then you have a shot at a happy marriage. Nobody else can make you happy; you must do that for yourself. That's why affairs happen. People are in real marriages, sharing bathrooms, in-laws, and bills. And they're thinking, "God, this is tedious, and not what I signed up for." Then they meet someone new and exciting, some fantasy person they have never lived with and don't really know. They have breathy affairs at seaside resorts, believing, "Wow, this person really understands me," when in fact, they really know very little about the person. Try living with Mr. Perfect, and the flame is often quickly doused.

When I was going through the difficult first years of my own marriage, hit with the grind of the ordinary, several of my friends were getting divorced. They would say, "You know, this marriage just isn't making me happy." I must admit, I thought of leaving my own marriage for the same reason. But thankfully, I realized that those same people often find themselves in second marriages, saying, "You know, this person is not making me happy, either. Maybe I was better off with bucket number one." And people on third and fourth marriages say things like, "Gee, why can't I get this right?"

Well, it's not a big head scratcher. You take yourself with you. Marriage wasn't designed to make you happy—you must do that for yourself. Happiness comes from the wellspring of your heart, not from another person, even if you have the greatest husband on Earth, which I happen to think I have got. Today, I think that. Ha! Tomorrow, it may be a different story, and so goes real marriage, heaven one day, hell the next. My father always used to tell me when times got tough, "Iris, you gotta swing with it." And that's my approach to marriage, you gotta swing with it, and you gotta have an unshakable faith that when you're down, you're going to eventually swing upward.

● ROSANNA ARQUETTE
ACTOR AND DIRECTOR

AT 30 . . .
Rosanna Arquette had gained early acclaim as an actress for her appearances in films such as *The Executioner's Song*, *Baby, It's You*, and *After Hours*.

TODAY . . .

Rosanna Arquette has marked her directorial debut with the critically acclaimed 2003 film *Searching for Debra Winger*, a documentary exploring the issue of aging in Hollywood. In the late 1980s and early 1990s, Arquette lived and worked in Europe for six years before returning to Hollywood and taking roles in films such as *Nowhere to Run*, *Pulp Fiction*, *Crash*, *Hope Floats*, *The Whole Nine Yards*, and *Big Bad Love*. She lives in California with her daughter.

Rosanna Arquette is a member of the New Girls' Club because she used her public platform to examine the paucity of roles for women over 40 in Hollywood and the pervasive cultural pressure to look physically perfect and artificially youthful. Moreover, as an actress, she continues to identify new venues for her talent.

I MADE THE MOVIE *Searching for Debra Winger* about women in Hollywood over 40 because as an aging actress, I think it's about time we all— as a culture—learned to embrace the sexiness that comes from within. I think aging affects all women's careers, but the pressure in Hollywood to stay frozen in time is outrageous. A few days ago, I was with a beautiful, little, young, gorgeous, 28-year-old who was getting Botox. I said, "What are you doing—why are you getting Botox? For what?" I have not succumbed to that stuff yet, as much as the pressure is on.

I am aging, yes, but I am terrified that women are also guilty of buying into this robotic way of looking—that we are not even allowed to be ourselves as we get older. In other cultures, you are allowed to have lines on your face and still be considered beautiful; in other places, you are allowed to visually reveal wisdom. And now, in this town and this business that I am in, unfortunately, you can't even go out without the possibility of being caught by a video camera. The reality is that when you're leaving a yoga class without makeup, no one looks glamorous! And this is actually something all women deal with because there is an entire beauty product industry out there telling us we have to look great—all the time. Even if the cameras are not there, the pressure is.

In Hollywood, people have to deal with this by leaving. I said, "I'm

just going to go behind the cameras, because I don't want this pressure."
I want to be able to age and not feel like I look like an old hag! But Frances
McDormand talks about not buying into it—that's why I love her so
much. And she hasn't! She is sexy and amazing and herself and says that
if we just hold off and don't buy into this, there will be parts for 53-year-
old women, and we'll get them because we really look the part. Women
have to realize that we are like a tribe, and if we stick together we can
make things happen and change the way people think about these issues.

● GAIL EVANS

AUTHOR AND CNN'S FIRST FEMALE SENIOR EXECUTIVE VICE PRESIDENT

AT 30 . . .
Gail Evans was a stay-at-home mother.

TODAY . . .
Gail Evans is the author of *Play like a Man, Win like a Woman*, which
has been translated into 18 languages and has been a best-seller
around the world. Her latest book, *She Wins, You Win,* was published
in May 2003.

Evans worked at the White House in the Office of the Special
Counsel to the President during the Lyndon B. Johnson Administration and was instrumental in the creation of the president's Committee on Equal Employment Opportunity and the 1966 Civil
Rights Act. She took a break to raise her three children, then relaunched her career at CNN in the early 1980s, where she quickly
rose through the ranks. Upon her retirement in 2001, Evans was responsible for program and talent development of all CNN domestic
networks, overseeing national and international talk shows and the
network guest bookings department, which schedules about 25,000
guests each year. She is currently a visiting professor in the Dupree
School of Management at Georgia State University, and her weekly
syndicated radio segment "It's Not Just a Man's World" is syndicated
to 1,900 radio stations throughout the United States.

Gail Evans is a member of the New Girls' Club because throughout her entire career, she has made mentoring women a top priority. Moreover, she took risks and learned that perfection is not a prerequisite for success.

THE BIGGEST RISK I EVER TOOK—internally for me—was being willing to stand up publicly, first in meetings and now in front of audiences and on television and in classrooms, and not be beautiful. Not being beautiful has always been the hardest thing for me. If you look at the women who have been my friends for my entire life, most of them are very beautiful. I always thought my looks were the greatest detriment about who I was, and that is the honest truth. And I really do believe that the times it was hardest for me to break through professionally were always about my looks.

For years, the biggest battle I had at CNN was over getting a publicity shot taken. My secretary Robin would tell you how—forever—it somehow never got scheduled. I think it was all on purpose. All of the beauty stuff is so hard for women. One of the observations I have absolutely made over time is that when you look at a group of successful women, they are almost always attractive. You just never see a really ugly woman in the executive suite. You see guys who are fat slobs and pigs—but the women are rarely that way. So this has always been an issue for me, although it's much less of an issue today than it was when I was younger. Now, I look younger than my age, and I always get complimented when people find out I have five grandchildren. It soothes what I've felt before, but I had to wait until I was older to let that go.

My way of winning in life was always to be smartest one in the room. Yet when I came to CNN, television was new ground for me, and I definitely didn't know as much as everyone else in the room. And of course, television is a business where image really matters, so it was very hard. I don't think I ever really got over that feeling of inferiority, but I just kept on plowing through. I just kept on going. Ultimately, the excitement of the challenge was bigger than the terror of "Oh, my God, what am I am doing here?"

Another big risk I took repeatedly over the years was that I did not get it perfect a lot of times. I have learned to say to myself, "I have done as much work as I am doing on this project. I've got other things to do, and I am moving on." All of my girl training told me to make it perfect, but believing that I knew enough about a topic and then *walking away from it* proved to be the key difference between me and my female colleagues who didn't get as far ahead as I did at CNN. I was also that way as a student, which was very frustrating to everyone I was involved with at school. I believed firmly that the difference between a B and an A is nothing I would ever need to know in life. What gets you from a B to an A is a lot of irrelevant material that you will have to look up one day anyway if you ever need it, so what I did was settle for a B-plus. It used to make my parents nuts. They would always say, "But Gail—you could be brilliant," and I would say, "But then I couldn't learn as much." In my career, I am certain I wouldn't be as broadly accomplished if I were always going for an A. And I tended not to hire people who only wanted the A as well. All "perfect" does is absolutely force you to waste time, because you'll never get there. That is one of the places I think that women really get stuck.

● JUDY BLUME

AUTHOR

See page 176 for her profile.

Judy Blume is a member of the New Girls' Club because she realized that true happiness is often found through failure, false starts, and hard work—and by abandoning a life that looks "perfect" but feels wrong.

MY TWENTIES WERE MY WORST DECADE. Maybe it was because my beloved father died suddenly when I was 21, just weeks before my wedding, and I didn't know how to deal with that loss. Maybe because I thought I had to be perfect, even though I knew I wasn't. Maybe because growing up in the '50s, women didn't have many choices (at least I didn't think they did), and I remember my mother telling me, "You'd better find yourself a husband while you're in college, because where are you going to meet one otherwise?" So, like a good girl, I married before the end of my junior year at NYU.

I was such a baby, and soon I was having babies of my own. I was thrilled with my two small children, but at the same time, I felt trapped in a suburban marriage where women were responsible not only for the children but also for running the household and making sure their husbands (the breadwinners) were free to concentrate on work. I wasn't an equal partner in my marriage (who thought of equal partnerships back then?), but I felt I had chosen this life, I had been raised to lead this life, and I tried desperately to live up to my mother's and my husband's expectations, though I didn't have the self-awareness at the time to understand any of this.

All the other women in the neighborhood were living the same kinds of lives I was, except they seemed happy. I'm a very good mimic, so I tried to be like them, pretending to be happy and fulfilled. I later learned they thought I had a model marriage and family life. The girlfriends I'd grown up with who were such an important part of my life before marriage were all busy role-playing, too. Raising children is the ultimate adult responsibility, we were all in over our heads, and we held everything inside. Somehow we muddled through, but it would have been so much better for us and our kids if we could have been truthful with one another. You know, call each other up and say, "I'm feeling unbearably lonely and isolated today. I don't know what to do." But there was an unwritten rule at the time, leading us to believe we couldn't admit that anything was wrong. That, I think, is what really did me in. Pretending to be happy all the time was so exhausting—and it was such a lie.

Depression wasn't a word in any of our vocabularies then. It wasn't until years later that I found out three of my childhood friends were hospitalized with depression during those early years of our marriages. We were unprepared for marriage, motherhood, and responsibilities.

I started to write when I was 27, out of desperation, though I don't think I knew that at the time. My children were two and four years old. I signed up for a course in writing for children at the School of Continuing Education at NYU, and I lived for that one night of class a week. I was excited about the possibilities, writing every morning while my children were at preschool. My first stories were accepted for publication during the second semester of that course, and my first book about a year later.

Writing saved my life, and I'm speaking literally as well as figuratively. If I hadn't found my creative outlet, I honestly don't know what would have happened to me. I was sick all the time. Some of it was psychosomatic and some of it wasn't. The worst of my exotic illnesses started on my thirtieth birthday with a rash that covered my body, a temperature of 105°, and aches and pains in my joints. My eyes were swollen shut. I felt so sick I didn't care if I lived or died. The doctor was never able to diagnose that illness. I got well when he prescribed cortisone, but it took months to gain back the weight I'd lost and even longer to regain my strength. My husband didn't like it when I rocked his boat—and being sick definitely rocked his boat.

The biggest risk I ever took in my personal life was to admit failure—*twice*. I packed up the kids (they were 12 and 14) and left my marriage after 16 years. It wasn't that my husband was a bad person. It was just that it was time to admit we were wrong for each other. By then it was 1975. I had such fantasies of freedom! But so ill-prepared was I for life without a man that I married the first guy who came along. I wish it had just been an affair, but I believed I could make this marriage work. It wasn't long before I realized making marriage work has everything to do with choosing the right partner. And for the second time, I hadn't taken the time to get to know him. To be divorced once was bad enough; twice was unthinkable. But I lived through it. So did my kids.

It's not easy to admit to yourself and the world that you've made a mistake, but admitting it can also be a freeing experience. It doesn't kill you any more than rejection does, although in the beginning, you're sure you'll never get over it. Life is a series of ups and downs no matter how successful you are. You can't plan your life, because you never know what's just around the corner. For me, understanding and accepting that concept was a profoundly adult experience.

Today, I live in the present. I've been with the same man for 24 years. This time we got to know each other before we married. My life, both personal and professional, is so much better than I could ever have imagined when I was 30.

● RIKKI KLIEMAN
COURT TV ANALYST AND TOP TRIAL ATTORNEY

AT 30 . . .
Rikki Klieman was working as an assistant district attorney in Cambridge, Massachusetts, for (now Senator) John Kerry.

TODAY . . .
Rikki Klieman is a Los Angeles–based legal analyst for Court TV and NBC's *Today Show* and is author of the *Los Angeles Times* best-seller *Fairy Tales Can Come True: How a Driven Woman Changed Her Destiny*. She served as an anchor for Court TV in New York from 1994 through 2003, analyzing trials and legal proceedings throughout the country. A practicing attorney for 28 years and a member of the adjunct faculty at Columbia University Law School, Klieman was named one of the five most outstanding woman trial lawyers in the country by *Time* magazine. She remains counsel to the Boston law firm of Klieman, Lyons, Schindler, and Gross and lives in Los Angeles with her husband, Los Angeles Chief of Police Bill Bratton.

Rikki Klieman is a member of the New Girls' Club because she recognized when to make short-term personal and professional compromises that would allow her marriage and career to flourish in the long run.

IN 2003, I SOLD MY BEACH HOUSE and my apartment in New York City and left the job that I loved to move across the country when my husband accepted the job of L.A. chief of police. I left a position of substantial financial well-being with no real job on the other side. In essence, I jumped off a cliff, in total freefall.

Throughout my adult life, I always chose my career over my personal life. Although I gave lip service to the fact that I was changing that tune, and articles appeared at intervals on "the new Rikki Klieman" or "the new and improved Rikki Klieman," the truth was that I talked a good game, but I returned to my pattern of work first, happiness later. In many ways, I treated my spouse or significant other in the manner that men traditionally treated women—they did precisely what they wanted when they wanted to do it.

When I married my husband, Bill Bratton, in 1999, I knew that I had worked hard to reach a place in my own life where I was ready for a truly committed relationship—a true partnership. He was certainly my professional and intellectual equal; we were two of the most ambitious people on the planet, and we were thought of as leaders and role models. Our courtship blossomed during his years in the private sector. He had been chief of the New York Transit Police, Boston police commissioner, and New York City police commissioner at an earlier time. When we fell in love at the age of 50, we were both ready for a real commitment—for a relationship where each person took 100 percent responsibility for the happiness of the other. Our jobs became just that—jobs, not all-consuming occupations. Our priority was "us," and that was a source of joy, sometimes ecstasy, and always contentment.

At sunset by the pool on July 4th weekend of 2002, I said to Bill and my closest friends that I thought my life was perfect . . . that I never wanted anything to change. I was totally at peace with all aspects of my life. We were in the house where we would grow old. My job at Court TV would be my life's work, along with teaching at Columbia Law School. My friends were accessible. Bill's family, which became my family, was a moment away in Boston. What could be better?

One week later, Bill returned from a business trip to Los Angeles and said that he had been approached about applying to become the chief of police there. He had one week to apply—or not. I retreated into a shell and wouldn't speak. For the weekend, I alternated between silence and open rage. How could he do this to our lives? How could he want to do this? Why would he want to do this? What we had was everything anyone could want. Why would he turn our lives upside down for the sake of one job? What about my house, my house, my house, my job, my job, my job?

At some point, I came to my senses and did what I do best—I

tackled the situation as I would a business issue. I got a yellow pad and wrote out pros and cons, questions and answers. Then we switched roles. He returned from a tennis lesson and said he would not apply—that he had not considered me and us sufficiently—and he meant it. This strong leader would really not go forward. By that time, I was ready for him to proceed, so I asked him why he wanted the job. He explained that he felt powerless after September 11, that he didn't know what his identity was anymore, and that he could do this job, turn this department around, make those police officers proud again, change people's lives, and save hundreds of lives. I then knew that this was his destiny, just as other roads had been mine. Then I simultaneously understood that this was my destiny to do this with him—to be part of the change.

Of course, he got the job, and he is the right person for it. He is thriving. He moved to Los Angeles in October 2002. I commuted virtually every weekend for nine months, arriving in L.A. on Friday night at 9:00 P.M., going through a swirl of events till I boarded the red-eye at 10:00 on Sunday night, arriving in New York at 6:00 A.M. on Monday, running home to take a shower, then going to work to do live television five days a week and start all over again. We lived in a hotel in L.A. until we found a new home. It was my responsibility, since I remained in New York, to sell the apartment, sell the house, keep working, and be scintillating seven days a week. Once I sold the apartment, I actually rented one apartment in my building from a judge and his wife who were in town only 7 to 10 days a month. Then I would take a clothing rack with a bag of lingerie and a bag of cosmetics across the hall to sleep with my de facto godmother, who is 86 years old.

I could have been a basket case. I could have given up or given in. I could have looked at all of this and done what I always did—choose my own job as a substitute for the hard work of a relationship. I didn't. I chose life; I chose love; I chose an "us" over a "me."

And what grand rewards I am having. I am finally in our new home with my magnificent husband. It's really "our" new home, not just mine. It is so beautiful, so peaceful.

On the professional side, I am more and more fulfilled every day.

Would I be without work? Would no one come to my door? If you let go of fear, it all works out. I am continuing as a legal analyst with Court TV, something that wasn't possible until my employer and I created it this spring. You can create what you want and what you need. I will be contributing to a major television network—a job others said would be impossible from Los Angeles. I have published a book and continue to speak to groups around the country. In L.A., I'm being approached to be the keynote speaker at various charitable and public service events. I am joining boards that fulfill my needs of mentoring youth and fighting domestic violence. I am working with my husband in the community and am so proud to be in his light; he says he is proud to be in mine, and he means it. Together, we are working to change this city for the better, and we can see how others appreciate it.

CHAPTER ELEVEN

Guts and Grace
Staying on Course When It Counts

MARTHA WASHINGTON ONCE SAID, "I have learned from experience that the greater part of our happiness or misery depends on our dispositions and not on our circumstances." The remarkable strength, courage, and clarity that carried these members of the New Girls' Club through the very hardest of times proves that statement to be true. Precisely at the moment when nothing seemed possible, these brave and classy women showed that anything really is possible when you stay true to who you are.

● GERALDINE FERRARO
FORMER CONGRESSWOMAN AND VICE-PRESIDENTIAL CANDIDATE

AT 30 . . .
Geraldine Ferraro was a stay-at-home mother.

TODAY . . .
Geraldine Ferraro has earned a place in history as the first woman vice-presidential candidate on a national party ticket. She was first elected to Congress from New York's 9th Congressional District in

257

Queens in 1978 and served three terms in the House of Representatives. In Congress, she spearheaded efforts to achieve passage of
the Equal Rights Amendment. She was appointed by President
Clinton to lead the U.S. delegation to the United Nations Human
Rights Commission. An active participant in the nation's foreign
policy debate, she serves as a board member of the National Democratic Institute of International Affairs and is a member of the
Council on Foreign Relations. In addition to numerous articles, Ferraro has written two books, *Ferraro: My Story*, which recounts the
1984 campaign, and *Geraldine Ferraro: Changing History*. She is a political analyst for the Fox network.

*Geraldine Ferraro is a member of the New Girls' Club because she fights
all battles—political, professional, and personal—with passion and dignity.*

WHEN I FIRST FOUND OUT I HAD CANCER, it was like getting
hit in the head with a bat—it was totally unexpected. I had just come off
a Senate campaign, and though I had been too tired too get up in the
morning to do a subway stop at 6:30 A.M. and was really exhausted by the
end of the day, I didn't give it much thought. I figured, "It's been six years
since I last ran, and six years can make a difference." I attributed my fa-
tigue to just getting older.

After the campaign, I went to see my doctor for my annual checkup.
Over the years, he had always told me that I wouldn't hear from him
about my tests if everything was normal, but if there was anything wrong,
he would call. This time he did. He said it looked like I had either
leukemia, lymphoma, or multiple myeloma. I had heard of leukemia and
lymphoma, but not multiple myeloma. When he explained to me that like
the others, it was a blood cancer, I was stunned. I went into my husband's
office—which was right next to mine—and I said, "I have to talk to you."

The tests came back the following week, and they confirmed that it
was multiple myeloma. My first reaction was, "Thank God it's me and not
one of my kids." Then I asked, "How much time do I have?" and he said,
"The usual prognosis is three to five years, but I have many patients who
are living well past that." It was like getting hit with a bat again, and that

bat was my own mortality. As hard as it was for me to accept, in some ways the shock was worse for my husband—he was completely distraught.

When I saw my husband's reaction, I was determined I was not going to tell my kids until after Christmas. So I waited until after the New Year, after we were back home from a vacation, and I sat them each down and told them one at a time. It was extremely difficult; we are a very close family. Ultimately, they each dealt with it in their own way, very much in step with their own experience and training. Donna was, at the time, a producer of the *Today Show*. She immediately went to the Web and did research. She found the Multiple Myeloma Research Foundation, called them to learn all she could about the disease, and volunteered to help them in fundraising. Eventually, she got the *Today Show* to do a segment on multiple myeloma. My son is a lawyer in business with my husband. Since John was accompanying me to all of my doctor's visits, our son said, "Don't worry about anything at work. I will take care of everything." And he did. Laura, my youngest, is a doctor, so she immediately got in touch with the specialists to keep an eye on my care. She also accompanied me on my hospital visits in Boston. We raised our children to be people of action, and they are.

For several years, I didn't discuss my condition with anybody except my family and a few very close friends. When you are in public office, people are entitled to know everything about you. But I was no longer in public office, so I considered my private life private, and that included my illness. When you get a disease like cancer, you invariably want to say something like, "Why me?" I don't have cancer in my immediate family, but I was concerned. Was it genetic nonetheless, and might I have already passed it on to my kids and my grandkids? Was it environmental?

About two and a half years after my diagnosis, I received a call from the head of the Multiple Myeloma Research Foundation. She was having a hard time getting Congress to hold a hearing on blood cancer research. She asked me if there was anything I could do, and I said, "Tell the Senate staffer to tell the senator quietly that if he has a hearing, I will testify." My Donna asked me, "Are you sure you want to do this?" I told her I was ready.

I couldn't get over the number of people who got in touch with me—and continue to contact me—after my testimony. There is not one person who has asked to speak to me about multiple myeloma whom I have not spoken to. They call to tell me how they're doing. They ask about how I'm doing. You should hear what some of the doctors are recommending! And it's not that their doctors are not smart, but many are not myeloma specialists, so they go for the most aggressive treatment because they don't know other ways to approach it. The hearings also resulted in a bill authorizing $250 million for blood cancer research and $25 million for blood cancer education. I am very proud of that.

About two months ago, after receiving the results of my blood tests, my Laura called me to go over my numbers, and she said, "You know, Mom, cancer sucks." I laughed and asked her if that was a medical diagnosis, and she said, "No, but it really does. Nonetheless, when you think about it—you're lucky. Research in the past three years has really made a difference." And it's true. Since I was diagnosed, there are new therapies available. I am currently in a clinical trial for a new drug. But I also have the best specialists and the best care—which makes me feel a little guilty because not everyone has access to the same care I do. That's why I keep nagging to get cancer drugs funded by Medicare and insurance. These drugs can make a difference in how you live your life. I am lucky. I work a full-time job. I travel. I work for Fox. I do all these things, and I feel great. Many multiple myeloma patients are not as fortunate as I am.

I have had the opportunity over the past 25 years to meet with heads of state throughout the world and lots of movers and shakers in this country. But to me, the greatest advice I got was from my mother, who had an eighth-grade education. She told me that when something bad happens, take a look at what has happened, and if it's something that you can correct—fine. If not, learn from it and move on. And that is exactly how I face life. I don't look back and say, "Gee, if only I had done this, or if only that hadn't happened." Well, it happened, so move on. I think that is the only way to deal with loss. It's the only way to deal with personal tragedy. My mother's advice is what helps me deal with cancer, too. I am not sitting here wallowing. I am not dying of cancer, I am living with cancer. And I am moving on.

So getting back to the question of "Why me?" and going beyond what caused my cancer: I really do think that one of the reasons I have this disease is because God is using me. I would never say I am glad that I have multiple myeloma, but I am pleased that I am able to use my illness as a vehicle to help others. It's my mother's voice telling me, "Don't sit here and brood. Move on and see what you can do to make things better."

● NANCY GRACE
COURT TV ANCHOR AND FORMER PROSECUTOR

AT 30 . . .
Nancy Grace was prosecuting felony cases in Georgia and working as a litigation instructor at a Georgia law school.

TODAY . . .
Nancy Grace is the anchor for Court TV's daily trial coverage program *Closing Arguments*. Previously, she clerked with a federal court judge and practiced antitrust and consumer protection law with the Federal Trade Commission. She serves as a legal commentator and frequent guest host on *Larry King Live* on CNN, as well as CNBC, MSNBC, Fox News Channel, NBC's *Today Show*, and ABC's *Good Morning America*, and *The View*.

A lover of Shakespearean literature, Grace's plan to become an English professor was derailed by the random murder of her fiancé. The incident propelled her to enroll in law school and set her on the path to becoming a felony prosecutor and an outspoken victims' rights advocate. She helped staff the hotline at an Atlanta battered women's center for 10 years. As a district attorney in Atlanta, she tried more than 100 cases and never lost one.

Nancy Grace is a member of the New Girls' Club because she always stays focused on what is truly important—regardless of attempts to undermine her efforts or distract her from her goal.

PROSECUTING VIOLENT FELONIES as a young, blonde female in Southern courtrooms posed its own challenges—being hit on by judges, putdowns in open court, snide comments—just like other women encounter in the workplace. I believed, however, that I was in the unique position of having more than just myself to consider when responding. My case had to come first; in no way could I jeopardize the outcome of the trial. Sometimes a quick comeback could put another attorney in their place, or sometimes I simply pretended I hadn't noticed a thing and focused on defeating the defense. Why waste energy on a snarky lawyer when a jury verdict speaks for itself? Gotta keep your eye on the prize . . . the true verdict.

But I remember a particularly offensive defense attorney, the over-the-top, macho B.S. type, who actually filed a written motion to preclude me from wearing short skirts or low-cut blouses in court and from bending over in front of the jury. Defense counsel filed the motion during a violent rape-murder case turning on very complicated DNA evidence found in a quickly decomposing body. I was working late in my office that night when I heard the "whoosh" of papers being shot under my door. I picked them up and read them, then I sat in my office and hot tears came to my eyes. I was embarrassed that someone would publicly allege such a thing, that I would use sexuality to win a case. How demeaning not only to me but to the memory of the victim—that her life meant so little.

For the most part, I always wore simple black shift dresses in court for freedom of movement, covered neck to wrist to knee. The motion was an attempt to ruin my focus, to humiliate me, and to take the attention, even if for a moment, off the accused. The next day in court, I didn't mention a thing about the motion and pretended I didn't notice the fleet of reporters and others there to hear the motion addressed. The judge was one I had tried my very first case before nearly 10 years earlier. When arguing motions in the South, lawyers typically stand to address the issues. I recall refusing to stand for the motion and simply looking the judge square in the face, waiting. He looked down at the documents and dismissed the motion with no discussion, totally thwarting the defense attempt. P.S.: I won the case.

● LT. GENERAL CLAUDIA KENNEDY
U.S. ARMY (RETIRED)
See page 159 for her profile.

Lt. General Claudia Kennedy is a member of the New Girls' Club because throughout her 32-year career in the military, she was known as a formidable advocate for women soldiers. She gained national recognition for successfully blocking the promotion of another general on the grounds of his having sexually harassed her. During our interview, she described how she found the courage to blow the whistle on General Smith, risking her entire professional reputation on the eve of her retirement.

AT FIRST I THOUGHT OF WHAT HAPPENED that day in my office with General Smith as an individual issue, and the way I handled it initially was to just make sure I stayed away from him. I called my executive officer, who was the person responsible for my schedule, and said to her, "There are a couple of people we are not going to allow in my office anymore." I buried him among one or two other names because she would have asked what was going on, and I didn't want anyone to know. You don't tell anyone something that you want to be kept a secret. I knew even then if I was not to report it, it was possible he was doing the same thing to others. But I also felt like we were going through enough in the army at that time. We had Aberdeen; we had Sergeant Major of the Army McKinney; we had it all. What we didn't need was a general-on-general case of harassment.

I watched him get promoted from one-star to two-star general, and I thought, "It's their business, not mine." But when General Smith was nominated to be deputy inspector general—a position which is pivotal in matters of general officer misconduct in the army—I thought, "Well, we have gone waaay too far on this one. It's got to be dealt with." He was about to be put in a position of sacred trust, and I couldn't let that happen without giving the army the information from my experience with him. Then it just became a question of how to deal with it. Should I confront him personally? Should I tell someone who would tell someone? Should I write an anonymous note? I imagined every possible scenario to avoid having to get my name attached to it. I ultimately decided that because the charge was so serious, I had to be accountable for it.

I waited a few weeks to see if someone else would come forward—perhaps someone with a more egregious story or more courage than I had to get right out there and tell it—but no one did. And then I finally said to myself, "Well, guess what? It's on you, Kennedy." And so I consulted a senior lawyer in the army, who happened to be a civilian, and I knew that there would be no turning back at that point, because no lawyer was going to listen to what I said and respond by saying, "Oh, keep that quiet, General Kennedy. You don't have to tell anybody." Nor did I expect they would give me a protected position from which to make this report.

It was a huge risk for me to come forward, and the risk played out. I paid for that in a lot of ways. Some people were real ugly and wrote horrible letters and said terrible things. There were death threats. I remember one person wrote a letter to me that said, "You will see people back away and you will be ostracized." And I felt in many ways that is exactly what happened. Most people do not want to do that, but they are exhausted by their own loads to carry, so I don't blame them for not rallying around me. People are not very discerning when they are under pressure. They become very black-and-white and think, "Well, if I'm friendly to you, I have to own everything you have said or done publicly." Guess what? It doesn't work that way. At the other end of the spectrum of reactions, there were many heartwarming moments in which peers and younger officers and NCOs reached out in quiet, meaningful support. Those were of priceless value to me and, after all, are what I remember with the most emotional clarity—the sense that through it all, they were faithful to the soldiers' vow of mutual loyalty.

I have thought about this a lot over the years, and I have asked myself, "How could I have handled it differently? How could I have minimized all the publicity?" But the truth is that I could not have been more discreet. I could not have been more careful. I could not have chosen my words more sparsely. I was as sparing in my public and private comments as any human could have been. When it turned into a public event, I knew that was really the result of the people who wanted to talk. I got through it all because I have a real strong internal core. You have to know what you own and what you do not own. I owned the event and my own personal participation in what I said about it—but I did not own all the other ramifications.

Sometimes you can't look at the consequences, you have to just look at the action required. So often, when you hear about someone who did something criminal or ethically wrong, people will say, "Oh, not good old Joe. I go golfing with him every Saturday. No way would he do that; he is a good family man." What's wrong with that reaction is that they are judging *him* when they should be judging *the event*. If something bad happens to you at work, the issue to focus on is whether the *event* is something your institution or your company disapproves of, and do they say in their written policy that they don't want this to happen? If so, then the institution must live up to its own rules and guidelines. Whether or not they are good at that, you are going to improve the institution by bringing this forward and forcing accountability.

● GINNY BAUER

EXECUTIVE DIRECTOR, NEW JERSEY STATE LOTTERY

AT 30 . . .
Ginny Bauer had just left her job as a stockbroker to stay at home with her infant son.

TODAY . . .
Ginny Bauer, mother of three and widow of a victim of the September 11, 2001, attacks on the World Trade Center, has been a key activist on behalf of the families of the 9/11 victims. She spearheaded efforts to enact federal tax relief legislation for surviving

family members and is assisting in the creation of a new development plan for the WTC site in lower Manhattan. She was recently appointed executive director of the New Jersey Lottery, which in fiscal year 2002 distributed a record $754 million to support higher education and programs for the developmentally disabled and veterans.

Ginny Bauer is a member of the New Girls' Club because she defines resilience and embodies the potential we all share for powerful second acts.

SADLY, SOMETIMES IN LIFE, you have to go through a major trauma in order to better understand yourself and your calling. My life can be divided into two very distinct parts—before 9/11 and after 9/11.

I met my husband in grammar school, so we had been friends since we were kids. We started to date when we were seniors in college. We knew immediately we belonged together. We got married a year later, when I was 23 years old.

During my twenties, I was a financial consultant at Merrill Lynch. I was one of only a few young women at the firm and the top producer in my group. I knew I wasn't a financial genius, a stock jockey, but I was very good at what I did, I think in large part because I never pretended to be someone I was not. My job was to study the research they provided at Merrill and relate it to my clients. I understood my role. People would see me and at first be hesitant because I was pretty and young and a woman. But I never tried to be someone I was not, and I believe that is what propelled me forward. My professional success gave me a lot of confidence back then.

Fast-forward a few years, and we decided we wanted to have a family. It would have been almost impossible for me to continue working at the same level (there was no telecommuting back then), and we knew we wanted more than one child. So, bottom line, we made the choice that I would stay home and take care of the family.

By the time I was 30, I was a stay-at-home mom with a little baby. It was a big change, and there were times I was left scratching my head about it all, but overall I was very happy. And a lot of that was because my husband was so wonderful. Dave never, ever made me feel like my job at home was not important. He also understood that it could be frustrating at times. Sometimes when I think about our life together, I just think it was too good to be true. My husband adored me, and he adored our children. We had enormous respect and love for each other. We lived in the perfect suburban community—the same one where we grew up. Ours really was the American Dream.

Then 9/11 happened.

I remember it was a beautiful day outside, and I was doing what I always did in the mornings—cleaning my kitchen and getting ready to go play tennis with some girlfriends. I spoke to David at about 8:20 A.M. about nothing in particular, and he mentioned he had a 10 o'clock sales meeting in the office. I had the TV on in the kitchen. I'll never forget when I looked up and saw the plane hit that tower. I just dropped to my knees. I knew he was there. I knew he was on the 105th floor. I knew he was hurt, best case. Right away, I did.

The rest of the week was a total blur. My first instinct was to get my kids home from school. I never lied to them. I told them that it didn't look good, that we hadn't heard from Daddy, and that I knew he was there. By the end of the week, we were reconciled that he was definitely dead.

You can't believe that one day, your gorgeous husband is going to leave for work and never come home again. And you never, ever, ever think that he could be blown off the face of the Earth by a terrorist attack. It was a nightmare. Somehow, I got through the next few weeks . . . the memorial service. In some way, I did almost feel like he was with me.

So, it was the beginning of October, and suddenly I was a 45-year-old, widowed housewife with three teenagers to take care of. My husband had been a very good provider. There was charity money available, but I had always been the kind of person who *gave* to charity. I was too proud to take it. But I knew that I had to do something; I didn't want my kids to have to worry. They were going through enough. I wanted them to know that Mommy could take of them, too.

I came across this idea. The federal government gives the families of soldiers killed in action tax rebates for the year they died and the year prior to that. And I thought, "We deserve the same relief." It just seemed fair. After all, it's your money that you put into the system, which technically should protect and secure you. My husband had a high-paying job at Cantor Fitzgerald, so we paid more than a third of his salary in taxes. That money would make a big difference. So I grabbed onto the idea.

I guess sometimes in life you are made quarterback of something, even if you didn't ask for the position. Like it or not, this time, I had the ball, and I felt I had no other choice but to run with it. So I rallied the other widows together, and we ended up going down to Washington. We sat with some of the top leaders in the Senate and explained to them why they needed to sign this bill right away. Now, nothing happens fast in politics. But I pushed hard, and I said, "You can't let us sit around and have another what-if in our lives. We need this to happen *right now*."

While our family had always been socially aware, I had never been politically active. Yet there I was, a month after my husband's death, this dopey little housewife doing all of this lobbying and public relations. But I surprised myself, because I was really *good* at it. Again, I think it worked because I never pretended to be anyone I was not. I didn't pretend to be a tax expert or a politician or an attorney. I kept my message simple by just explaining how this bill would help me and the other women like me. And you know what? No one can argue with that. When you know who you are, and your message is clear, people will listen to you.

It was December 21, and I was at home, cleaning up my kitchen, when Congressman Dennis Hastert's office called and said, "Mrs. Bauer, turn on C-Span, because your bill is being passed." It was amazing. And that is when I started to realize that I was so much more than just a wife and mother—I was a woman who could negotiate with some of the most well respected senators in Washington. The experience woke something up in me that had been sleeping since I left my job when I was 30. It elevated my confidence and reminded me what else I could do with my life.

My husband lived life so fully—he was successful in every possible way. At times, I looked at him with awe, because I don't think I ever felt totally fulfilled, like he did. I was entirely fulfilled as a mother, and I was entirely fulfilled as a wife, but my whole life was largely defined by those roles.

The White House invited us to meet the president and be with him when he signed the bill into law. When my eldest son shook his hand, the president said to him, "Take good care of your Momma."

David was very polite, as I raised him to be. Then he nodded his head and said, "Yes, sir, I will. But I want you to get Osama."

And the president's eyes teared up, because he knew that this 16-year-old kid who lost his father was essentially saying to him, "I am going to do my job, but I need you to do yours, too." It was a very powerful moment—and one of my proudest.

I miss my husband every single day, but I know that the greatest tribute I could give to him is to live my life bigger and better than I ever did before. We can all get back at the terrorists by living our lives more fully, without taking anything for granted. I do have very bad days, but whenever I start to feel at the bottom, I just remind myself that time is really a gift. I will not accept that the best years of my life are behind me. I am moving in a different direction now. It's not one that I would have predicted, and it's certainly not one that I would have chosen, but this is my life, and it is what I have. I am going to make the most of it.

Notes

Introduction

1. Catalyst. "The Next Generation: Today's Professionals, Tomorrow's Leaders" (New York: Catalyst, 2001).

Chapter 1

1. Barbara Dafoe Whitehead, *Why There Are No Good Men Left* (New York: Broadway, 2002), p. 10.

2. Andrew Hacker, *Mismatch: The Growing Gulf between Women and Men* (New York: Scribner, 2003), p. 70.

3. U.S. Census Bureau, "Fertility of American Women" (Washington, D.C.: Government Printing Office, 2000).

4. U.S. Census Bureau, "America's Families and Living Arrangements, 2000" (Washington, D.C.: Government Printing Office, 2001); some information in press release for study.

5. U.S. Census Bureau, "Statistical Abstract of the United States, 2000" (Washington, D.C.: Government Printing Office, 2001), p. 52.

6. Betty Friedan, *The Feminine Mystique* (New York: Norton, 2001), pp. 19–20.

7. Daniel Levinson, *The Seasons of a Woman's Life* (New York: Knopf, 1996), p. 302.

8. Interview with Helen Fisher, Ph.D., July 18, 2003.

9. Beverly Beyette, "Ms. Finds Some Muscle," *Los Angeles Times*, July 11, 2002, p. E-1.

10. Marlo Thomas, *Free to Be . . . You and Me* (Philadelphia: Running Press, 1974), back cover.

11. Katti Gray, "Courteous Crusader," *Newsday*, July 26, 2001, p. B-6.

12. Women's Sports Foundation, *Title IX: What Is It?* womenssportsfoundation.org.

13. ————, "Significant Events in Women's Sports History: Post–Title IX History," womenssportsfoundation.org.

14. Interview with Donna Lopiano, July 1, 2003.

15. Pamela Paul, "Meet the Parents," *American Demographics*, January 2002.

16. Whitehead, *No Good Men*, p. 79.

17. Walter Kirn, "Should You Stay Together for the Kids?" *Time*, September 22, 2000, p. 4.

18. Yomi Wronge, "Debate Continues on Impact of Divorce on Children," *San Jose (Calif.) Mercury News*, September 6, 2000, p. 1-B.

19. Nancy Gibbs, "Making Time for a Baby," *Time*, April 15, 2002, p. 2.

20. Ilene Philipson, *Married to the Job* (New York: Free Press, 2002), p. 48.

21. National Marriage Project survey, in David Popenoe and Barbara Dafoe Whitehead, "The State of Our Unions: The Social Health of Marriage in America, 2001" (New Brunswick, N.J.: National Marriage Project, 2001).

22. Kathleen Gerson, "Children of the Gender Revolution: Some Theoretical Questions and Findings from the Field," in *Family in Transition*, 12th ed., ed. Arlene Skolnick and Jerome Skolnick (Upper Saddle River, N.J.: Allyn & Bacon, 2002), reading 8.

23. Interview with Cheryl Gould, November 2003.

24. Kay Long, "Leave It to Gen-X," *Chicago Daily Herald*, November 7, 2002, p. 3.

25. Ibid, p. 1.

26. Amy Keller, "Senate Has at Least 42 Millionaires," *Roll Call*, June 16, 2003.

27. Barbara Walters, speech at Gracie Awards Luncheon for Female Radio and Television Executives, New York City, April 13, 2002.

28. "Babies vs. Career," *Time*, April 15, 2002, cover story inspired by Sylvia Ann Hewlett, *Creating a Life: Professional Women and the Quest for Children* (New York: Talk/Miramax, 2002). Statistics cited in Hewlett, pp. 87, 90.

29. Dianne Prather, "Biography: J. K. Rowling, Author of Harry Potter Books—From Single Mom Writer to Global Phenomenon," About.com, Single Parents.

30. Sheryl Crow bio, "Tuesday Night Music Club" CD (Fort Worth, Texas: ASM Records, 1994).

31. J. E. Bourgoyne, "Being a Sex Object Nice Change of Pace for *Basic Instinct* Star," *New Orleans Times-Picayune*, May 1, 1992; Laura Miller, "Stone Rocks," Salon.com, June 20, 1992.

Chapter 2

1. Carolyn Jacobson, "Women at Work," *American Federationist*, April 5, 1985. p. 5.

2. Ilene Philipson, *Married to the Job* (New York: Free Press, 2002), pp. 45–46.

3. U.S. Census Bureau, "Women's History Month Fast Facts," press release, February 14, 2003.

4. Jean Sahadi, "When She Makes More Than He," CNN/money.com, March 3, 2003.

5. "What Younger Women Think of Older Women," *Oprah Winfrey Show*, January 16, 2002.

6. Oxford English Dictionary, OED Online.

7. Lee Scheier, "Call It a Day, America," *Chicago Tribune*, May 5, 2002, p. 1.

8. CNN, "Study: U.S. Employees Put in the Most Hours," CNN.com, August 31, 2001.

9. Juliet Schor, *The Overworked American: The Unexpected Decline of Leisure* (New York: Basic, 1992), p. 22.

10. Billy Cheng, "Gen-X Women: Moving Up," BusinessWeek Online, June 17, 2002.

11. U.S. Census Bureau, "Fertility of American Women" (Washington, D.C.: Government Printing Office, 2000).

12. Karl Shinn, "Four Generations of Workers Have Much to Offer Bosses," *Fort Lauderdale Sun-Sentinel*, August 28, 2000, p. 8.

13. *Keywords: Magazine*, headline, February 2003.

14. Philipson, *Married*, p. 3.

15. Rikki Klieman, *Fairy Tales Can Come True: How a Driven Woman Changed her Destiny* (New York: HarperCollins, 2003), pp. 287–88.

16. Interview with Rikki Klieman, June 23, 2003.

17. Joyce Purnick, commencement address, Barnard College, 1998.

18. Peggy Orenstein, *Flux: Women on Sex, Work, Love, Kids, and Life in a Half-Changed World* (New York: Knopf, 2001), p. 97.

19. Radcliffe Public Policy Center with Harris Interactive, Inc., "Life's Work: Generational Attitudes toward Work and Life Integration" (Cambridge, Mass.: Radcliffe Public Policy Center).

20. Census Bureau, "Infertility."

21. Michelle Conlin with Jennifer Merritt and Linda Himelstein, "Mommy Is Really Home from Work," *BusinessWeek*, November 25, 2002, p. 101.

22. Patricia Sellers, "Power: Do Women Really Want It?" *Fortune*, October 13, 2003, p. 80.

23. Ibid.

24. Ibid.

25. Ibid.

26. Lisa Belkin, "The Opt-Out Revolution: Why Women Don't Rule," *New York Times Magazine*, October 26, 2003.

27. Sellers, "Power."

28. Belkin, "Revolution."

29. Video presentation, Women's Leadership Exchange conference, New York City, November 14, 2003.

Chapter 3

1. Pat Heim and Susan A. Murphy with Susan K. Golant, *In the Company of Women* (New York: Tarcher, 2001), p. 9.

2. Ibid.

3. Phyllis Chesler, *Woman's Inhumanity to Woman* (New York: Thunder's Mouth Press/Nation Books, 2002), p. 16.

4. Cindy Lord, "The Secret Life of Girls," *Queensland (Australia) Courier Mail*, February 3, 2002.

5. Helen Fisher, *The First Sex: The Natural Talents of Women and How They Are Changing the World* (New York: Random House, 1999), p. 44.

6. Suzanne Braun Levine, "'You Ruined Men!' and Other Outrageous, Annoying, and Maybe Truthful Things Younger Women Are Saying about Us," *More*, October 2001, p. 102.

7. Ibid.

Chapter 4

1. Gallup Organization, "Young Adults' Attitudes toward Marriage," April 2001. Unpublished report; results in David Popenoe and Barbara Dafoe Whitehead, "The State of Our Unions: The Social Health of Marriage in America, 2001" (New Brunswick, N.J.: National Marriage Project, 2001).

2. Ibid.

3. Ibid.

4. Ibid.

5. Ibid.

6. Lisa Berenson, "The State of the Union: A Special Report," *Ladies Home Journal*, March 2003, p. 112.

7. Tamela Edwards, "Single by Choice" *Time*, August 28, 2000, p. 46.

8. Interview with Helen Fisher, Ph.D., July 18, 2003.

9. Iris Krasnow, *Surrendering to Marriage* (New York: Talk/Miramax, 2001), p. 23.

10. U.S. Census Bureau, "America's Families and Living Arrangements, 2000" (Washington, D.C.: Government Printing Office, 2001); some information in press release for study.

11. Edwards, "Single."

12. Census Bureau, "America's Families," pp. 10–11.

13. Barbara Dafoe Whitehead, *Why There Are No Good Men Left* (New York: Broadway, 2002), pp. 99–102.

14. Gallup, "Attitudes," in David Popenoe and Barbara Dafoe Whitehead, "Should We Live Together? What Young Adults Need to Know about Cohabitation before Marriage," (New Brunswick, N.J.: National Marriage Project, 2002).

15. Andrew Hacker, *Mismatch: The Growing Gulf between Women and Men* (New York: Scribner, 2003), pp. 24–25.

16. Ibid.

17. Ibid.

18. Gallup, "Attitudes," in Popenoe and Whitehead, "Should We Live Together?"

19. Marie Brenner, "Not Their Mothers' Choices," *Newsweek*, August 13, 2001, p. 48.

20. Naomi Wolf, *Misconceptions: Truth, Lies, and the Unexpected on the Journey to Motherhood* (New York: Random House, 2003), p. 4.

21. Peggy Orenstein, *Flux: Women on Sex, Work, Love, Kids, and Life in a Half-Changed World* (New York: Knopf, 2001), p. 178.

22. Kellyanne Fitzpatrick, "The Pro-Life Movement at 30," speech at Family Research Council, January 2003.

23. Kay Long, "Leave It to Gen-X," *Chicago Daily Herald*, November 7, 2002, p. 1 (suburban living).

24. Hacker, *Mismatch*, p. 81.

25. Danielle Crittenden, *What Our Mothers Didn't Tell Us* (New York: Simon & Schuster, 1999).

26. Eloise Salhotz, "Too Late for Prince Charming?" Newsweek, June 6, 1986, p. 54.

27. Vanessa Grigoriadis, "Baby Panic," *New York*, May 20, 2002.

28. Census Bureau, "America's Families."

29. Ibid.

30. Michelle Conlin, "Unmarried America," *BusinessWeek*, October 20, 2003, p. 106.

31. Karen M. Thomas, "Adoption Fills Need for Nurturing Singles," *Tallahassee Democrat*, July 22, 2003, p. 3.

32. Dolores Hayden, *The Grand Domestic Revolution* (Cambridge, Mass.: MIT Press, 1992), pp. 196–97.

33. "More Wives Earning More Than Their Husbands," *Washington Post*, February 29, 2000.

34. Ibid.

35. Anna Quindlen, *A Short Guide to a Happy Life* (New York: Random House, 2000), p. 10.

Chapter 5

1. Gail Evans, *She Wins, You Win: The Most Important Rule In Business Every Woman Should Know* (New York: Gotham, 2003), p. 11.

2. Radcliffe Public Policy Center with Harris Interactive, Inc., "Life's Work: Generational Attitudes toward Work and Life Integration" (Cambridge, Mass.: Radcliffe Public Policy Center, 2000), pp. 2–3.

3. Suzanne Braun Levine, *Father Courage: What Happens When Men Put Family First* (New York: Harcourt, 2000), pp. xii–xiii.

4. Interview with Roland Warren, May 9, 2003.

5. Celeste Freeman, "What Our Sons Think of Us," *More*, March 2003, p. 99.

6. "The Mission Calendar," *O, the Oprah Magazine*, June 2003, p. 35.

7. Freeman, "Our Sons."

8. Deborah Tannen, *You Just Don't Understand: Men and Women in Conversation* (New York: Morrow, 1990).

9. Andrew Hacker, *Mismatch: The Growing Gulf between Women and Men* (New York: Scribner. 2003), p. 77.

10. "Married Couples Have to Work Harder to Make it Work When Career Paths Get Out of Sync," *San Francisco Examiner*, October 10, 1999.

11. Ibid.

12. Patricia Schroeder, *24 Years of Housework . . . And the Place Is Still a Mess: My Life In Politics* (New York: Andrews McMeel, 1998), in Levine, *Father Courage.*

13. Ibid.

14. Hacker, *Mismatch*, p. 165.

15. Arlie Russell Hochschild with Anne Machung, *The Second Shift* (New York: Viking Penguin, 1989), p. 7.

16. University of Michigan Institute for Social Research, "U.S. Husbands Are Doing More Housework while Wives Are Doing Less," press release, March 2002.

17. Hacker, *Mismatch*, p. 12.

18. M. L. Lyke, "Fathers of Invention," *Seattle Post-Intelligencer*, June 17, 2000, p. E-1.

19. U.S. Census Bureau, "Current Population Reports, Series P20-537" (Washington, D.C.: Government Printing Office, 2001), tables CH1–CH4.

20. Jennifer E. Lansford et al., "Does Family Structure Matter? A Comparison of Adoptive, Two-Parent Biological, Single-Mother, Stepfather, and Stepmother Households," *Journal of Marriage and the Family* 63 (August 2001), pp. 840–51.

21. Wade F. Horn and Tom Sylvester, *Father Facts*, 4th ed. (Washington, D.C.: National Fatherhood Initiative, 2002), p. 12.

22. Lyke, "Fathers."

23. Catalyst, "The Next Generation: Today's Professionals, Tomorrow's Leaders" (New York: Catalyst, 2001).

24. Nancy Hatch Woodward, "Make Room for Daddy," *HR* 46, no. 7 (July 1, 2001), p. 101.

25. Ibid.

26. Diane Stafford, "New Parents Often Don't Use Family-Leave Laws," *Chicago Tribune*, February 26, 2003, p. C-3.

27. Sharman Stein, "Make Room for Daddy," *Working Mother*, October 2002, p. 49.

28. Ibid, p. 47.

29. Interview with Roland Warren.

30. Levine, *Father Courage*, p. 224.

31. Stephanie Coontz, *The Way We Never Were: American Families and the Nostalgia Trap* (New York: HarperCollins, 1992).

Beyond 30

1. Catalyst, "The Next Generation: Today's Professionals, Tomorrow's Leaders" (New York: Catalyst, 2001), p. 25.

2. Ibid, p. 33.

3. Interview with Deborah Rosado Shaw, October 8, 2003.

Index